State of
the World's
Minorities
2008

Acknowledgements

Minority Rights Group International (MRG) gratefully acknowledges the support of all organizations and individuals who gave financial and other assistance to this publication, including the European Commission, the Sigrid Rausing Trust and Matrix Causes Fund.

Minority Rights Group International

Minority Rights Group International (MRG) is a non-governmental organization (NGO) working to secure the rights of ethnic, religious and linguistic minorities and indigenous peoples worldwide, and to promote cooperation and understanding between communities. Our activities are focused on international advocacy, training, publishing and outreach. We are guided by the needs expressed by our worldwide partner network of organizations which represent minority and indigenous peoples.

MRG works with over 150 organizations in nearly 50 countries. Our governing Council, which meets twice a year, has members from 10 different countries. MRG has consultative status with the United Nations Economic and Social Council (ECOSOC), and observer status with the African Commission on Human and People's Rights. MRG is registered as a charity and a company limited by guarantee under English law. Registered charity no. 282305, limited company no. 1544957.

ISBN 978-1-904584-72-8
Published February 2008
Design by Texture +44(0)20 7739 7123
Printed in the UK

Cover photo: A Hindu woman seeks shelter after her home in Siranganj, Bangladesh, was submerged during the 2007 floods. Over 5 million people have been displaced in Bangladesh and many have lost their lives. G.M.B. Akash/Panos Pictures

Inside cover photo: The remains of houses damaged when Hurricane Katrina struck New Orleans in August 2005. Alvaro Leiva/Panos Pictures

Minority Rights Group International
54 Commercial Street, London, E1 6LT, United Kingdom. Tel +44 (0)20 7422 4200, Fax +44 (0)20 7422 4201, Email minority.rights@mrgmail.org Website www.minorityrights.org

Getting involved

MRG relies on the generous support of institutions and individuals to further our work. All donations received contribute directly to our projects with minorities and indigenous peoples.

One valuable way to support us is to subscribe to our report series. Subscribers receive regular MRG reports and our annual review. We also have over 100 titles which can be purchased from our publications catalogue. In addition, MRG publications are available to minority and indigenous peoples' organizations through our library scheme.

MRG's unique publications provide well-researched, accurate and impartial information on minority and indigenous peoples' rights worldwide. We offer critical analysis and new perspectives on international issues. Our specialist training materials include essential guides for NGOs and others on international human rights instruments, and on accessing international bodies. Many MRG publications have been translated into several languages.

If you would like to know more about MRG, how to support us and how to work with us, please visit our website www.minorityrights.org.

Select MRG publications:
- *Assimilation, Exodus, Eradication: Iraq's Minority Communities since 2003*
- *China: Minority Exclusion, Marginalization and Rising Tensions*
- *Minority Rights: The Key to Conflict Prevention*
- *A Quest for Equality: Minorities in Turkey*

This document has been produced with the financial assistance of the European Union. The contents of this document are the sole responsibility of Minority Rights Group International and can under no circumstances be regarded as reflecting the position of the European Union.

State of the World's Minorities

2008

Events of 2007

With a Preface by Professor Wangari Maathai, founder of the Green Belt Movement and 2004 Nobel Peace Prize winner

Edited by Ishbel Matheson

Preface

Professor Wangari Maathai, founder of the Green Belt Movement and 2004 Nobel Peace Prize winner

When I started the Green Belt Movement in Kenya in the 1970s, the idea was simple. By mobilizing rural African women to plant trees we could protect our fragile and rapidly degrading environment. We have now planted more than 35 million trees. Through this simple act, we went on to build a consciousness of the importance of conserving our natural resources for future generations, and helped people stand up for their rights, for the fair and equitable distribution of national wealth to all.

Three decades on, this campaign is as relevant as ever, because it is apparent that the global abuse of the natural world is finally taking its terrible toll. The debate about whether climate change is real or not is over. Unless the carbon-polluting lifestyles of the Northern hemisphere and the massive deforestation in the South are dramatically curbed, our climate is set to change – permanently. And so too, inevitably, will our way of life. If even the more modest scientific predictions come true, warmer temperatures will lead to rising water levels and increased flooding, more frequent droughts, increased disease, changes in the fish-stock and mammals in our oceans, and threats to our global flora and fauna. We will be confronted with massive ecological and economic challenges, and the risk of conflict over dwindling resources will increase.

Africa is the continent that will be hit hardest by climate change and, as I noticed in Kenya 30 years ago, the impact of environmental destruction hits the most vulnerable first – and hardest. Already communities in Kenya are witnessing – and feeling – changes in local and regional climates. In this special edition of *State of the World's Minorities*, you will read personal testimonies from communities across the world. All face immense challenges, as the landscape which they – and their ancestors – have depended upon, is changing before their very eyes.

But if the effects are already being felt, the responses from governments are – as yet – remarkably low-key. Some policy-making initiatives to combat climate change are under way. For example, under the auspices of the UN, 50 Least Developed Countries are now drawing up National Adaptation Plans of Action. In theory, these plans should take on the principles of equity and justice, taking account of the needs of all sectors of society. But all too often vulnerable communities are not consulted by governments. Often marginalized from political power, minority groups have little or no voice when it comes to having their interests reflected in national decision-making. We saw this all too clearly, when Hurricane Katrina hit New Orleans.

But it is not only governments which have to act – we all have a part to play. Activists might wonder why, in light of all the other challenges facing them, they should pick up the issue of climate change too. But the connection is obvious: unless the unfolding disaster is addressed, all the problems currently facing these communities – poverty, discrimination, marginalization and, at worst, persecution – are likely to be magnified a hundred-fold. Already local groups are acting in diverse parts of the world, but more needs to be done to influence negotiations over the successor to the Kyoto Treaty, which will run out in 2012.

Finally, at an individual level, minorities need to mobilize. Just as I urged rural women to plant trees and protect their deteriorating environment 30 years ago, so too must we encourage individuals and their communities to come up with their own adaptation plans and coping strategies. In the otherwise gloomy report published by the Intergovernmental Panel on Climate Change (IPCC) in 2007, it was pointed out that those who live close to the land, such as pastoralists in particular, with their dependence on the vagaries of the weather, may be better placed to adapt than most.

It is a reminder that the response to this global challenge is far too important to be left to politicians and policy-makers alone. Everyone, whoever and wherever they are, can make a difference by engaging less in rhetoric and more in action. ▪

Climate Change and Minorities

Rachel Baird

Climate change is attracting ever more attention from the media, academics, politicians and even businesses, as evidence mounts about its scale and seriousness, and the speed at which it is affecting the world. But rarely do its impacts on minorities and indigenous groups get a mention, even though they among the worst affected.

The effects of the changing climate are bad enough in themselves – more frequent hurricanes and droughts, burning temperatures, new plagues of diseases and worse floods, for instance. But the general failure to recognize and respond to minorities' resulting problems greatly exacerbates their suffering. Disadvantage and discrimination affect them at every stage, including in the immediate aftermath of climate-related disasters and during official planning at local, national and international levels for coping with the current and future impacts of climate change.

The close relationship of some indigenous peoples and minorities with their natural environments makes them especially sensitive to the effects of global warming. In some cases, peoples' ways of life and even their very existence are being threatened by climate change, and by the rapidly increasing cultivation of biofuels, which are being touted as part of the 'solution'.

This chapter sets out some of the evidence on how minorities and indigenous people are being affected by climate change. It shows how discrimination against them means that they are not getting the help they need, or influence over governments' plans for combating and adapting to climate change. Finally, it highlights some of the opportunities for change.

The chapter uses the term 'minority' to refer to groups that are normally numerically smaller groups who share a common religious, ethnic or linguistic identity. Examples are the Roma across Europe, Dalits and Muslims in India and Afro-descendants in Colombia. 'Indigenous peoples' refers to groups who have a special connection with the natural environment and who are often seen as the 'first people' to inhabit a particular territory. Examples include the Sami of the Arctic and the Miskitu of Nicaragua.

When we contacted groups working with minorities as part of the research for this chapter, it was striking that, in three countries, they were caught up in weather-related crises. In India, the National Campaign on Dalit Human Rights was urging greater attention to the plight of Dalits, Muslims and Adivasis in India, following unusually severe monsoon floods in 2007. In Nicaragua, Oxfam staff were tackling the devastation left by Hurricane Felix on the Atlantic coast, while in the Czech Republic, staff at the Roma rights group Life Together feared major floods in the north-east of the country following three days of rain. In the event, the rivers carried the water away safely.

It is impossible to attribute any single instance of extreme weather to climate change, so none of these examples can be blamed on it. However, the world's climate is clearly changing. As the Intergovernmental Panel on Climate Change (IPCC) states in its latest Synthesis report, published in November 2007: 'Warming of the climate system is unequivocal, as is now evident from observations of increases in global average air and ocean temperatures, widespread melting of snow and ice, and rising global average sea level.'[1]

In addition to these relatively gradual changes, climate change also has sudden impacts, in the form of more weather-related disasters. The toll of emergencies caused by hurricanes, floods, droughts and other forms of extreme weather has more than doubled over the last decade, from 175 in 1996 to 391 in 2005, according to the International Federation of the Red Cross and Red Crescent's *World Disasters Report.*[2]

Mind the gap: climate change, minorities and indigenous peoples

Despite consulting with climate change and development specialists within NGOs, academia and intergovernmental organizations, we failed to find any English-language research about how global warming is affecting minority groups and indigenous peoples in different countries around the world. The only exception to this was the recent Tyndall Centre for Climate Change conference report on indigenous peoples (but not minorities) and climate change.[3]

Where minorities are mentioned in reports on climate change, it tends to be incidentally, during studies of particular countries. In addition, some academic, non-governmental organization (NGO) and media reporting of specific disasters has clearly acknowledged that minority communities have fared worse than others. Examples are the reporting of the

Poverty in New Orleans		
People living in poverty, 2000 (%)	**New Orleans**	**United States**
Total population	28	12
Children 18 years and younger	38	18
Whites	12	9
African-Americans	35	25 Source: UNDP, HDR 2007

New Orleans floods which followed Hurricane Katrina in August 2005, and of the Indian floods in the summer of 2007, in which African-Americans and Dalits respectively suffered especially badly.[4]

Part of the problem is that climate change research tends to focus on economic sectors – water, infrastructure, agriculture, settlements and so on – rather than human groups, says Rachel Roach, Climate Change Policy Officer at the development agency Tearfund. 'Often, climate change is thought of sectorally, in terms of agriculture, water and so on, rather than in terms of a people, group or livelihood.'[5] This is evident in major reports on climate change, such as those by the IPCC, as well as in countries' National Adaptation Programmes of Action (see p. 16 for more details about NAPAs).

The recent Tyndall Centre conference report[6] begins by stating that indigenous peoples 'are only rarely considered in academic, policy and public discourses on climate change'. However, indigenous peoples have won more attention than other minorities for the ways in which climate change is harming them.

One reason for this is that indigenous peoples are relatively well organized at national and international levels, through organizations that represent them to politicians, bureaucrats and journalists. The Inuit, who live in the fast-melting Arctic, have gone so far as to launch a precedent-setting case against the United States in the Inter-American Commission on Human Rights (see pp. 17, 133–4). It is making slow, if any, progress, but has greatly increased awareness of the Inuits' plight.

The United Nations Permanent Forum on Indigenous Issues will further highlight the issue for all indigenous peoples in 2008, when it holds a session on 'climate change and the stewardship role

of indigenous people: bio-cultural diversity, livelihoods and new challenges'. In addition to the session, the Forum has also appointed two of its members to produce a report on the 'impact of climate change mitigation measures on the territories and lands of indigenous peoples'. The activism of the indigenous lobby provides lessons for campaigners for minority rights. They might wonder why – given the host of disadvantages their communities face – they should take on this issue too. The answer is clear: not only is global warming changing our world – but, as we shall see from the following sections, minorities and indigenous people are among the worst off at every stage in the climate change story.

Minorities tend to live in places that are worst hit by the impacts of climate change – their poverty exacerbates their vulnerability

John Magrath, programme researcher at Oxfam, says:

'Minorities tend to live in the more marginal areas, exposed areas, that seem to be seeing more climate changes and are more susceptible to climate impacts because they have got less, and get less, from governments.... It is a characteristic of all the studies that I have seen, that the ethnic communities are the people who suffer most from climate impacts and are the most vulnerable.'

The IPCC's latest impacts report also clearly acknowledges that some groups are especially vulnerable, although it rarely uses the term 'minority'. For example, it states:

'Impacts of climate change are like to be felt most acutely not only by the poor, but also by certain

segments of the population, such as the elderly, the very young, the powerless, indigenous peoples, and recent immigrants, particularly if they are linguistically isolated, i.e. those most dependent on public support. Impacts will also differ according to gender.'[7]

One of the most shocking examples of minorities' greater exposure to climate change is in India, where some 170 million people known as Dalits are physically, socially and economically excluded from the rest of society. As a result they and two other minorities, Adivasis and Muslims, were worst hit by the unusually severe monsoon floods in 2007.

Many Dalits lived in rickety homes in flood-prone areas outside main villages, leaving them especially exposed. They were often last to get emergency relief, if they received it at all, because relief workers did not realize that Dalits live outside the main villages, or because dominant groups took control of distribution or were given priority.

A survey by Dalit organizations of 51 villages on 8–9 August 2007 found, among other things, that 60 per cent of the dead were Dalits, that none of the Dalit colonies (or *tolas*) attached to the main villages had been visited by government relief officials and that Dalits' housing had suffered the worst damage because most was of poor quality and in low-lying areas. These findings were set out in a letter from N. Paul Divakar, convenor of the National Campaign for Dalit Human Rights, to the Governor of Bihar.[8]

African-Americans living in New Orleans were also disproportionately badly hit by the floods caused by Hurricane Katrina in 2005. A Brookings Institution report on the disaster found that: 'those areas hit hardest by the flood were disproportionately non-white. Overall, blacks and other minority residents made up 58 percent of those whose neighborhoods were flooded, though they encompassed just 45 percent of the metropolitan population.'[9] Within the city itself, 80 per cent of people who had lived in the flooded areas were non-white. Escaping the stricken city was harder for people in the flooded areas, because one in five of them had no access to a car, compared to one in ten without access in the dry areas.

In Europe, Roma communities' housing conditions are notoriously unpleasant and unhealthy. That some are at high risk of flooding has been less widely noted, perhaps because of the more obvious hazards they face.

However, a few studies have found that Roma people suffered especially badly during floods. One, in *Making the Case for Environmental Justice in Central and Eastern Europe*, examines events in the Slovakian Roma community of Jarovnice, which suffered the worst floods in its history in June 1998.

Some 140 Roma homes were affected, compared with 25 non-Roma homes, and of the 47 people who were killed, 45 were Roma. Of those who died, 42 had lived in a shanty town in the valley of the River Svinka, which had flooded, while non-Roma lived in the village above the valley. The report notes: 'The public, shocked over the fatalities associated with the flood, forced the Government to take action, However, while housing for 20 families was eventually constructed in 2006, the vast majority of the residents still wait for safer housing.'[10]

In the Dominican Republic, Haitian migrants' poverty leads them to live in the rural areas bordering the capital, Santo Domingo, where they work on sugar plantations. When Hurricane Georges struck in 1998, there were severe delays before they received any help from the civil defence authorities or local Red Cross. Dr Mark Pelling, chair of the Climate Change Research Group at the Royal Geographical Society, outlines how entrenched discrimination means that the unfair treatment is rarely questioned, or even noticed, by mainstream society. He says: 'It is accepted [by the majority] that Haitians will be living in poorly paid jobs, in difficult conditions, and because they are poor, it's also accepted that their losses will be higher after any sort of disaster.'

The close relationship of many indigenous peoples and some minorities to their environments makes them especially sensitive to the impacts of climate change – and also to the cultivation of biofuels, which are being presented as part of the 'solution' to global warming

Indigenous peoples tend to live close to nature, in relatively natural environments, rather than in cities, growing and making much of the food and other products that they need to survive. This gives them an extraordinarily intimate knowledge of local weather and plant and animal life. Traditional wisdom on matters such as when to plant crops or where to hunt for food has been accumulated over many generations, but now that the climate is shifting, some of those understandings are proving to be no longer valid. Climate change, and the rapidly increasing amount of land being converted into plantations of biofuel crops, threatens the very existence of some cultures.

In the Arctic, where the atmosphere is warming twice as quickly as in the rest of the world, there are currently some 400,000 indigenous peoples. They include the Sami people of northern Norway, Sweden, Finland and Russia, who traditionally herd reindeer as a way of life.[11]

Olav Mathis-Eira, a herder and vice-chair of the executive board of the Sami Council, says people first noticed signs of climate change in the mid-1980s, when winter rainfall increased. Now, higher temperatures and increased rainfall are making it harder for reindeer to reach the lichen they eat, which in winter can be covered in ice. 'There are a lot of starving reindeer in some years,' he says.

The thinning of the Arctic ice has also made reindeer herding tracks dangerous, forcing people to find new routes. 'Old people used to tell us how to move the herds and where it was safe to go,' says Mathis-Eira. 'Now they are not sure if they can do that any more ... because conditions are so different.' The loss of their ability has damaged old people's status, he adds: 'Suddenly, they are nothing.'

Many aspects of Sami culture – language, songs, marriage, child-rearing and the treatment of older people, for instance – are intimately linked with reindeer herding, says Mathis-Eira. 'If the reindeer herding disappears it will have a devastating effect on the whole culture of the Sami people.... In that way, I think that climate change is threatening the entire Sami, as a people.'

Climate change has also played havoc with the lives of indigenous people living on Nicaragua's remote North Atlantic coast, where groups such as the Mayangna, Miskitu and Rama peoples live.

Rainfall patterns have changed in line with what climate change scientists are predicting for the region and, as a result, people's traditional knowledge about when to plant crops is no longer reliable. Their ability to correctly identify the rainy season has suffered, leading them to plant crops prematurely. Then, when the rain stops, they lose what they have planted and have to start all over again. Even when the main rainy season does arrive, it is shorter than before, inflicting further economic

and psychological damage. 'To see something growing really nicely is going to make the community optimistic,' says Carlos Ling, a Nicaraguan who is humanitarian officer for Oxfam in the region. 'In the middle of that [rainy] season, they see things rotting away, so collective confidence is being damaged.'

Without surplus crops to exchange with others for goods such as soap and cloth, indigenous peoples have become less prepared to take risks and try new methods, says Ling. 'They are going to be even more prone to extinction because they are not going to survive in a changing environment when they are not changing themselves,' he warns.

As in the Arctic, the increasingly unpredictable weather has also undermined older people's ability to interpret their environment and make decisions such as when to plant crops. This, in turn, has damaged community respect for them, and reduced people's confidence that their community's intimate knowledge of their environment will guarantee their livelihoods. Instead they have become more interested in alternative means of survival, such as helping drug-traffickers or allowing gold prospectors and loggers into the forest.

'They are being pressured, more and more, to give away the forests,' says Ling. While the amounts of money on offer seem small – $300 for a big tree, say – they are huge to people who might make $40 in an entire a year. According to the Nicaraguan government, people living on the Atlantic coast are among the nation's poorest.[12]

In northern Kenya, increasingly severe and frequent droughts, as well as major floods, have had a devastating impact on pastoralists. Traditionally, they have survived by herding animals, in an already harsh and dry environment. However, the drought of 2005–6 led to a 70 per cent fall in the size of their herds of cattle, goats and camels, leaving some 80 per cent of pastoralists dependent on international food aid, according to Mohamed Adow. He is regional programme manager for Northern Aid, a Muslim organization based in Mandera in north-east Kenya, which does development and advocacy work with pastoralists.

Droughts force them to travel long distances in search of water and have also sparked deadly conflicts over water. The deaths of so many livestock in 2005–6 reduced pastoralists' food supplies and damaged their health. Around one-third of the pastoralists of northern Kenya are now 'living on the periphery of their way of life' – in villages and small communities, where they work for money, having given up their small numbers of remaining livestock to family or kinsmen, says Adow.[13]

The biofuels connection

Across the world, meanwhile, the biofuel crops being championed as part of the solution to climate change are also severely affecting forest-dwelling indigenous peoples and minorities, threatening or destroying their land rights, traditional ways of life and even their survival.

Biofuels are liquid or gas fuels produced from plant (or animal) matter such as corn, oil palm, rapeseed, sugar cane, soya and wheat. The European Union (EU), the UK and other governments are promoting their use, partly because biofuels generally produce lower emissions of carbon dioxide than fossil fuels. The profits to be made from biofuels has led to a rapid increase in the amount of land devoted to their cultivation. Oil palm plantations, for instance, have become one of the fastest growing monocrops in the tropics.

A report produced by two members of the United Nations Permanent Forum on Indigenous Issues (UNPFII) in 2007 warns that the expansion of oil palm and other biofuel plantations is having a devastating effect on indigenous peoples and other forest dwellers.[14] It gives a long list of abuses documented in relation to plantations and logging on indigenous people's lands, which includes forced evictions; the denial of rights to lands and resources; habitat loss which has led to the destruction of livelihoods, cultures and traditional forest-related knowledge; food insecurity; higher incidence of diseases; increases in rates of prostitution and sexually transmitted diseases and the creation of exploitative, corrupt relationships between forestry officials and indigenous peoples.

In Colombia, which has the world's second largest population of internally displaced people (after Sudan), oil palm companies employ armed guards and paramilitaries to drive people off their land using intimidation, violence and murder. A recent report by the Internal Displacement Monitoring Centre paints a shocking picture of two communities Jiguamiandó and Curvaradó in the department of Chocó in the north-west of the country.[15]

By March 2005, more than 90 per cent of the land planted with oil palms in the two communities belonged to displaced Afro-Colombian communities, according to the report. 'There is sufficient evidence to suggest that the [oil palm] companies have taken advantage of the violent displacements committed by paramilitary groups to encroach on collective land belonging to Afro-Colombian communities,' it states. Furthermore, the authors say there is evidence that judicial authorities have been pressured not to investigate such abuses, while the Colombian government, through its Agrarian Bank and international aid agency, has subsidized one of the major groups of companies charged by the Ombudsman's office with taking advantage of the paramilitary activities and forced displacements in the area.

'A solution to this conflict rests on the clarification of ownership in the collective territories and the political will to suspend support to companies operating on land whose inhabitants were forcibly displaced,' the report argues.

Aparicio Rios, an indigenous activist from Colombia's Nasa people and leader of the Cauca Indigenous Regional Council, believes that the outside world also needs to act. 'This is a critical situation, practically the same as genocide,' he told *SWM*. 'We ask that the international community pressure the Colombian government to provide comprehensive protection for indigenous communities and live up to its promises of buying and setting aside land for indigenous reservations so that we can preserve our traditional way of life.'

Violent evictions from ancestral lands are also taking place in Argentina, to make way for soya plantations. In Brazil, soya bean farmers are hiring gunmen and erecting barbed wire fences to exclude Afro-indigenous and Afro-descendant people from the areas where they have traditionally collected nuts from the babaçú tree.

In Indonesia, another of the world's major palm oil producers, the possibility of a further vast expansion in Kalimantan, on the border with Malaysia, threatens to have grave consequences for indigenous peoples. This government plan prompted activists in July 2007 to apply to the UN Committee on the Elimination of Racial Discrimination (CERD), under its early warning and urgent actions procedure, to get the Committee to institute its urgent action procedures in order to halt the mega-project (see pp. 28–9).[16]

Forest-dwelling minorities and indigenous peoples will also bear the brunt of another plan to combat climate change. Under so-called 'Avoided Deforestation' (AD), rich countries will pay poor countries to reduce forest clearance, again to reduce the rate of climate change. Advocates of AD want the concept enshrined in the next commitment period of the Kyoto Protocol, which governments are currently negotiating. But if this is to happen, then indigenous peoples will need to ensure that it includes explicit safeguards of their rights, because AD – while helping the environment – may erode forest-dwelling peoples' rights even further. This was highlighted in a recent report by the Forest Peoples' Programme, which warns that, 'Such practices may violate people's right to culture and livelihood, weaken food security and undermine their traditional practices.'[17] They also warn that such action on the part of governments would be in contravention of a raft of human rights conventions, including CERD, as well as participating states' obligations 'to protect customary use of biological resources and traditional knowledge under the Convention on Biological Diversity'.

Discrimination against minorities and indigenous peoples makes it harder for them to cope with the impacts of climate change

As already mentioned, even during the severe monsoon floods of 2007, Dalits were often excluded from emergency shelters and camps, in line with their routine exclusion from the rest of Indian society. As a result, many Dalits died from snake bites.

In his letter to the Governor of the State of Bihar, N. Paul Divakar, convenor of the National Campaign for Dalit Human Rights, described the many ways in which discrimination against Dalits, Adivasis and Muslims continued as usual during and after the disaster:

'These social dynamics are manifested in failure to identify Dalit communities affected, registering death and loss, not taking cognizance of their situation of hunger, not registering barriers and prohibitions in accessing relief. The non-recognition and under-recognition of the loss and destruction suffered by my Dalit communities in disaster results in scanty relief measures to them and limited provisioning in rehabilitation. This has serious implications for their ability to get back to normal.'[18]

Discrimination was also overt in New Orleans, following Hurricane Katrina in 2005. African-Americans seeking to rent homes throughout the Gulf Coast suffered clearly worse treatment than their white counterparts, according to a group of advocacy organizations' report *Housing in New Orleans: One Year After Katrina*: 'In phone tests that had white and African American individuals call numerous housing complexes, white home seekers were more likely to be told about apartment availability, rent and discounts. Their African American counterparts were often denied this information.'[19]

In the city of Ostrava in the north-east Czech Republic, which suffered severe flooding in 1997, Roma families were treated very differently from 'white' families. The clearest example of this was that while evacuated white families were given flats outside the flood-affected Hru?ov district, Roma families were sent to makeshift cabins of the sort used by construction workers, or back to homes that had been flooded. This was despite the fact that the Main Office of the Architect of the City of Ostrava declared parts of the Hru?ov district unfit for habitation A 2002 report by human rights lawyer Barbora Bukovska states: 'While non-Roma residents of the flooded area were resettled elsewhere, only these flooded apartments were made available to Roma residents. The apartments were in severe disrepair and clearly uninhabitable.'[20]

Campaigners worked with the Czech National Ombudsman to get dozens of families moved out of the area. However, a decade after the 1997 floods, some 65 Roma families are still living in the condemned areas.

While Nicaragua's government has committed itself to helping the indigenous people of the North Atlantic coast to cope with the impacts of climate change, it has done little, says Oxfam officer Carlos Ling: 'Almost nothing has come to reality, not real, concrete support.' So there is a danger that indigenous people will migrate to other, wealthier regions or move into activities such as gold prospecting. Then, says Ling, they will be unable to maintain the current balance between people and nature. Loss of the forests will exacerbate climate change, with consequences for the entire world. Perhaps if foreigners took more interest, he concludes, the Nicaraguan government would do more to help the indigenous peoples.

Minorities and indigenous people have less influence than other groups over local, national and international decision-making on mitigating and adapting to climate change

This should not be surprising, given their more general political marginalization. However, it will need to be recognized and addressed if minorities and indigenous peoples are to get the support and protection they need in relation to global warming.

The question of influence over decision-makers is highly topical, as the world's governments negotiate new commitments under the Kyoto Protocol – the international treaty on climate change. At the same time, the world's Least Developed Countries are drawing up National Adaptation Programmes of Action (NAPAs), which set out their immediate plans for coping with climate change. Meanwhile biofuel plantations are expanding fast, with official support, and Avoided Deforestation (AD) projects may follow.

Global warming is here and is 'locked in' for decades to come, as a result of past emissions, so adaptation is vital. Adaptation means actions that reduce the actual and expected effects of climate change – a simple example is switching from one crop variety to another that copes better with a shorter rainy season.

Adaptation actually takes place at local level and people are already making the changes they can, independently of government. In the Arctic, for example, Sami reindeer herders are transporting food to the reindeer in winters when the animals cannot reach the lichen. They are also starting to reverse their traditional pattern and take their animals inland during the summer and to the coast in winter, where there is no snow and so grazing is better.

But individuals' and communities' ability to adapt is limited, for instance by lack of financial resources and technical expertise, and by the sheer scale of some of the changes that are needed. There is only so much that they can do without government backing.

For instance, the Sami want Norway's Reindeer Husbandry Act made more flexible, so that it permits new practices that they need to adopt in the face of climate change. But when *SWM* asked the government of Norway how it is helping the Sami cope, the answer we received suggests that, in terms of practical action, very little has actually happened. This is despite the fact that scientists have been

reporting rapid warming in the Arctic for years. In a statement, the Norwegian Ministry of Labour and Social Inclusion told *SWM*:

'We have conducted extensive research on the effects of climate change, and how these changes will affect societies. It is now fundamental to transform this knowledge into action. To aid in this process on a national level, we have designated a small task group within the Directorate for Civil Protection and Emergency Planning with special responsibilities to aid the adaptation process. One key task for this new group will be to aid in the process of converting scientific conclusions into useful policy advice.'

In Kenya, some pastoralists have adapted to climate change by growing livestock fodder crops in wetter areas near rivers, selling some of their livestock rather than allowing them to die during droughts, fencing off areas of rangeland to grow grass for private use or for sale, and using plastic rather than grass to cover worn out parts of huts.

But their inadequate representation in national politics has damaged their ability to cope with the increasingly harsh climate. 'It is primarily politics that explains the increasing inability of many pastoralists to cope with what the climate throws at them,' a group of international development and environment NGOs argued in a 2004 case study of pastoralists in Turkana district in north-west Kenya.[21] In *Africa Up in Smoke 2*, the authors say:

'If the Kenyan Government makes good on its promises to promote sustainable development in the arid and semi-arid lands, and also creates a national drought contingency fund, pastoralism could still, despite climate change, be not only a viable way of life but a profitable one too.'[22]

In Bangladesh, minorities were not included in consultations about the country's official plan for coping with climate change – the NAPA. Tom Tanner, research fellow at the Institute of Development Studies Climate Change and Disasters Group, helped prepare the country's NAPA. Asked whether ethnic and religious minorities were involved, he says: 'I think we can safely say that they weren't. They certainly weren't explicitly considered.' Even at a stakeholder consultation meeting held in the Chittagong, Tanner does not recall the presence of anyone representing the Chittagong Hill Tribes. He points out that developing countries are given only a limited amount of money to spend on NAPA preparation and that 'it is very difficult, in a country so big, to be totally inclusive'. Overall, however, he feels that Bangladesh could have done better.[23]

Speaking about the preparation of NAPAs more generally, he suggests that minorities will tend to be ignored, just as they are in other matters. 'Minority groups are not targeted and it's very likely that they are excluded on the same grounds that they often are from development projects and interventions, just because they are unseen,' he says.

Worse still, some climate change specialists argue that, if carried out naively, then adaptation has the potential to reinforce existing disadvantages. 'Evidence suggests that adaptation decisions and plans do not benefit all stakeholders equally,' say Adger, Mace, Paalova and Razzaque in a paper for the website:

'Rather, they often benefit those who are not particularly vulnerable and those who are well placed to take advantage of planning and regulatory processes. For example, when recovering from the impacts of weather-related hazards, the status quo in terms of wealth and access to decision making is often reinforced.... The political economy of adaptation is, in fact, directly tied to the underlying determinants and drivers of vulnerability. Adaptation to climate change can potentially heap further injustice on past injustice.' (*Our emphasis.*)[24]

Opportunities for minorities and indigenous peoples to be heard

National Adaptation Programmes of Action and national communications
Despite such warnings, the NAPAs that are being drawn up by some 50 Least Developed Countries also have the potential to benefit the most vulnerable. NAPAs provide: 'an opportunity for applying principles of equity and justice to ensure that the voices and priorities of the communities that are most vulnerable to climate change are incorporated into the UNFCCC process on adaptation.'[25]

NAPAs are being drawn up under the UN Framework Convention on Climate Change (UNFCCC) – the existing international agreement on climate change which entered into force in 1994,

and to which the Kyoto Protocol is linked. The Kyoto Protocol entered into force in 2005. It is very much in the news because governments are now negotiating a second 'commitment period', which will follow on from the current one and which runs up to 2012.

NAPAs are documents which identify countries' most urgently needed adaptation projects. By mid-September 2007, 20 countries had submitted their plans to the Secretariat of the UNFCCC, which places all completed plans on the UNFCCC website.[26]

During the development of their plans, countries are supposed to consult with local communities about how climate change is affecting them and what adaptation activities they consider most vital. As we have seen, this often does not happen in practice, but, officially, the UNFCCC secretariat says that: 'In the NAPA process, prominence is given to community-level input as an important source of information, recognizing that grassroots communities are the main stakeholders.'[27] In addition to NAPAs, the UNFCCC also requires all countries to produce 'national communications' every few years, with more complex and demanding requirements for developed countries. These communications set out what countries are doing to implement the Convention. They also state the expected impacts of climate change and what countries are doing about adaptation.

During the formation of these new domestic and international plans and standards, it is plainly vital that minorities and indigenous groups are represented. While the main obligation rests with the government to include minorities and indigenous peoples in these processes, it also presents a challenge to international and local NGOs. They will have a vital role to play, raising awareness of this new realm of policy-making at the grassroots, mobilizing support and pressurizing governments. Only by participating in these critical processes, can marginalized communities hope to have their concerns reflected and their livelihoods protected.

Climate change and human rights
Climate change is just beginning to be articulated as a human rights issue – rather than a purely development or environmental crisis. Yet the effects of global warming described above, go to the heart of minority rights, and the key issues of existence, identity, discrimination and participation. If

marginalized communities experience systemic discrimination, then they are less likely to survive the upheavals of global warming. If a minority's lifestyle is being eroded by environmental changes, then their unique culture and language are also under threat. If they cannot participate in the decisions that will affect the outcomes of global warming, then the chances are that their needs will be ignored or sidelined. These outcomes are violations of a state's obligations to minorities, under international human rights law – a fact already being utilized by some indigenous groups seeking to hold their government to account for climate change-related impacts on their communities.

The most famous attempt to use human rights law so far has been the petition submitted to the Inter-American Commission on Human Rights on behalf of the Inuit in Alaska and Canada. This was submitted by Sheila Watt-Cloutier, supported by the Inuit Circumpolar Council (ICC) against the United States in 2005. Their 175-page petition argued that the Arctic was more severely affected by climate change than any other place on earth and that the US, as the world's largest greenhouse gas emitter, bore more responsibility for this than any other nation.

It asked the Commission to recommend that the US should adopt mandatory measures to limit its greenhouse gas emissions and to cooperate with other countries to limit global emissions (the US has not so far signed the Kyoto Protocol or committed itself to emissions reductions). It also sought recommendations that the US should take into account the impact on the Arctic of all major government actions, implement a plan to protect Inuit culture and natural resources, and help the Inuit to adapt to the unavoidable effects of climate change.

One year on, in December 2006, the Commission said it could not accept the petition, but declined to give specific reasons for doing so. Nevertheless, it granted a thematic hearing in March 2007, where it heard about the issue generally, rather than about the Inuit in particular. Lawyer Donald Goldberg, who worked on the case, says it was evident from the questions at the hearing that the Commission was anxious about assigning responsibility for global warming to any one particular state – especially when the effects of global warming were cumulative, and a collective failure on the part of carbon-producing nations.

However, he also notes that the precedent-setting

nature of the case, may have contributed to the Commission's reluctance. 'They have never had a case of this magnitude before,' he told SWM. 'If they were to take it on, they would be changing human rights law [as] it could open the door to thousands of other groups.' He points out, 'If Inuit rights are violated, what about [those] in Bangladesh, [the] Ganges and Pacific Islands?' However, the door is not entirely closed on this route. The information gathered at the thematic hearing, will inform the Commission's thinking on any further cases they receive on climate change. A Commission official also told SWM that: 'It is such a new topic for the Commission that they want to go slowly and really when they make a decision they want to be very sure because it will be a precedent.' And of course, from the Inuit point of view, the publicity that accompanied the filing of their petition dramatically drew attention to their plight, even if it did not, in the short term, deliver a legal victory.

The Inuit case centred on a state's responsibility for the direct cause of climate change – namely, the warming gases emitted by carbon-polluting industries – but a submission to CERD in July 2007, challenged a state's responsibility for its policy responses to the climate change. The threat of new oil palm plantations totaling 1.8 million hectares in Kalimantan, Indonesia, prompted 12 NGOs to request action under the CERD's Urgent Action and Early Warning Procedures.[28] Their submission coincided the Geneva-based body's examination of Indonesia's compliance with the International Convention on the Elimination of Racial Discrimination.

The document drawn up by the NGOs lays out starkly the impact of the mega-project. In it, they warn that between 1 million and 1.4 million indigenous people would be affected, with some 300,000 required to move from their ancestral territories:

'They will lose their traditional means of subsistence and become wage labourers and indebted farmers working for the companies that have assumed control of their ancestral lands. In short, they will suffer irreparable harm to their basic rights and well-being, to such an extent that their survival as distinct cultural entities will be severely threatened.... It will permanently render their traditional territories unsuitable for anything but cultivation of palm oil and destroy their traditional way of life.'

They requested that, under the Urgent Action and Early Warning Procedures, the Committee should recommend a number of measures, including that Indonesia not proceed with the mega-project, that Indonesia remedy the massive and ongoing rights violations occurring in existing oil palm plantations, as well as a range of legislative and administrative measures to realize the rights of indigenous peoples. In its concluding observations, CERD did not accede to the NGOs' request to make Indonesia the subject of its Urgent Action Procedures. However, it did recommend that: '[the] State party secure the possession and ownership rights of local communities before proceeding further with this Plan'. It also said that the state should ensure that meaningful consultation with the communities should take place, with a view to obtaining their consent and participation.

While not going as far as the NGOs requested, the Committee's observations nevertheless have given the campaigners ammunition that they can use to argue their case with the government more effectively. The submission also drew valuable publicity to their opposition to the mega-project beyond Indonesia. The Inuit and the Kalimantan examples are both early instances of how human rights law, and the mechanisms for enforcing it, are likely to become increasingly important as the effects of climate change begin to bite, and the real impacts on the livelihoods of minorities and indigenous peoples are seen.

Standing up for minority rights after disasters

Although states have the primary obligation to protect, respect and fulfil the rights of minorities and indigenous peoples – other agents also have a role to play. New guidelines aimed at international relief organizations, which emphasize the need to protect the rights of minorities and indigenous peoples in the aftermath of disasters, provide a further opportunity to improve the treatment of people affected by climate change.

In June 2006, the Brookings–Bern Project on Internal Displacement published new guidelines called *Protecting Persons Affected by Natural Disasters*.[29] These have been adopted by the Inter-Agency Standing Committee, which coordinates NGOs and UN bodies doing humanitarian work.

They are informed by international human rights

law, existing standards and policies on humanitarian action and human rights guidelines relating to natural disasters. And they acknowledge that, all too often, disaster victims' human rights are neglected.

The special vulnerability of minority groups and indigenous peoples is explicitly and repeatedly recognized. For instance, paragraph B1.3 states:

'Safe and non-discriminatory access to available humanitarian assistance should be secured for all persons in need. In particular, measures should be taken to grant priority access to such vulnerable groups as minorities, single-headed households, elderly, people with disabilities, and unaccompanied and separated children.'

In a section on property and possessions, paragraph C2.7 states: 'Specific arrangements should be made to enable and facilitate recognition of claims to land ownership based on prolonged possession, in the absence of formal land titles, especially for indigenous peoples.'

While the laws and principles on which they are based are well established, the guidelines themselves are less than two years old. Yet if even the most minimal effects predicted for climate change are realized, international relief and the agencies which deliver it, are likely to become increasingly important to the survival of many minorities and indigenous people. It is vital therefore, that these guidelines are implemented in practice. A gap in the current guidelines, in fact, relates to the monitoring of their application. Although the guidelines say this should be done, they do not spell out *how* – although the document says vaguely that it would be 'essential to establish effective monitoring mechanisms, benchmarks and indicators'. Nevertheless, awareness among minority and indigenous activists of the existence of these guidelines, may lead to better, more equal treatment, as well as, over time, remind governments, UN agencies and NGOs of their obligations towards all groups, on a non-discriminatory basis.

Conclusions

It should not be surprising that minority groups and indigenous peoples are especially badly hit by climate change, that they get less help coping with its effects and that they have to fight harder to influence decisions about mitigating and adapting to climate change. Their needs, problems and voices are all too easily ignored at every stage.

The lack of research into the ways in which minorities and indigenous peoples are being affected by climate change only exacerbates their disadvantage and vulnerability. For them to get the help they need, their situation must first be documented and recognized – by academics, development and environment NGOs, governments and intergovernmental organizations.

Minorities' and indigenous peoples' own organizations can contribute to such a shift in awareness, using all the institutional, media and legal avenues open to them.

One immediate opportunity is governments' ongoing negotiation of a new commitment period under the Kyoto Protocol. This is attracting a vast amount of political, media and academic attention, and provides a good chance to start putting minority and indigenous concerns on the climate change map.

Minorities and indigenous peoples will add weight to their demands if they emphasize their role (where appropriate) as stewards of precious natural environments – notably tropical forests, which are major carbon sinks and biodiversity hotspots that benefit the entire world.

Finally, taking legal action to uphold people's human rights can only reinforce the impact of minorities' and indigenous peoples' efforts in other spheres. Even though the Inuit case against the US floundered, it won massive publicity for their arguments and, conceptually, it prepared the way for more successful actions in future. ■

Flashpoint
Pakistan in Crisis: Religious Minorities under Pressure

Kamila Hyat

To approach Rabwah, home to Pakistan's minority Ahmadi sect, it is necessary to pass through Chiniot, an ancient town said to have been first populated by Alexander the Great of Macedonia, in 326 BC.

Today, Chiniot, which stands amidst the lush green countryside of the Punjab province, is known chiefly for its skilled furniture craftsmen. The town is a bustling, but run-down urban centre – the cascading monsoon rain failing to wash away the grime and squalor that hangs all around.

It is on the peeling, yellow-plastered walls of Chiniot that the first signs of the hatred directed against the Ahmadi community appear. The movement – named for its founder, Mirza Ghulam Ahmad of Qadian (located in the Indian Punjab) – broke away from mainstream Islam in 1889. The slogans, etched out in the flowing Urdu script, call on Muslims to 'Kill Ahmadi non-believers'.

Rabwah, a town of some 50,000 people, houses the largest concentration of Ahmadis in Pakistan. Overall, there are an estimated 1.5 million Ahmadis in the country amongst a population of 55 million people. Rabwah was built on 1,000 acres of land purchased from the Pakistan government in 1948 by the Ahmaddiya Muslim community, to house Ahmadis who were forced to leave India amidst the tumultuous partition of the subcontinent in 1947, which resulted in the creation of the mainly Muslim state of Pakistan. Today the country is an Islamic Republic with Islam as its state religion.

While theological opposition to the Ahmadi school of thought, and its offshoot, the Lahore Ahmaddiya Movement, created in 1914, has existed for over a century, and centres on its founder's claims to be a messiah, it was in 1974 that the community's difficulties began in earnest. At the time, Prime Minister Zulfikar Ali Bhutto, caving in to pressure from orthodox Islamist forces, declared the group 'constitutionally non-Muslim', effectively making them, as per law, a minority in Pakistan where over 95 per cent of the population is Muslim.

'It was absurd; a government deciding on the faith of people. The problems created by that decision have lingered on,' said Qamar Suleiman, the articulate media spokesperson for the Central Ahmaddiya Organization at Rabwah. The well-maintained office is surrounded by greenery – all planted after Ahmadis moved onto the previously barren stretch of land in 1948. Incongruously, amidst the oasis-like setting, it soon becomes

apparent every official building is heavily fortified – even the holy places and the parks – testifying to the fact that Rabwah remains a town under siege.

While the 1974 decision against Ahmadis was met by anger within the community, worse was to come. In 1984, military dictator General Zia ul-Haq, as part of policies aimed at 'Islamizing' the country, introduced a set of laws that, among other restrictions, barred Ahmadis from preaching their faith, calling their places of worship 'masjids' (the term used by mainstream Muslims) and from calling themselves Muslim. The situation was aggravated by the toughening of anti-blasphemy laws in 1986, with section 295-C introducing the death penalty for 'defiling' the name of the Prophet Muhammad. A term of life imprisonment for defiling the Qur'an, the book believed by Muslims to be of divine origin, was already in place.

Victimization of Ahmadis

Since then, hundreds have fallen victim to these laws. They are most often misused by accusing a person of defiling the Qur'an or uttering words against the Prophet Muhammad, often to settle a petty dispute over business, property or a personal matter. Orthodox clerics typically jump swiftly into the fray, with police, more often than not, immediately arresting the accused person. Non-Muslims remain most vulnerable to such accusations, though they have increasingly been used against Muslims as well.

Among the victims of the blasphemy laws is Mansoor Ahmed, 35, an Ahmadi who has recently come to live in Rabwah after being in prison for two and a half years. In 2004, he was accused of blasphemy.

'I was caretaker of an Ahmadi masjid in the town of Hafizabad in the Punjab. While cleaning the area, I burnt some old magazines lying there. I was accused by a rival sect of setting the Holy Qur'an on fire,' said Mansoor.

What followed was sheer hell. Mansoor, facing a life term, was jailed. He says that he was beaten, abused and for many months held in small 'punishment cells', into which no light filtered and where prisoners were held in isolation.

'Jail officials said this was to protect me from other prisoners, who would beat me up, since I was accused of blasphemy,' said Mansoor.

Today, finally freed on bail, he is still recovering from his ordeal and trying to rebuild his life, as is his wife, Kausar Perveen, and their three children aged 13, 12 and 9 years.

'We suffered terribly when Mansoor was in jail. In Hafizabad neighbours taunted us, and teachers victimized my children,' said Kausar. She adds, 'My youngest daughter, Qamar Nisar, still wakes up screaming because of the nightmares she has.'

Mansoor however is among the more fortunate. Others have been beaten, maimed or killed because of their belief.

According to the Central Ahmaddiya Organization, in April 2007, in a village in Kasur district in the Punjab, an elderly Ahmadi, Chaudhry Habibullah Sial, 82, was found strangled, his arms and legs bound together. Ahmadi groups stated his home had been used regularly as a prayer centre by Ahmadis and alleged he had been killed by local extremists. The incident is not an isolated one. The Human Rights Commission of Pakistan (HRCP) reported that in 2006, three Ahmadis were killed and at least four others escaped attempts on their lives.

Over the past two decades, according to records maintained by HRCP, an autonomous rights monitoring body, hundreds of Ahmadis have been murdered, assaulted or intimidated. Graveyards and holy places belonging to the community have been attacked and Ahmadis denied jobs, education or promotion on the basis of their faith.

Ahmadis face 'worst discrimination'

'The Ahmadis, among Pakistan's minority communities, face the worst discrimination,' said I.A. Rehman, director of the HRCP.

The situation for Ahmadis is aggravated by the official attitude to their problems. In April 2007, attempts by Ahmadis in Lahore to fence a piece of land they had bought to build a graveyard, were violently stopped by local orthodox clerics. Police claimed they could 'do nothing'. Similar incidents are reported each year.

Indeed, in 1999, Rabwah was re-named 'Chenabnagar' by the Punjab government, against the will of the community. Community leaders say that the neglect of the infrastructure in the town is due to 'official indifference' – and the fact that Ahmadis have no representation on local government councils.

Ahmadis have not voted in any election in Pakistan since 1985, when they were asked to enrol as non-Muslims under a system introduced by General Zia, in which people of various religious beliefs voted only for candidates sharing the same faith. In this system of 'separate electorates', a set number of seats in assemblies were to be filled only by non-Muslim voters, effectively ousting minorities from the political mainstream. Separate voting lists were created on the basis of belief. When the joint electorate, in which all adult citizens voted collectively, was restored in 2002 by the government of President Pervez Musharraf, Ahmadis were optimistic they would now be able to take part in polls again. However, under pressure from orthodox religious groups, the government capitulated – and within months went back on its decision to retain a single voting list for all eligible citizens. Instead, a 'non-Muslim' list was reintroduced for Ahmadis, while all other groups remained on a combined list. Today, an affidavit as to religious belief must be signed by all Muslim voters – a measure to filter out Ahmadis.

'Because we refuse to vote as non-Muslims, we are the only community in Pakistan that is disenfranchised,' said Captain (retd) Shamim Khalid, who runs the human rights desk for the Ahmaddiya Movement.

'We have no voice,' said Abdul Qadeer Qamar, 35, a resident of Rabwah. He too has faced prison and years of litigation for preaching his faith.

Those who do have a voice are the fanatically anti-Ahmadi groups, including the Khatm-e-Nabuwat (Finality of Prophethood) Movement headquartered in Chiniot. These organizations are permitted each year, by the district authorities, to hold a meeting in Rabwah – where the population

consists almost exclusively of Ahmadis. In contrast,
Ahmadis themselves are not allowed to organize
gatherings, within the town or elsewhere.

'We are forced to listen to the hatred these clerics
belch out. The cries to kill Ahmadis ring out across
this town each year,' said Qamar.

He also pointed out that while 'Ordinary
Pakistanis are not against Ahmadis and live
peacefully with them in many towns and villages,' it
is the fanatical groups who carry on, and try their
best to expand, the campaign of hatred against them.

Growing intolerance towards minorities

While the Ahmadis face the harshest discrimination,
under laws directed specifically against them, other
minority communities in Pakistan have also been
victims of increasing intolerance over recent decades.
Historically speaking, Pakistan, which until 1947
included a Hindu and Sikh population of at least 15
per cent, underwent a kind of ethnic cleansing when
the Indian subcontinent was divided at the end of
British colonial rule. The sectarian tensions that
broke out in the run-up to the creation of Pakistan, a
separate country demanded by India's Muslims, saw a
series of massacres. Most Hindus and Sikhs fled over
the new border to India, while tens of thousands of
Muslims moved in the opposite direction.

Yet, despite this wave of hatred, in many parts of
Pakistan – which today comprises a Muslim
population of over 95 percent, with Christians,
Hindus and Ahmadis making up most of the rest –
communities continued to live harmoniously
together. This was particularly true in Sindh, which
has significant Hindu populations, and in the Punjab,
where there are scattered pockets of Christians.

'Islamization' policies

Much of this changed under the harsh,
'Islamization' policies introduced by Zia ul-Haq in
the 1980s. The content of schoolroom curriculums
was altered, reflecting the new, hard-line tone of
government. Dr A.H. Nayyar and Ahmad Saleem,
the authors of a much quoted 2003 report, titled
*The Subtle Subversion: A Report on Curricula and
Textbooks in Pakistan*, released by the Sustainable
Policy Development Institute (SPDI) in Islamabad,

found that, among other issues, textbooks
promoted 'insensitivity to religious diversity' and
encouraged bigotry.

Madrassahs (seminary schools) began to spring up
across the country. According to Arnaud de
Borchgrave, director of the Transnational Threats
Initiative at the Washington-based Center for
Strategic and International Studies, most of these are
funded from Saudi Arabia and number at least
10,000. Other estimates suggest the seminaries, the
growth of which has been encouraged by the sharp
decline since the 1970s of Pakistan's public sector
school system, could number twice or even three
times as many. In 1947, the year Pakistan appeared
on the map of the world, there were only a few
hundred seminaries in the country.

Since the 1980s, hard-line factions within
Islam, including the Salafis and the Deobandis,
have also opened up many madrassahs. This has
introduced a new dimension to religion in a part
of the world where Islam, influenced over the
centuries by its close contact with other religions
in the Indian subcontinent, traditionally followed
a tolerant path incorporating much from a shared
past with other faiths. Today, the Salafi and
Deobandi seminaries are believed to be the most
proactive in preaching militancy.

'In the schools, children are taught that Muslims
are good, and those of other faiths bad,' said
Amarnath Motumal, a lawyer and President of the
Hindu Panchayat (Gathering), Karachi division.

He believes the biggest problem Hindus suffer
today is that of forced conversion. 'We have on

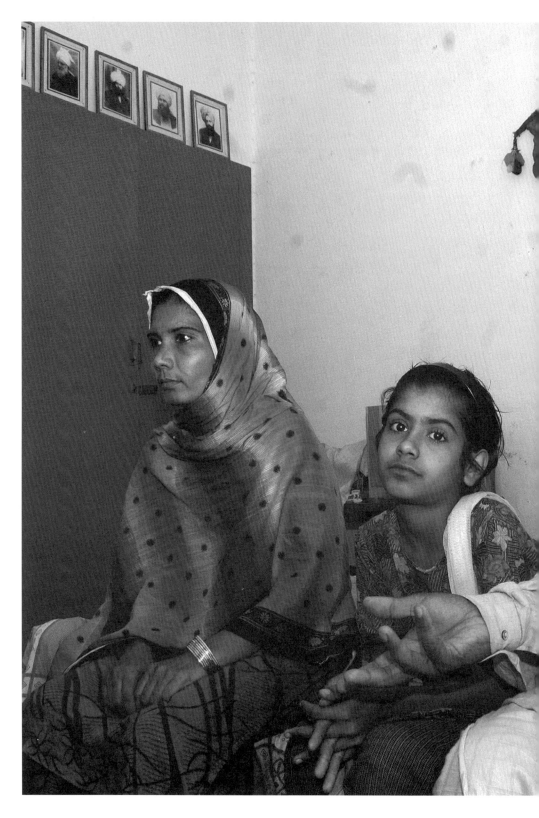

average 70–80 cases each year of Hindu girls, aged under 18, being lured away, and coerced into converting to Islam,' he said.

One such girl was Deepa, 17, the daughter of Besham Das, allegedly taken away in December 2006 from the town of Islamkot in Tharparkar, Sindh. Das said his daughter had been 'kidnapped by her tutor, Ashraf Khaskheli, a Muslim'. Ayub Jan Sarhandi, who runs a seminary in the area and sheltered Deepa and Ashraf, was quoted by the Press at the time of the incident as saying that she 'married of her free will and accepted Islam'.

Hindu community leaders, such as Motumal, point out that 'when girls who are minors are taken away, authorities should intervene'. He also says that due to the 'pressure of extremists', the 2.5 million or so Hindus living in Pakistan are 'unable to play any prominent role'.

There are at least as many Christians in Pakistan as Hindus. Historically, while they have suffered acute social and economic discrimination, often relegated to the lowest-earning jobs in society, violent attacks have been relatively rare.

Impact of 9/11

This changed quite dramatically following the events of 11 September 2001. As the Muslim world found itself plunged into conflict with the West in the aftermath of the deadly terrorist attacks in New York, Christians in Pakistan were unexpectedly cast as villains and labelled as allies of leaders in powerful world capitals such as Washington or London. Through 2002, as the global conflict accelerated, attacks were staged on the consulates of Western governments, churches, Christian-run organizations and on foreign visitors. At least 36 Christians were killed. Suddenly, as a result of events quite beyond its control, the Christian community found itself in the sights of militants' guns.

Though this terrifying surge of hatred has partially receded, violent attacks on Christians still occur. The site of one such outbreak was the innocuous looking town of Sangla Hill, located around an hour's drive from Lahore, and named for the isolated hillock that looms over it.

Sangla Hill attacks on Christians

In November 2005, the town , with a population of around 10,000, hit world headlines after a mob set ablaze three churches, a missionary school and several Christian homes. The violence was triggered by the accusation that a Christian man, Yousaf Masih, had committed blasphemy. As a frenzied mob of around 2,000 Muslims rampaged through the streets, the town's 1,000 or so Christians cowered in terror within their homes. The Punjab government ordered an inquiry and the HRCP blamed police for failing to prevent the violence.

In the weeks that followed, peace was restored, blasphemy charges – apparently motivated by a gambling dispute – dropped and the damaged churches rebuilt. But the wounds remain. Perhaps they will never heal.

It is Sunday in Sangla Hill and small groups of Christians, dressed in their best *shalwar kameez* (tunic and pants worn throughout Pakistan) or pressed suits, walk to church in the warm, late September sunshine – some attend Roman Catholic services, others go to the large Presbyterian church. The children laugh and play, kicking a stray pebble along the dusty road, ignoring rebukes from their mothers, until, on reaching the church compound, they fall into a respectful silence and file quietly into the building.

But beneath the calm façade, there is fear. 'Pakistan is too dangerous for us Christians. When I grow up, I will shift to Australia and take my mother as well,' says Dilawar Masih, aged 10, one of the children in the church. He can recall vividly the terror of that day two years ago when frenzied men banged on the doors of Christian homes.

Misapplication of laws and forced conversions

Dilawar's talk of moving overseas is rooted in reality. Thousands of non-Muslims moved away in the 1980s, at the height of the Islamist zeal inspired by General Zia ul-Haq. Under the relatively more liberal regime of President Musharraf, there have been some concessions to minorities, including the restoration of the joint electorate and an administrative change introduced in the blasphemy law in 2004, intended to make it harder to press criminal charges.

But leaders of the Christian community, such as Joseph Francis, National Director of the Centre for Legal Aid, Assistance and Settlement (CLAAS), a non-governmental organization (NGO) which works for the rights of minorities, maintain that things are no better.

'More Christians have been killed and more blasphemy cases registered against them under Musharraf than ever before,' Francis asserted. In July 2005, the Pakistani Catholic bishops' Justice and Peace Commission reported that, since 1998, some 650 people had been falsely accused and arrested under the blasphemy law. Francis also identified forced conversion as a major problem for Christians: 'At least 10 cases have been reported this year alone. Many others go unreported.'

Two of the most recent incidents took place in the giant, textile manufacturing centre of Faisalabad, the second largest city in the Punjab province. On 5 August 2007, an 11-year-old Christian girl, Zunaira, was kidnapped, allegedly by a Muslim man, Muhammad Adnan, who was helped by his sister. The child was reported to have been forcibly converted to Islam and made to marry her kidnapper.

In an interview with Asia News Network, a Bangkok-based online publication, her mother, Abida, alleged that police refused to help. Just 10 days later in the same city, another Christian girl, Shumaila Tabussam, 16, was allegedly lured away by a Muslim man identified as Mazher. Her father, Salamat Masih, who immediately reported the abduction to police, stated he believed his daughter had been kidnapped and forcibly converted.

Christians also face other risks. In May 2007, Walter Fazal Khan, 79, a wealthy car salesman in Lahore, the Punjab's capital city, was accused of blasphemy by an employee, Raja Riaz. Walter was jailed for over a week, but subsequently bailed by the sessions court, which found no evidence against him. Investigations suggested the charges had been brought in an attempt to seize valuable property.

Work and educational progress impeded

Christians also face entrenched discrimination that holds up their ability to access better jobs and better education. Francis traces this discrimination back to 1965, when Pakistan went to war with its neighbour, India. 'At the time, there were many Christians who were accused of being Indian agents, and that approach continued into the post-war days,' he said.

Such attitudes have been key factors in the fate of Pakistan's religious minorities. Apart from Ahmadis,

Christians and Hindus, these include small populations of Sikhs, Parsis (Zoroastrians), Buddhists and Baha'is – a breakaway faction from Islam with roots in Iran – each of which numbers around 20,000 to 30,000. In most cases, they have stayed out of the spotlight by consciously assuming a low profile. Despite this, there have been incidents of violence. In September 2004, the Gurudwara Janam Asthan in Nankana Sahib close to Lahore, one of the holiest Sikh temples in the region, was attacked by an angry mob and at least two Sikhs injured. The rioters were protesting a move to hand over a government-run college to the Sikh community to house pilgrims. A number of arrests were made and the unrest faded away.

Campaigners for minority rights

While growing intolerance and discriminatory laws have worked greatly to the disadvantage of Pakistan's religious minorities, there are also brave campaigners who have spoken up for them. Indeed, in their efforts, these activists often cite Mohammad Ali Jinnah, the man known as the founder of Pakistan and the country's first Governor General. Until his death in 1948, only a year after the birth of Pakistan, Jinnah, a man who held liberal, secular views, consistently called for all citizens to be treated equally, regardless of belief.

As the tide of obscurantism began to close in around Pakistan in the decades after the 1970s, other activists have taken up the same plea. They include the late Justice (retd) Dorab Patel, one of Pakistan's most respected jurists. A Zoroastrian by birth, Patel led the battle against intolerance during the Zia years – a period that marked Pakistan's descent into the abyss of religious extremism that has today emerged as among its most critical problems.

More recently, leading lawyer and chairperson of the HRCP, Asma Jahangir, also the UN Special Rapporteur on Freedom of Religion or Belief, has spearheaded the struggle. She has faced death threats and a constant barrage of criticism from orthodox elements for taking on cases of those accused under blasphemy laws or insisting that the state not favour a particular religious faith. Indeed, Asma Jahangir, with her reputation for bold dissent, was one of the first persons to be detained at her home when a state of emergency rule was declared in Pakistan on 3 November 2007 by President Musharraf, and many basic rights suspended.

State discrimination

Prominent members of non-Muslim communities remain immensely angry and dissatisfied with the structure of this state. 'The thing about the political system in Pakistan is that, as a non-Muslim, I cannot contest the poll for president. I am barred from doing so by law,' said Joseph Francis of CLAAS.

The situation in Pakistan has attracted consistent international concern. The US State Department, in its *International Religious Freedom Report* for 2007, released in September, noted that while the government took 'some steps' to improve its treatment of religious minorities over the past year, 'serious problems remained'.

The political uncertainty that has persisted in Pakistan since November 2007, with all the major political players caught up in the turmoil, of course makes it more unlikely that sufficient attention will be given to such concerns.

Other organizations have taken a tougher line. Also in September 2007, the UN's International Convention on Elimination of Racial Discrimination (ICERD) secretariat asked Pakistan to submit by 31 December reports on efforts to purge its society of racial discrimination, which have been pending since 1998. ICERD warned that a further failure to hand them in could lead to 'necessary' action – since, as an ICERD signatory, the country is bound to submit biannual reports.

But, for non-Muslims, who face day-to-day hostility from the society within which they live, this means little. 'Today, my son, aged 6, was told by a teacher he would burn in hell because we are Christian. I do not know how to comfort him,' said Bertha Jones, 34, a nurse. She scoffs at the talk of reform in Pakistan, saying bleakly, 'For us, the only reality is constant fear and constant pain. This is the reality I know, that my children know, and I very much fear that it will be all that the generations that come after us will know – if, at all, they are allowed to live in this country we call our home.' ▪

Trouble in Paradise Tourism and Minorities: A Kenya Case Study

Lucy Hannan

Tourism is promoted worldwide as a key to development. It often constitutes one of the main foreign exchange earners in developing economies, and is routinely perceived as an important provider of employment and business opportunities for indigenous communities. In Kenya, for example, indirect and direct revenues from wildlife-related tourism alone have been estimated at 10 per cent of GDP. Its world-famous parks and coastline are among the top holiday destinations worldwide. Tourism creates jobs, and provides markets for suppliers of goods and services, most of which are domestic. It provides revenue to the state in the form of tax and visa fees, as well as other forms of income from land rent, rates and concession payments.

Economic measurements alone would confirm that tourism is beneficial; but economic activity and growth do not indicate development. In developing countries, goals include aspirations to social welfare, social justice and equitable use of natural resources, as well as a commitment, enshrined in international treaties, to protecting the human rights of all those affected by the development process.

Yet the tourist industry all too often leads to land loss, destruction of traditional livelihoods, impoverishment of indigenous communities and violations of human rights. Although 'promoting' local culture has become a standard aspect of tourism in developing countries – through local dances, artifacts and general 'showcasing' – the impact on traditional culture is in reality often detrimental.

But tourism is not without accountability. Trends in international opinion have influenced the tourist trade to be increasingly sensitive to the environment, which has encouraged 'high end' tourism to demand certain standards. Worldwide, the ecotourism concept aims at a healthy and mutually beneficial relationship between the tourist and the environment. More recently, this is supposed to include a beneficial and harmonious relationship between the tourist and the local community. But emphasis at present is more on the community as an *extension* of the environment – meaning how the local community functions within and contributes to the local environment – than as an informed concern for the rights of the indigenous communities themselves.

Attempts have been made to bridge the gap through programmes of 'community participation' as part of an ethical ecotourism movement. But documentation widely available showing the impact of tourism on minority groups demonstrates the industry has a long way to go. Tokenism is rife. Participation is desultory. In this chapter we will explore these issues through the lens of the Kenyan experience. But in fact, much of what is written here is equally relevant to minorities affected by tourism around the world.

The Kenyan coast

Take *The Voyager*, a ship which has everything necessary for a luxury holiday on the Kenyan coast – restaurants, discos, massage parlours and hairdressers, dancers, gift shops and every imaginable entertainment under the sun – but it's not at sea. It's in the middle of Mombasa, surrounded by shacks and traffic, where tour buses battle for space with men pushing hand-carts on the pot-holed roads. *The Voyager*, a themed hotel offering the all-inclusive tourist package *par excellence*, is seen by indigenous coastal communities as a typical example of Kenya's inaccessible tourist industry.

'Tourists don't even step outside the hotel,' laments Isembwa, who sells paintings and curios in a small local market. Isembwa is a member of one of Kenya's coastal minorities, the Giriama, one of the largest of the nine ethnic groups that make up the Mikikenda, who occupy the Kenyan coastal strip. The Giriama, who have their own Bantu language dialect and distinctive cultural practices, are primarily subsistence farmers and fishermen.

'We live in different worlds.'

Traders like Isembwa say small businesses are being starved by the trend in package holidays, where earnings are monopolized by hotels. Hotel representatives counter that a fair quota of local workers from the area are employed inside the hotels, creating jobs in catering and service industries – but coastal communities point out these are typically poorly paid, low-grade jobs, without access to decision-making positions.

'Tourism itself is not bad, but it needs to be managed in a different way. If you are part of it, you support it; but when it is like an enemy, you start to fight it,' says Isembwa.

The traditional lifestyle of minority communities on the coast has been changed significantly by the growth of tourism and the legacy of colonial land policies. Isembwa's father used to be a fisherman, and the family owned a small market garden with coconut, mango and lemon trees. Much of the family land had already been lost when colonial agreements with chiefs turned many local communities into squatters on their own land. Individual notions of ownership were introduced, which discriminated against indigenous communities whose social and economic systems were communally based. The notion of private, individual ownership was imported into Kenyan legislation at independence, making later claims to ancestral land legally vague and unenforceable. Tourism has fed off this exploitation: community land was vulnerable to being seized by officials and wealthy individuals and sold on to developers. Large swathes of beach and coastal land became privatized.

As hotels and holiday sites multiplied on the coastline, access to traditional fishing grounds became restricted. Isembwa said he was encouraged by his father to leave school and reap the benefits of tourism through petty trade and small business. It was good at first, he said, when there was plenty of access to foreign visitors.

But then trade around the hotels and on the beach became more strictly regulated, to control harassment of tourists. Tourists are now actively dissuaded from going out of the hotels and encouraged to buy either from the hotels, or from selected merchants confined to areas of hotel-owned beach. This has increased the revenue of hotels and boosted coastal tourism, but impoverished indigenous communities who are already relatively disadvantaged compared with other Kenyan groups, says Ole Taiko Lemayian, executive director of Kenya Community-Based Tourism (KECOBAT) network, which promotes community participation in the tourist industry. Statistics that show that the poorest, most underdeveloped communities are frequently in areas where tourist revenue is highest – like the coastal towns of Kilifi, Kwale and Malindi. In Kenya, official statistics demonstrate that poverty has increased in recent years, with some 70 per cent of the population below the poverty line, while tourist earnings have expanded by 14.9 per cent to 56.2 billion Kenyan shillings (KS) in 2006, which accounts for more than 10 per cent of Kenya's GDP.

Dispossessed
Uncontrolled development of the coast has dispossessed indigenous communities of much of their ancestral land.

Hamisi Omari, from the Digo community in Kwale, lost his ancestral land in what has become a prime tourist spot on the coastal strip north of Mombasa. His family cultivated sesame seed and cotton after Digo land was divided up between European settlers in 1914. The community was allowed to remain as squatters, continuing to plant and fish along the coast. The Digo are part of the greater Mikikenda Bantu group, and are a distinct linguistic and ethnic group on the Kenyan–Tanzania coastline, estimated at about 300,000 people. They suffered the same fate as the Giriama under the colonial government and lost ancestral land when land rights became based on individual ownership. As squatters, the Digo remained on their ancestral land, but without any legal entitlement or ownership.

Then a survey in the area carried out by the independent government in 1970s allocated 960 acres to build the Diani Beach Complex, offering 600 Kenyan shillings (now about US $9) per acre as compensation to those residing on the land. Many refused, including Hamisi, but people were violently evicted by armed police. Hamisi was arrested and jailed for trespass.

In a ruling by Kwale District Magistrate's Court on 11 September 1978 Hamasi and others were released after they testified it was their ancestral land. They said they had planted lemon and mango trees, and farmed and lived on the land for generations without being challenged. The court dismissed the case on the grounds there was not sufficient evidence that the land belonged to someone else.

But Hamisi was never able to return to his home. His case demonstrates how difficult it is for non-dominant minorities – lacking education, resources and political influence – to seek justice through official and legal channels.

Holiday apartments, hotels and a shopping complex now stand where his lemon trees used to grow. Hamisi has diligently pursued his case over two decades through letters and appeals to police and government officials, copies of which were given to MRG. On 12 September 2007 he received a letter from the District Commissioner, Kwale, which said: 'your ancestral claim over this land is in order [but] it is your burden to legally prove legitimacy of the claim [and] demonstrate your ancestral rights over that specific land'. Since the eviction, Hamasi's land has been sold on, and now belongs to the current

Trouble in Paradise

owner through 'outright purchase through a valid process', said the letter.

He has been told by officials and lawyers there are no records in Kenya of the original agreement with the colonial government. 'Historical injustices' like this warrant a special section in the country's Draft Land policy, which calls for attention to 'land grievances which stretch back to colonial land polices and laws that resulted in mass disinheritance of communities of their land'.

Land and loss

In the Kenya Draft National Lands Policy, the coast is described as 'potentially explosive' in its widespread land exploitation. 'The abuse of [the] Land Titles Act has had a great negative impact on coastal land leading to the area having the largest single concentration of landless indigenous people.'

Kenya has not had a clear land policy since independence, and land is administered haphazardly under a mix of British, Indian and customary law, rural and urban. Colonial laws and legacies still shape the policies, laws and institutions charged with the management of public land in Kenya; and, in principle, the president enjoys similar powers over land to those held by the colonial governor when the country was a colony. Through the Government Lands Act, the president may make grants of public land to individuals and corporate entities – powers that have been taken advantage of by successive governments, resulting in a highly exploitative and undemocratic use of land.

There has been a pressing need for reform and, in 2007, the government published the Draft National Land Policy, aimed at overhauling the existing piecemeal structure and identifying key areas for reform. The document was the outcome of a long consultation, which has been linked to a constitutional review process, and it will need parliamentary approval, and legislative and possibly constitutional changes, if it is to be implemented. These might be hard to attain if the political elite perceive the policy's measures to go against their own vested interests. However, there are strong reasons why Kenya's minorities should be pressing for its implementation: in particular, because it explicitly recognizes the rights of minorities regarding communal, farm and individual land ownership. Moreover, it also acknowledges the long-standing difficulties created by tourism and conservation – both on the coast and in the displacement and impoverishment of pastoralist communities through the creation of national reserves. For many minorities, the establishment of the latter has had a severe effect on their culture and economic existence.

National reserves: 'conservation refugees'

Pastoralist communities in Kenya like the Borana, Masai and Somalis have been among those most affected by the creation of national parks. National parks have been carved out of areas typically occupied by pastoralists, who graze free-range livestock on swathes of dry land important for both conservation and tourism. Fenced-off areas and animal corridors have put pressure on indigenous communities by reducing access to water and the size of areas available for grazing and firewood collection. Domestic animals found in game parks are impounded and fines imposed. Problems of 'illegal grazing' are especially acute during periods of stress and drought, when livestock are more likely to be taken into the park in desperation.

The Report of the Special Rapporteur on Indigenous Rights said of the situation in Kenya in 2006 that:

'Most of the human rights violations experienced by pastoralists and hunter-gatherers are related to their access to and control over land and natural resources…. Historical injustices derived from colonial times, linked to conflicting laws and lack of clear policies, mismanagement and land-grabbing, have led to the present crisis of the country's land tenure system.'

The colonial authorities and European settlers seized agriculturally rich lands, displacing the original owners to 'native reserves' or leaving them as squatters on their own land, i.e. without ownership rights. Most of the worst land-related abuses after independence took place in former native reserves and Trust Land, which were administered by the county councils on behalf of communities.

The growth of the tourist industry has made this worse, the Special Rapporteur's report says, as the 'establishment of natural areas has created additional problems for these communities … local indigenous communities do not participate in the management of the parks and reserves and do not benefit from the revenue'.

Some minorities, like the Masai, have as a consequence been evicted from large areas of ancestral land. Their grazing areas were split by the Kenya–Tanzania border, and an estimated one-third of their territory was lost through coercive treaties – for which they received no compensation. In Masai Mara, private tourist resorts and lodges have resulted in territory being fenced off, with loss of critical water sources and grazing areas.

Without access to these areas, periods of hardship mean that indigenous communities are more likely to resort to small-scale killing of game, like antelope. 'And why not, when an antelope can feed your family for three days?' said a local warden from one of the conservancies.

Consequently, game parks, designed to operate as

a protective exclusion zone, have effectively *provoked* survival poaching among minorities who have been deprived of their traditional livelihoods. Small-scale killing of game for survival and traditional purposes is very different from organized poaching for profit, and is one of the critical considerations in motivating indigenous communities to establish sustainable conservation.

The counter-productive nature of exclusion of indigenous communities is underlined by Professor Michael Cernea in his paper 'National parks and poverty risks: is population resettlement the solution?' He says the creation of national parks has inflicted systems of impoverishment on minority communities, and forced many to adapt or abandon their traditional livelihoods and economic systems,

pastoralist lifestyle to small-scale farming find they have to spend time and money guarding their crops from wild animals. The vast majority of people living on the boundaries of a national park or in a conservancy interviewed by MRG complained they faced delay or negligence when they attempted to get attention from the Kenya Wildlife Service (KWS) after animals had invaded homes and gardens, or had attacked members of the community.

'If an animal gets killed, helicopters and vehicles appear immediately. If a person gets injured or killed, it takes days to get a response,' confirmed one park warden.

If gaining adequate compensation for the loss of a life is hard in Kenya, it is even more difficult to seek restitution for a people's loss of their traditional land. However, the Endorois community, evicted from their ancestral land round Lake Bogoria in the Rift Valley is attempting to do just that. Under colonial legislation, the Endorois land was asserted to be 'vacant' or 'ownerless'. 'Native areas' with ethnic boundaries were held as a title by the Native Lands Trust Board in London. Kenya imported this notion of property law. At independence, it substituted county councils for the Native Lands Trust Board, making Baringo County Council trustees of the Endorois land. The county council was able to use constitutional powers to deprive the indigenous community of their land for the purposes of establishing a national park.

As a result, the Endorois – a distinct pastoralist minority – have been evicted and impoverished, cut off from access to vital grazing lands. Lack of access to the lake has serious cultural consequences for the community, who link many of their ancestral beliefs and social rituals to the lake. They face further displacement by mineral mining. The Endorois first sought legal redress under domestic law. However, the High Court of Kenya in Nakuru ruled in 2002 that all the necessary provisions of the law had been adhered to when the land was set aside as a game reserve. Attempts to appeal met with various obstacles, so the community has taken its case to the African Commission on Human and People's Rights in the Gambia. Among other

creating 'conservation refugees'. Cernea points out that the expansion of national parks and protected habitats has often been accompanied by a *decline* in wildlife as a result of human exclusion: because displacement from national parks can alienate indigenous communities from conservation objectives, and because eviction of resident minority communities has the effect of removing 'the customary protector'.

Indigenous peoples often perceive that, when it comes to tourism, wildlife is valued more than human life. In Kenya, this is literally the case. Wildlife that attracts tourists also injures and kills local inhabitants and their livestock. Indigenous communities take up the costs but don't get the benefits. People who try to adapt their restricted things, the Endorois are arguing that indigenous peoples have a right to property in their ancestral lands – including collective ownership of such lands – and the mass eviction of a people, without adequate consultation or compensation, is a violation of the Charter.

The Commission's ruling will be important – partly because the Endorois' experience has been replicated across the continent. For example, in Uganda in 2007, the plight of the pastoralist Basongora people came to public attention. Historically, their land was in the area of the Queen Elizabeth National Park, but they were pushed out after the reserve was created. Attempts to re-occupy it this year were initially met with force by the wildlife authorities. The government said that domesticated animals were bringing disease to the wild animals and that tourists wanted to see wildlife, not cows, in the national park. Similar cases have been reported in Botswana, Ethiopia and Namibia.

Community-based tourism

Under international human rights law, the right of participation is extremely important (see pp. 41–3) in establishing the legitimacy of a state's actions, with regard to its treatment of minorities. However, outside the legal realm, the idea of community participation is also gaining ground as a component of ecotourism. Trends in international opinion have influenced the tourist trade, making it increasingly sensitive to the environment, and this concept is increasingly being stretched to embrace the idea of community involvement. For example, Skal International – the largest association for travel and tourism professionals – makes an annual award for ecotourism, based on criteria which indicate the 'conservation of nature and cultural heritage, community involvement, educational features, business viability and innovation'. Prestigious international awards like this have forced tour operators to address these issues; it promotes business, enabling tour operators to charge a premium for these specialist services.

However, the benefits are not simply on the side of the tour operator. Involving indigenous groups in the management and benefits of a conservation and tourist strategy is likely to improve its sustainability, activists argue. Noah Sitati, a conservation expert on the Mara ecosystem, believes that community-based tourism plays a positive role in development if

managed effectively and sensitively, and directly contributes to reducing people–animal conflict.

'The best way we can stop conflict is by encouraging these areas to become ecotourism destinations, where the community gets direct benefits.' Ecotourism returns 'could be very high if money is used properly', says Sitati. It needs to go hand in hand with development to motivate those living in and around the conservation areas. The Masai were actually 'natural conservers' of their own environment, points out Sitati. Traditionally they co-habited successfully with wildlife, and hunting was limited, confined to some specific clans or rituals.

What is effective participation?

The question is, what is effective community participation? And who is the community? 'We have to ask, who is benefiting? What does "community" mean? Who says this is "good practice"?' says Taiko Lemayian of KECOBAT regarding ecotourism schemes to improve participation.

The intrinsic assumption of community-based participation is that decisions have been made freely and fairly regarding consent over use and management of land and resources, and of revenues and benefits. However, involving 'the community' is not always what it seems; decision-making is often left to a handful of elders, and women and the youth may be traditionally excluded from active participation. The difficulties with establishing a fair and equitable community participation model are highlighted in the management of one of the world's most famous safari parks – Masai Mara.

Masai Mara: poor returns

Some 350 km north-west of Mombasa, the road to the Masai Mara runs through wilderness of magnetic beauty. Rutted and almost impassable, the road is one of the worst in Kenya. Yet this is the route to one of the most productive areas of tourist revenue, and home to one of the most romanticized and marketed cultures on the continent.

The image of the willowy frame of the Masai man wrapped in a red *shuka* cloak and silhouetted with his cattle against the orange sunset, is sold from one end of the country to the other. Difficult sometimes to separate fact from fantasy: the Masai have capitalized on marketing their tradition, but have enjoyed very few modern benefits in return. Although consisting of only about 2 per cent of the total population, the Masai are probably the best-known ethnic group outside Kenya and have fiercely held on to much of their traditional culture. The absence of basic development is 'their greatest asset and their greatest curse', says Tiamaren Ole Riamit, a local human rights activist, who lives in the unattractive bustle and grime of the Masai town of Narok, seat of the district administration and local services. The nearest town to the national park, it has the highest rate of illiteracy in the area.

The Mara ecosystem is famous for its wildebeest and lions and there are over 60 lodges and camps within the reserve, and seven lodges inside the game park itself. Most of the tourist revenue is generated from inside the park, but there are also eight community-held, county council-funded, group ranches surrounding the park. Community-held ranches were established early 1990s when the government, with the support of the World Bank, attempted to address the rampant corruption and exploitation by county councils. Of the revenue from the park, 19 per cent goes back to the community through the county council, divided equally between the eight group ranches; committees in the group ranches decide what to do with the community revenue.

But the high tourist revenue plainly fails to bring development to the area – roads, schools and clinics are rudimentary; illiteracy is high; skills and market opportunities are few. What happens to the 19 per cent? Local corruption and exploitation are to blame, complained 9 out of 10 Masai interviewed in the area. Community benefits from tourism are seized by 'first among equals'. Poor management of resources means lack of accountability in a country notorious for corruption at all levels, including the county councils. 'The 19 per cent revenue adds up to a decent amount of money but it doesn't trickle down to the common person,' says Michael Koikai, senior warden in the Masai Mara reserve.

Without proper management and protection, earning money from tourists is more gamble than enterprise. In the Mara, 'cultural bomas' (show homesteads) have been established for tourists to visit, where the Masai showcase their culture and sell traditional artifacts. These traditional Masai compounds, seen from the tour bus window along the road to the entrance of the game park, are literally open house. Women and children sit around on dusty animal hides next to mud huts,

cooking on an open fire, surrounded by gourds and goats. Tourists can stop the bus and walk right into a Masai bedroom for just a few dollars. In the situation of impoverished and dispossessed minorities, this raises questions about choice, informed consent and basic human rights. One Kenyan tour guide explained how, when on a training course, his group of 20 trainee guides were taken into a Masai woman's bedroom early in the morning when two small children were still sleeping on the floor, and she dutifully showed them where she and her husband slept. 'It was an eye opener to me,' he told MRG. 'I felt like an intruder. What choice did that mother have?'

Cultural bomas bring direct cash benefits, but not always to the people who have to keep their door open. Tour drivers are known to charge up to $30 per tourist, with only a nominal amount – about $2 per tourist – paid to a select group of elders. Recent attempts to control exploitation by the tour drivers include making tourists pay the visiting fees through hotels and lodges, which are then paid directly to the bomas. But guides are in a unique position as 'middle men' to work with corrupt elders and opportunistic members of the community. Prostitution services, including young girls and boys from the bomas, are run out of the curio shops in the lodges, say human rights activists based in Nairobi.

'Tourism has impacted both negatively and positively on our culture. There are benefits, but the way the young embrace tourism is not good – they leave school and hang around to dance for the tourists. They take alcohol, lose respect for their parents, and issues of HIV come in because tourists romanticize our culture and actually seek sexual favours,' says local activist Tiamaren Ole Riamit. Employment opportunities counts as a positive, but the majority of Masai interviewed believed there should be more training opportunities and more commitment to promoting indigenous people to managerial positions. Rangers, clerical workers, warders and tour guides are locally recruited, and about 20–30 per cent of workers in the lodges inside the park are Masai.

Asking the right questions

Johnson Ngila, a local guide from Lewa Downs conservancy in Northern Kenya, says donors and well-wishers who support community-based tourist enterprises should be diligent in looking behind the marketing of 'community' as a fundraising strategy. 'Community participation' needs careful scrutiny, as it has become required terminology for eco-marketing and proposal writing. 'Community' becomes meaningless in huge swathes of territory inhabited by different ethnic groups and clans.

Ben Ole Koissaba, of the Indigenous Concerns Resource Centre, agrees. He says much depends on 'who is talking to who'. Policies can be put to uneducated and artless decision-makers who do not understand the impact on the community or the legal implications. 'Basically, these people do not discuss as equal parties and whoever has the idea has the upper hand, and presents himself as a saviour to a poor community. People accept unknowingly terms and conditions,' says Koissaba.

The process is replicated within the community itself – with elders effectively coercing members of the community who lack the social status to refuse. Ester Letorongos, from the Ngwesi clan of the Masai, said she was told to move from her family home to a cultural *boma* by elders who had made an agreement with a nearby lodge. She said she had no choice but to move.

'A senior elder came and told us to move here. He said we were coming for a job and me and my husband would be paid…. My duties are to show tourists how we build houses, how we live, clean gourds, and make beads.' Her husband demonstrates hunting and honey-gathering techniques, and dances for tourist groups. Ester said the work from tourism provides critical income and she would not go back to her old life. 'We used to have to sell goats one by one to get food; now we are saving our goats and not selling them.'

But her standard of living remains well below the poverty line, and she struggles to educate, feed and adequately clothe her five children. She shrugs off questions about privacy, only saying it is better to get advance notice when tourists are coming.

The overwhelming majority of indigenous people living in tourist destinations told MRG they didn't feel they were benefiting directly. Real benefits – as opposed to the general assumption of general benefits – were seen to be, specifically, new business opportunities, improved protection from wildlife and displacement, visible community development and participation in critical decision-making.

Better practice: awards and indicators

One way forward is to revise the way ratings are awarded to ecotourism operators. Tourists who buy into these packages should be able to clearly see that not only are environmental concerns being addressed, but local social concerns are also taken into account. These ratings have been successfully devised in some countries, like South Africa, which demands acceptable standards in tourist destinations of education, health, employment, infrastructure and services, as well as improving on poverty indicators and respecting relevant human rights treaties. Fair Trade in Tourism South Africa (FTTSA) encourages responsible business practice by South African tourism establishments, including fair wages, good working conditions, ethical business practices, and respect for human rights and the environment.

Taiko Lemayian of KECOBAT believes local ratings could play an important part in keeping check on international ratings. Acclaimed eco-destinations should be measured against a system of agreed local ratings, he says, 'as a way of controlling eco-ratings as a marketing tool, and show any disconnect between international and local assessments'.

In the long run, says Ben Ole Koissaba, of the Indigenous Resource Centre: 'Community participation requires "thinking outside the paradigm" '. It requires effort on the part of owners and managers to increase local training. This is a pragmatic business decision as well as an ethical one – it is more cost effective and reduces hostility. For example, most lodges in Kenya habitually bring in food and necessities from established supply lines in the capital, Nairobi, as managers consider it easier to tap into established supply lines and credit facilities. This practice of 'importing' makes for a costly process by road and air, instead of encouraging locally grown produce, and establishing local systems of slaughter and meat inspection. Most lodges also rely on a transitory and more costly pool of skilled and educated 'outsiders' from the more developed central and western provinces, instead of investing in training, educating and promoting local personnel.

Welcoming tourism

The Shompole group ranch, situated in southern Kenya on the Kenya–Tanzania border, has taken many of these steps and received international awards for ecotourism achievements. In an area inhabited by the Loodokilani clan of the Masai, Shompole is considered a model of community participation. It is a group ranch communally owned, with members holding the title and the right to use the land. Although some skilled personnel have been brought in from other areas, Shompole's aim is to be entirely community-run by local members trained to reach managerial level. The lodge has partnered where necessary with private investors to bring in technical and marketing skills, and has attracted high-profile clients like Bill Gates. Visitors to the luxury eco-lodge also pay an entrance fee for the larger conservation area, which goes directly to the community.

Shompole members 'make actual decisions on a daily basis', says Ole Petenya Shani, of Shompole Community Trust. 'If we raise KS1,000 or US $1000 that all goes into our kitty and we disburse that money where we think the priority need is.' He says this is in contrast to the Mara, where the county council absorbs the bulk of the proceeds. Shompole also has a good record on local employment and training: 70 per cent of employees in Shompole are locally recruited, with about 30 per cent of skills brought in from outside the area to ensure effective running of the business. The community decides what facilities to build, like tented camps, and fences and land divisions have been removed to let wildlife move freely.

Over time, the intention is for the community to buy equity from private investors with the aim of full community ownership.

Shompole is by no means the only good practice example in Kenya. Further north, about 160 km north-east of the capital Nairobi, is Il Ngwesi Group Ranch. 'Il Ngwesi' means 'people of wildlife' in Masai – and it was built in 1996 after local Masai elders were persuaded to allocate a large area of pastoralist land to wildlife conservation. The idea was floated by Ian Craig of Lewa conservancy, originally a white settler ranch of some 64,000 acres. Craig worked through the local elders to turn the land into a conservancy, and tried to persuade as many neighbouring communities as possible to turn land over for conservation. Il Ngwesi elders gave 16,500 acres of community land, in the conviction that tourism was the only way to bring development and business opportunities to the community. Initially, the idea was greeted with much suspicion, particularly from the youth, that this was the scheme of a '*mzungu*' – white man – to steal more land.

'There is no Masai word for tourist, and we had no idea what tourism was all about at that time,' says Ochen Sakila Mayiani, the lodge manager. Representatives from all age groups went to see lodges in the Masai Mara to learn how tourism worked – and to develop a vision of how it could work better. People were successfully convinced that genuine community-based tourism could bring benefits and development, and would improve standards of living.

All revenue from the lodge is ploughed back into the community, in way of salaries, water points, road construction, bursaries, training and business ventures, says the manager. This is very different from the small percentage ploughed back through the county council in the Masai Mara.

A 5 sq km no-go zone was cleared around the lodge for use by the animals and tourists alone, and suitable areas of settlement and grazing identified for community use. Done with community agreement, this meant that, unlike in conventional game parks, the Masai could remain in the vast lands of the conservancy, apart from the relatively small exclusion zone. The balance between human habitation and conservation is managed through consensus. The Natural Resource Management and Community Development Committee controls grazing movements and access to land on the conservancy, allowing for grazing in certain prime areas in times of stress and drought.

Since Il Ngwesi was established, some 14 more conservancies have been set up using it as a model of good practice. Local Il Ngwesi elder Simpai says the decision to build the lodge was a good one and was done with the full participation of the community: 'I am happy with the decision because now I am personally earning money as a result.' One of the benefits to the community is that more children are being encouraged to go school by a generation of parents who are mostly illiterate, and medical treatment is available through local clinics. Masai interviewed in Il Ngwesi by MRG expressed confidence that the land and the benefits belonged to the community.

But there have been some disappointments, too. Although the Il Ngwesi system means the Masai remain on their land – unlike the Masai Mara model – and share benefits at a certain level, more ambitious development projects have yet to be achieved. Commercially there is insufficient independence, and the conservancy is still driven by donations. 'We have not managed to get enough for development projects. We still need to rely on funding and donations because the population is increasing and what we generate is not adequate enough to improve living standards,' says Ochen, the lodge manager.

Tensions: conservation and power
Even with this good practice example, there are tensions between those concerned with wildlife conservation and community needs. The Ngwesi conservancy is under pressure to fence the land by the owners of Lewa Downs, despite opposition from the community, as the area includes endangered species like the black rhino, Grevy's zebra, elephant and sitatunga. Situated in a volatile part of Kenya, where banditry, poaching and illegal firearms are always a threat, Lewa states in its literature the need for an 'extremely effective security system to protect wildlife and people'. White settlers are a minority group with disproportionate access to land, wealth and influence, who are feeling pressure to establish good relationships with their pastoralist neighbours, in order to retain huge swathes of land originally acquired through the colonial system. Community-based ecotourism is one of the ways forward; but there is enormous imbalance between the two groups. The obvious vulnerability of indigenous communities within this relationship is their lack of political and economic standing, and the ease with which they can be exploited.

The Lewa conservation vision incorporates a huge area of land known as the Northern Rangeland Trust, and is a good example of how diverse the notion of 'community' can be. It includes the Mugokogodo and Laikipia Masai, the Borana, Rendile, Samburu and Turkana pastoralist minorities. It also includes small farming communities, like the Soboyga Meru – who were recently pushed out of land declared an animal corridor by local landowners.

'We ran without anything'
According to the Soboyga, the declaration was made when a local government official arrived in a government vehicle in the company of 'a white person'. The order to evict was given as a verbal declaration only. About 500 families now live in destitution on a road reserve outside the Lewa Downs electric fence. It is a sight that is not compatible with the expectations – or assumptions – of tourists visiting the lodge, who would likely be ignorant of the fact that the people living in misery around the electrified boundary had been brutally evicted in the name of conservation. Tourists who feel reassured by the impact of marketing of 'community participation' would not connect their enjoyment of the wildlife with the situation of the Soboyga.

'Government officials and *mzungus* [white people] came to tell us it was an animal corridor. Then a group of armed guards came on 10 September 1999 and forced us out,' says a young woman, Karimi. The area of eviction is known as 'Bosnia' by the community because of the violence used.

'When the guards arrived in the morning in a vehicle with the District Officer they started burning our houses with paraffin, shouting at us to leave.' Muremi, an elderly man, says he had to flee without any possessions. 'We ran, without anything, and came here. Now we can't dig because this land belongs to someone else.'

They are able to use a water point next to the fence, and get access to the school and health clinic on the boundary of the conservancy. No longer able to cultivate, they survive on what casual labour they are able to get from the conservancy, like digging trenches or clearing bush. The women harvest reeds in a nearby swamp, and sell them by the bundle to the Lewa Downs lodge or for making furniture. They make about KS500 (about US $6) in three days.

'We have to stand in water to collect the big reeds, and there is danger from the wild animals. The reeds cut our hands, and the water is very cold,' says Karimi. The community has long been landless: they lost family land in Meru immediately after independence, when they discovered they were not entitled to property rights. They were originally brought into the conservancy by a local politician who unilaterally promised the group government land as an election promise. Absence of legal rights to land does not justify eviction – the government has committed itself to this, through ratifying international treaties to protect an individual's security and right to life; the government also has to fulfil its obligations by providing for the basic needs of all its citizens, such as shelter and healthcare.

And, although the primary obligation rests with the government, Kenyan minority rights activists point out that it is also the responsibility of large landowners and tourist companies marketing 'community participation' to seek humane solutions for affected groups like the Soboyga rather than resorting to, or supporting, illegal evictions.

What future?

Increasing global concern about the environment and the growing awareness of development and poverty issues, especially among younger people, creates new and important opportunities for tourism to set basic standards in observing the rights of minorities. New tourist markets in developing economies have an obligation to take into account historical injustices and to address them rather than exploit them. In much the same way, ecotourism has set minimum basic standards for good practice and positively markets schemes for improved and sustainable use of resources.

Community-based models should be improved to take into account the positive contribution of indigenous communities to their own environment – as protectors rather than detractors – and ensure that 'community' adequately addresses ethnic and socio-political differences in what are sometimes huge and diverse territories. There is a large variation in existing 'community-participation' schemes. Some are little more than cultural tokenism; some have established important approaches to genuine involvement. The development of social indicator ratings – taking account of fair wages, good working conditions, and provision of education, health and training opportunities – would raise awareness among tourists about the effectiveness of the participation schemes, while obviously also benefiting indigenous communities.

Governments should be held accountable by statistics as well as international treaties. Where tourist revenue is high, governments should be able to demonstrate an established level of development funds and projects in that area, and should be held accountable by donors and investors if they fail to do so.

'Ecotourism' has proved that tourists are not only willing to support models that aspire to contribute positively to 'the greater good', but actually demand it at the higher end of the market. Standards for indigenous communities should be an integral part of these demands – not simply viewing them as an extension of the environment; there should be an informed demand for the basic human rights of communities who are often the original inhabitants of the land.

If these steps are taken, minorities may begin to rightfully gain from an industry which all too often has failed to bring prosperity and opportunity to their communities, while actively contributing to cultural erosion, impoverishment and human rights abuses. Properly managed, ecotourism can benefit indigenous communities as well as visitors, from the land and resources being packaged as paradise. ∎

Trouble in Paradise
How Can the Law
Help? Minority
Rights and Tourism

Cynthia Morel

What protection does international human rights law afford to communities adversely affected by tourism development? MRG's legal cases officer, Cynthia Morel, outlines how international human rights law can be used to secure more sustainable practices.

While little case law as yet exists on the specific issue of indigenous and minority rights in the context of tourism, most of the relevant principles can be drawn from well established standards and jurisprudence relating to land, effective participation and the right to development. Striking an ethical balance between tourism development and the needs of local communities can only be possible when the tourism industry and local authorities actively engage in upholding these rights.

Land rights

Both minorities and indigenous peoples have a right to property, though the latter are understood to have a prior claim on both property and wider communal land rights due to their ancestral ties to these lands, and also due to the importance of these lands for the survival of their traditional way of life. The recognition of indigenous peoples' communal land rights as property rights has become increasingly established under international law. One of the leading cases on this principle stems from the *Mayagna (Sumo) Awas Tingni v. Nicaragua* case, where a community's ancestral lands were threatened by commercial logging. In this case, the Inter-American Court of Human Rights recognized that the American Convention on Human Rights protected property rights 'in a sense which includes, among others, the rights of members of the indigenous communities within the framework of communal property'.[1] Moreover, the Inter-American Court stated that possession of the land should suffice for indigenous communities lacking real title to obtain official recognition of that property.[2] The Awas Tingni case has set an important precedent that is now influencing legal systems globally. For example, many of the principles set out in that landmark case are currently under consideration by the African Commission on Human and Peoples' Rights, in a case dealing with the eviction of the Endorois pastoralist community from a nature reserve in Kenya.

It is important to note that these standards do not render all forms of encroachments on indigenous lands illegal. If encroachment of land is found to pursue a legitimate aim (i.e. that measures taken are in the interest of public need or in the general interest of the community), and that the measures taken are in accordance with the provisions of appropriate laws, no violation will arise unless the measures taken are deemed disproportionate to the aims sought. It is clear that the creation of nature and game reserves often is – or can be – in the general public interest. United Nations (UN) Expert Erica-Irene Daes nonetheless sets out some of the key parameters that help establish what factors must be taken into account when determining proportionality. Daes draws particular attention to the fact that 'limitations, if any, on the right to indigenous peoples to their natural resources must flow only from the *most urgent* and compelling interest of the state'.[3] She then stresses that:

'few, if any, limitations on indigenous resource rights are appropriate, because the indigenous ownership of the resources is associated with the most important and fundamental human rights, including the right to life, food, the right to self-determination, to shelter, and the right to exist as a people.'[4]

Recent jurisprudence has further confirmed the link between dispossession of indigenous peoples and right to life violations in instances where prompt relocation to land of equal value is not afforded.[5] As such, if displacement is deemed absolutely necessary – or restitution impossible – only prompt relocation to land which allows for the continuation of the indigenous community's traditional way of life will be deemed compatible with international legal standards.

Given the critical importance of traditional knowledge systems for sustainable ecotourism practices, and also for the support of conservation efforts of natural reserves, a worthwhile alternative to forcible displacement of indigenous peoples for the creation of these initiatives is to allow them to remain on their ancestral lands as living testaments of how to live in harmony with the environment. More will often be gained from indigenous peoples actively engaging in conservation efforts from within, rather than being disenfranchised and impoverished by the process. Failure to engage indigenous peoples has in many instances forced displaced families to resort to poaching of wildlife. The stalemate often resulting from forced displacement without adequate compensation therefore poses a serious risk to sustainable conservation efforts. The flourishing of a fruitful and dynamic ecotourism industry will depend on the industry's success in negotiating a delicate balance between its interests and those of affected communities.

Right to participation and right to development

While interest in the traditions and cultures of minorities and indigenous peoples is consistent with the wider ethical framework of ecotourism, the reality is that, under current prevailing models, local peoples are being overwhelmingly marginalized in the process of development. Some of the most widely ratified international instruments, such as the International Covenant on Civil and Political Rights, secure the right to participation. The right to participation has also been incorporated in more recent instruments, such as the 1986 UN Declaration on the Right to Development, where the right to development is defined as requiring 'active, free and meaningful participation in development'. The right to participation is also outlined in the 1993 Vienna Declaration and Programme of Action, a Declaration which marked the culmination of a long process of review and debate over the status of implementation of the body of human rights instruments developed since the 1948 Universal Declaration on Human Rights. Most recently, this is also an underlying tenet of the newly adopted UN Declaration on the Rights of Indigenous Peoples.

In this regard, the right to participation is often scrutinized by UN Treaty Bodies in the examination of state reports. For example, in light of its General Recommendation No. 23 on the rights of indigenous peoples, the UN Committee on the Elimination of Racial Discrimination (CERD) has explicitly requested in the review of state reports that:

'information [be provided] on the effective participation of indigenous communities in the decisions directly relating to their rights and interests, including their informed consent in the establishment of national parks, and as to how the effective management of those parks is carried out'.[6]

CERD has also recommended that states 'adopt all measures to guarantee that national parks established on ancestral lands of indigenous communities allow for sustainable economic and social development compatible with the cultural characteristics and living conditions of those indigenous communities'.[7]

Together, these standards firmly establish the right for minorities and indigenous peoples to be involved in collectively in decision-making, planning and implementation processes affecting their economic, social and cultural rights. Moreover, they are entitled to information that enables the decision-making process to be meaningful. It follows that states and non-state actors, particularly development agencies, have a duty to enable people affected by a development activity to participate in ways that can positively transform their social, political and economic conditions. Indeed, international development organizations have begun adopting participation and consultation standards with respect to indigenous peoples. A UN Development Programme policy paper notes that participation is 'essential in securing all other rights in development processes'.[8]

In this light, ecotourism practices that adversely affect a community's socio-economic or cultural well-being will be in violation of the right to development. The overriding goal of the substantive improvement in well-being of these communities would therefore require, at a minimum, that they receive a fair share of the income and employment opportunities generated by the industry, and that necessary training be afforded to local community members in order to facilitate access to administrative and management positions.

Free prior informed consent

One of the most important concepts regarding participation is that any consent given by communities directly affected by the creation of nature reserves and ecotourism centres should be free prior informed consent. The International Labour Organization (ILO) delineated consultation standards with respect to indigenous peoples in Convention No. 169. The relevant text of the Convention states: 'The consultations carried out in application of this Convention shall be undertaken, in good faith and in a form appropriate to the circumstances, with the objective of achieving agreement or consent to the proposed measures.' The most developed explanation of what free prior informed consent means has been made by the UN committee of experts monitoring the implementation of the key treaty prohibiting racial discrimination (ICERD).[9]

The requirement of prior informed consent has also been delineated in the case law of the Inter-American Commission on Human Rights (IACHR). In *Mary and Carrie Dann v. USA*, where the state had interfered with the indigenous community's use and occupation of their ancestral lands by purporting to have appropriated the lands as federal property through an unfair procedure before the Indian Claims Commission, the IACHR noted that convening meetings with the community 14 years after title extinguishment proceedings began constituted neither prior nor effective participation.[10] To have a process of consent that is fully informed 'requires at a minimum that all of the members of the Community are fully and accurately informed of the nature and consequences of the process and provided with an effective opportunity to participate individually or as collectives'.[11] It is again a principle enshrined in the newly adopted UN Declaration on the Rights of Indigenous Peoples and that formed an important part of the landmark San case won by the indigenous community at the Botswana High Court in 2006.[12]

Conclusion

The above standards are obligations imposed upon states under international law – both in terms of restricting state action against minorities and indigenous peoples, and requiring authorities to protect these communities from third parties, including private business interests linked to the tourism industry. Tourism also raises more complex issues, like whether or not the country of origin of international tourists has responsibilities under international human rights law vis-à-vis its tourists and the country of destination, or whether such rights are only enforceable against the home state of those adversely affected. While addressing such complex issues falls beyond the scope of this article, what remains clear is that the tourism industry must show leadership in using the standards set out as key guidelines for all of their dealings with minorities and indigenous peoples, particularly when their dealings directly impact on the relationship of indigenous communities with their ancestral lands. ■

Find out more about our Trouble in Paradise campaign at:
www.minorityrights.org/troubleinparadise

Peoples under Threat

Mark Lattimer

Is war contagious? The question is an old one, but the events of the last year have seen it posed with renewed urgency as the long-term decline in global rates of armed conflict has now stalled.

In the 1990s, many of the new conflicts that erupted shared the same proximate cause: the fall of the Soviet Union. Much of the killing on the ground was driven by policies of ethnic nationalism but as, one by one, those conflicts were resolved or contained, they appeared in retrospect as the death rattle of the bi-polar world, or even, in the words of some commentators, as the necessary price of democratization. Optimists also pointed to the communications revolution and claimed that the real-time transmission of images of terrible suffering on the world's television and computer screens had made it impossible for international leaders to avoid taking joint action to resolve conflict. In the last years of the century, there was a series of internationally mediated settlements and a huge increase in UN peacekeeping operations to contain conflict. Up close, war was just too terrible for us to allow it to continue. The steady overall decline in global conflict that followed – and that continued despite the launch of the 'war on terror' – provided comfort to that viewpoint.

But 2007 threatens to mark a turning point. Indeed, a dispassionate observer of world events over the last 18 months, watching the tentacular proliferation of conflict in the Horn and Central Africa, the Middle East and western Asia, might be forced to conclude, like the chaplain in *Mother Courage*, that 'war always finds a way'.

War certainly has its own dynamics, which cannot even be controlled by the world's superpower, as the US has tragically demonstrated in Iraq. In that country, as in most of the others where conflict has spread over the last year, it is the way in which those dynamics act on ethnic and religious divisions to engulf ever wider and larger populations, within and across borders, that has fuelled the killing. The lessons of the 1990s already seem to have been forgotten.

This is the third year that Minority Rights Group International (MRG) has compiled the Peoples under Threat table (see Reference section, Table 1, pp. 162–7). Based on recent advances in political science it seeks to identify which of the world's peoples are currently under most threat of genocide, mass killing or other systematic violent repression.

The spread of conflict and new threats in 2008

The major risers in the table this year are listed overleaf. In most of these cases, the states concerned border a state where there is an existing armed conflict. Well-known factors in the international spread of conflict include refugee flows and the proliferation of small arms. In many of the highlighted cases, however, including Chad, the Central African Republic, Ethiopia, Iran and Lebanon, the determining factor appears to be the export of the ethnic dynamics of conflict to kin populations across borders.

The continuing tragedy in Darfur in Sudan is exerting an ever greater impact on the neighbouring states of Chad and the Central African Republic. To the 240,000 Sudanese refugees currently in eastern Chad can be added a further 170,000 internally displaced Chadians. Yet while for a time the precarious situation in eastern Chad could be blamed primarily on the mass refugee flows that began in 2004, and cross-border attacks from Janjaweed horsemen, over the last year the fighting has increasingly been between local communities, nonetheless replicating a model familiar from Darfur. What started as a local reaction to Janjaweed attacks has become a generalized inter-communal conflict pitting 'black' *toroboro* militias against Arab fighters, with civilian communities on both sides bearing most of the casualties. As the conflict has escalated, both Chad and Sudan have accused each other of supporting rebel cross-border attacks. A bilateral agreement in May 2007 to stop such attacks appeared to have little effect. Chad's President Idriss Déby, who survived an armed rebellion in 2006, held talks with key rebels in October 2007 even as a state of emergency was declared over much of the east and north of the country.

Eastern Chad has also received tens of thousands of refugees fleeing fighting in the Central African Republic (CAR). The insurgency in the CAR dates from when President Bozize took power in a coup in 2003, but has gathered intensity over the last year with the involvement of militias supported by Sudan. CAR armed forces have responded with a campaign of violence against civilians in the north, often targeting the Kaba, the ethnic group of the former president. In all, some 270,000 people have been displaced.

Ethiopia has risen further up the table following its military involvement in Somalia. In December

2006 the Ethiopian army, supported by the USA, invaded Somalia in support of the Transitional Federal Government, in order to overthrow the *de facto* rule of the Islamic Courts Union (ICU). By February, the UNHCR (Office of the United Nations High Commissioner for Refugees) reported that some 50,000 Somali refugees fleeing the fighting had crossed the border into Ethiopia. With them came significant numbers of small arms and tales of what the Ethiopians were doing to their country, invigorating a long-running insurgency in the Ogaden region of Ethiopia bordering Somalia. Following increasingly daring attacks by the Ogaden National Liberation Front in April and May, Ethiopian armed forces mounted a major counter-insurgency campaign in the Ogaden in June, resulting in widespread allegations of abuses against ethnic Somali civilians. With the military involvement in Somalia continuing, and renewed tension in Ethiopia's long-running border dispute with Eritrea, the government is under pressure. At the same time, serious ethnic tension persists in other areas of the country. In her 2007 mission report on Ethiopia, the UN Independent Expert on Minority Issues highlighted the situation in Gambella state, bordering Sudan, where human rights violations continue, including against the Anuak.

The situation in Somalia and Ethiopia also threatens to have an impact on the small state of Djibouti, which was affected by drought in 2007. Djibouti has suffered in the past from inter-ethnic violence between Somali-speaking Issas and Afars, who have a kin population in Ethiopia. The security situation in the country is closely connected with the supply of foreign aid and the presence of large French and US military bases, but in 2006 a UN report accused Djibouti, as well as Eritrea, of illegally arming the ICU in Somalia. Although part of the rise is due to the absence of data on some of the indicators last year, Djibouti has still risen significantly in the Peoples under Threat table.

The cases of Iran and Uzbekistan, as well as Pakistan (which is now ranked seventh in the overall table), all affected by cross-border conflict, are considered below. Another striking riser in the table is Lebanon, already seriously destabilized by the 2006 Hezbollah–Israel war. Lebanon seems as far as ever from escaping the influence of its neighbours and the wider Arab–Israeli conflict. Fighting in May–September 2007 between the Lebanese army

and a new Sunni jihadist group named Fatah al-Islam, based in the Nahr al-Bared Palestinian refugee camp, claimed at least 450 lives and displaced up to 30,000 Palestinian refugees. The professed aim of Fatah al-Islam, which was composed of some Palestinians and a large proportion of foreign militants, was to bring religion back to the Palestinians, but the mainstream Palestinian leadership in the region distanced itself from the group. However, given the humanitarian impact of the fighting, the continuing disenfranchisement of Palestinians within Lebanon, and the possibility of communal conflict between Fatah al-Islam or a successor group and Shi'a supporters of Hezbollah, the situation remains of grave concern.

The continuing march up the table of Sri Lanka and Zimbabwe is mainly driven by endogenous factors. The conflict between the Sri Lankan government and the Liberation Tigers of Tamil Eelam escalated during 2007 with major Sri Lankan army operations in the east and north of the country in January, March and July leading to the displacement of tens of thousands of mainly Tamil civilians. A programme of expulsions of Tamils from the capital Colombo was halted by a court order in June.

The ethnic dimension of the crisis in Zimbabwe has received little comment but may be becoming more pronounced. Although the opposition Movement for Democratic Change emphasizes its inclusive character, it has a higher proportion of Ndebele among its activists than the ruling ZANU-PF, and there were noted cases of ethnic discrimination in both the government's slum clearance programmes and its distribution of food aid. In the mid-1980s between 10,000 and 20,000 Ndebele were believed killed in the course of Zimbabwean military operations in Matabeleland.

The inter-ethnic violence which commenced in Kenya following disputed results in the December presidential election was not widely anticipated, although MRG had warned of serious inter-ethnic tension in Kenya for a number of years, particularly following the failure to agree a new inclusive constitution. Opposition resentment at the dominance of the Kikuyu, the ethnic group of President Mwai Kibaki, drove the early violence, but the situation has quickly deteriorated. Inter-ethnic attacks, revenge killings and forced displacement have targeted a number of groups, including the Kikuyu, Luhya, Luo and Kalenjin, particularly in west Kenya and the Rift Valley, as long-running disputes over land use and ownership have been brought to a head. Indigenous groups such as the Ogiek have also suffered as militias, profiting from the general insecurity, have attempted land grabs. As a result of these events, former UN Secretary-General Kofi Annan was brought in to mediate reconciliation talks, and Kenya has risen 14 places in the PUT table. However, the probability of the situation deteriorating farther in the immediate future will partly depend on whether the police – already accused of using excessive violence against demonstrators – and the armed forces become drawn into the inter-ethnic conflict. In the long term, fair political participation for the different groups and a concerted attempt to resolve equitably the disputes over land will be the key.

In the overall Peoples under Threat table for 2008 (pp. 50, 161–7), the top six positions are taken by the same states as last year: Somalia, Iraq, Sudan, Afghanistan, Burma/Myanmar and the Democratic Republic of Congo. In each of these states, further major episodes of inter-ethnic, inter-clan or sectarian killing in 2008 are highly probable if not inevitable.

The situation in Somalia deteriorated further in 2007. Following the ouster of the ICU, the Transitional Federal Government, backed by the Ethiopian army, launched an offensive against ICU supporters in February. Indiscriminate shelling

Major risers since 2007				
Rank	**Rise in rank since 2007**	**Country**	**Group**	**Total**
7	1	Pakistan	Ahmaddiya, Baluchis, Hindus, Mohhajirs, Pashtun, Sindhis, other religious minorities	19.16
9	4	Ethiopia	Anuak, Afars, Oromo, Somalis, smaller minorities	17.77
10	14	Chad	'Black African' groups, Arabs, Southerners	17.62
11	3	Sri Lanka	Tamils, Muslims	16.63
12	8	Iran	Arabs, Azeris, Baha'is, Baluchis, Kurds, Turkomans	15.71
13	25	Central African Republic	Kaba (Sara), Mboum, Mbororo, Aka	15.59
14	21	Lebanon	Druze, Maronite Christians, Palestinians, Shia, Sunnis	15.29
22	3	Zimbabwe	Ndebele, Europeans, political/social targets	14.26
25	3	Uzbekistan	Tajiks, Islamic political groups, religious minorities, Karakalpaks, Russians	13.73
28	5	Yemen	Zaydi Shia	13.52
40	30*	Djibouti	Afars	11.64
51	14	Kenya	Borana, Kalenjin, Kikuyu, Luyha, Luo, Somalis, Turkana, Endorois, Masai, Ogiek, other indigenous groups	11.10

* Disproportionately high due to the absence of data on some of the indicators in 2007

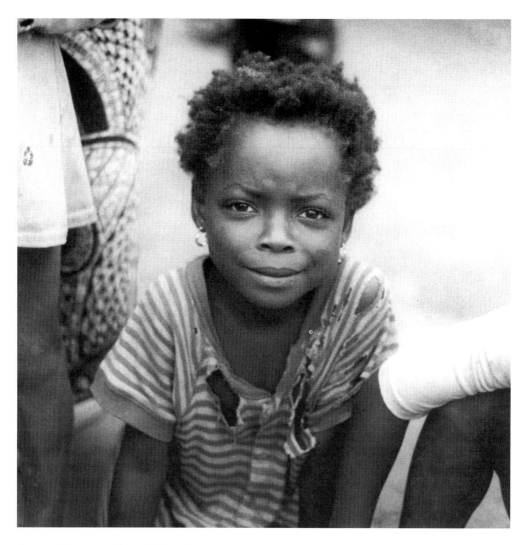

destroyed large parts of Mogadishu and over the following weeks some 340,000 people fled the capital. In fact, the anti-government fighters are dominated by the Hawiye clan, who fear what they see as an attempt by President Abdullahi Yusuf to advance the interests of his Darod clan. A further 80,000 people fled the latest fighting in November, causing leading UN officials to state that Mogadishu is facing a humanitarian catastrophe.

The fact that inter-clan violence in Somalia exhibits most of the characteristics of inter-ethnic or sectarian conflict in other countries means that it produces a very high score on nearly all the indicators used in the Peoples under Threat listing. In most cases, civilian victims are targeted simply because of their clan identity. However, also at

particular risk in Somalia are the country's ethnic minorities, the Bantu and caste groups such as the Midgan, Tumal and Yibir, who have been subjected to violence by all sides and whose social and economic marginalization makes them particularly vulnerable to the general effects of the conflict.

In Burma, demonstrations by Buddhist monks and the subsequent crackdown made the international headlines during 2007, but the continuing violent repression of minorities was barely reported. Both the UN Special Adviser on the Prevention of Genocide and the Special Rapporteur on Human Rights in Myanmar have drawn attention to serious human rights violations targeting ethnic groups including the Karen, Rohingya and Shan. In October the BBC reported that villagers in the increasingly militarized Chin state were being forced to take part in pro-government rallies, or face heavy fines, leading some to flee to neighbouring India.

Despite largely successful national elections in the Democratic Republic of Congo (DRC) in 2006, and the presence of the UN's largest peacekeeping force, armed conflict has escalated once again in the east of the country. Over 350,000 people have fled fighting in North Kivu with forces of the dissident General Laurent Nkunda, who claims to be protecting Congolese Tutsis. Nkunda points to the continued presence in the Kivus of Rwandan Hutu rebels, who typically live by pillaging from the local population, and most Congolese believe he is backed by the Rwandan government. The eastern DRC in fact presents a rather extreme case of exported conflict, with Rwanda itself enjoying peace and rapid development, attested by its fall of 15 places in the Peoples under Threat table.

Dropping out of the top of the table this year along with Rwanda is the Russian Federation, where the Chechen conflict has partly been contained. The situation remains precarious, however, as it does in Angola and Burundi, whose risk profile has improved on last year. More promising for the long-term is the situation in Liberia (which fell 23 places in the table since last year) and in Sierra Leone (15 places), both of which continue to recover from past conflicts.

The purpose of the Peoples under Threat table, as explained above, is to identify those country situations where there is a significant risk of mass killing or other systematic violent repression of particular ethnic or religious groups. This is not to say that such repression will occur, but that there is an increased probability that it *may* occur in the near or medium-term future (bearing in mind that for those countries at the head of the table, the violence is ongoing). But as this is now the third year that the Peoples under Threat table has been compiled, a brief assessment can be made of its performance as a predictive tool.

Pakistan and Sri Lanka, the top two countries in the table of major risers last year, faced a major increase in violent political instability and ethnic

killing in 2007. To a lesser degree, this was also the case with Turkey and Iran. In Lebanon, although violence did not reach the level of the international Hezbollah–Israel conflict of 2006, there was a major new upsurge of conflict in a Palestinian refugee camp. In Guinea, a political crisis led to a state of emergency being declared in early 2007. In three other situations, Yemen, Thailand and Israel/OPT, serious inter-ethnic or sectarian killing continued. Of the 10 states listed in the table of major risers, only in Haiti (where socio-political cleavages have been more prominent in conflict than ethnic or religious factors) could the situation be said to have partly stabilized.

US foreign policy and the spread of conflict

In 1937, in his so-called 'quarantine speech', President Franklin D. Roosevelt sought to counter the prevailing mood of isolationism in the United States. He argued that if war came again to Europe, 'let no one imagine that America will escape'. He went on:

'*Nations are fomenting and taking sides in civil warfare in nations that have never done them any harm. Nations claiming freedom for themselves deny it to others.... The peace-loving nations must make a concerted effort in opposition to those violations of treaties and those ignorings of human instincts which today are creating a state of international anarchy and instability.... When an epidemic of physical disease starts to spread, the community approves and joins in a quarantine of the patients in order to protect the health of the community. War is a contagion.... There must be positive endeavours to preserve peace.*'

His arguments resonate for US foreign policy today, although whether they provide more support for contemporary interventionists or multilateralists is not entirely clear. The dominant strand in US foreign policy after 9/11 was a belligerent interventionism which aimed at achieving a positive domino effect in world regions that were perceived as a threat. In November 2003, for example, President Bush claimed that: 'The establishment of a free Iraq in the heart of the Middle East will be a watershed event in the global democratic revolution' (speechwriters for President Bush often appeared consciously to echo Roosevelt's rhetoric, although notably FDR's 'peace-loving peoples' became Bush's 'freedom-loving peoples').

Rank	Country	Group	Total
	Peoples most under threat – highest rated countries 2008		
1	Somalia	Darood, Hawiye, Issaq and other clans; Ogadenis; Bantu; Gabooye (Midgan) and other 'caste' groups	22.81
2	Iraq	Shia, Sunnis, Kurds, Turkomans, Christians, Mandeans, Yezidis, Faili Kurds, Shabak, Baha'is, Palestinians	22.56
3	Sudan	Fur, Zaghawa, Massalit and others in Darfur; Dinka, Nuer and others in the South; Nuba, Beja	21.56
4	Afghanistan	Hazara, Pashtun, Tajiks, Uzbeks, Turkomans, Baluchis	20.89
5	Burma/ Myanmar	Kachin, Karenni, Karen, Mons, Rakhine, Rohingyas, Shan, Chin (Zomis), Wa	20.10
6	Dem. Rep. of the Congo	Hema and Lendu, Hunde, Hutu, Luba, Lunda, Tutsi/Banyamulenge, Twa/Mbuti	19.87
7	Pakistan	Ahmaddiya, Baluchis, Hindus, Mohhajirs, Pashtun, Sindhis, other religious minorities	19.16
8	Nigeria	Ibo, Ijaw, Ogoni, Yoruba, Hausa (Muslims) and Christians in the North	18.90
9	Ethiopia	Anuak, Afars, Oromo, Somalis, smaller minorities	17.77
10	Chad	'Black African' groups, Arabs, Southerners	17.62
11	Sri Lanka	Tamils, Muslims	16.63
12	Iran	Arabs, Azeris, Baha'is, Baluchis, Kurds, Turkomans	15.71
13	Central African Republic	Kaba (Sara), Mboum, Mbororo, Aka	15.59
14	Lebanon	Druze, Maronite Christians, Palestinians, Shia, Sunnis	15.29
15	Cote d'Ivoire	Northern Mande (Dioula), Senoufo, Bete, newly settled groups	15.26
16	Uganda	Acholi, Karamojong	15.25
17	Angola	Bakongo, Cabindans, Ovimbundu, pastoralists, San and Kwisi	15.25

Rank	Country	Group	Total
18	Philippines	Indigenous peoples, Moros (Muslims), Chinese	15.14
19	Burundi	Hutu, Tutsi, Twa	14.83
20	Haiti	Political/social targets	14.67
21	Nepal	Madheshis (Terai), Dalits, linguistic minorities	14.48
22	Zimbabwe	Ndebele, Europeans, political/social targets	14.26

Unfortunately it is conflict, rather than democracy, that has spread within and beyond the borders of Afghanistan, Iraq, Israel/Palestine, Pakistan and Somalia. Many critics, particularly in the countries affected, have moved beyond a condemnation of the US intervention in Iraq to seeing the hand of the superpower behind each and every negative development. Indeed, it can be argued that the sectarian nature of the conflict in Iraq was clearly aggravated by specific US policy errors, including: the early decision to dismantle the central state and divide power in the Iraqi polity along strict ethnic and sectarian quotas; the handling of an electoral process which effectively excluded Sunni Arabs from political power during the crucial constitution-making year in 2005; and the largely uncritical support for a new Iraqi government whose members were directly implicated in gross sectarian human rights abuses, including systematic torture and mass extra-judicial executions.

There is, however, a danger of seeing everything in terms of superpower influence, if only because it implies that a war can be stopped in the same way as it was started. The US neo-conservative movement and its most ardent critics, while disagreeing violently about US intentions, sometimes appear to share an almost idealist conception of superpower agency, as if the US can direct events on the ground at will. Yet, in Iraq, the sectarian violence is obviously also driven by factors that even the wilder conspiracy theories would acknowledge are clearly beyond the control of the US, not least the legacy of inter-communal hatred left by Saddam Hussein and the sectarian chauvinism of groups such as al-Qaeda in Mesopotamia or the Jaish al-Mahdi.

Over the past 18 months, sectarian or ethnic conflict has permeated every corner of Iraq and haemorrhaged across its borders. The huge escalation in sectarian and ethnic killing, which has supplanted the war against insurgents as the principal cause of fatalities in Iraq, is usually dated from the bombing of the al-Askari shrine in February 2006 but really started to grip the country after the inauguration of the permanent Iraqi government that May. At its peak the conflict has been responsible for over 3,000 civilian deaths a month, the majority Sunni victims of Shi'a death squads and the victims of suicide bombings by Sunni militants, but including casualties of Multinational Force operations. From summer 2007 the number of fatalities decreased to around 1,000 a month, following the 'surge' of US forces, particularly in the capital Baghdad, and the suspension of the military activities of the Jaish al-Mahdi. There are a number of reasons, however, to fear that this decrease will not continue: first, the pattern of past heavy US troop deployments, for example in the northern city of Mosul, has shown that improved security is rarely sustained when US troop levels fall again; second, the Jaish al-Mahdi remains very strong and the self-imposed suspension in its operations for a maximum period of six months may only be a tactical step; and, third, although violence is down, the flight of internally displaced persons and refugees has left many of Iraq's communities completely divided on sectarian and ethnic lines. Finally, the US tactic of co-opting Sunni tribal leaders in the fight against al-Qaeda may not last once the large financial incentives are no longer offered, and in any case continues the disastrous policy of arming and strengthening sectarian actors in Iraq at the expense of the central state.

How is the Peoples under Threat table constructed?

Since the genocide in Rwanda in 1994, our ability to identify those situations most likely to lead to genocide or mass killing has improved. A number of comparative studies of the factors preceding historic episodes of political mass killing had been undertaken since the 1970s, but it was not until the 1990s that researchers such as Helen Fein, Rudolf Rummel and Matthew Krain pioneered quantitative longitudinal analysis of a wide range of such factors, enabling the testing of different causal hypotheses. Rummel, for example, showed the very strong relationship between concentration of government power and state mass murder; Krain demonstrated the correlation between existing armed conflict or political instability and the onset and severity of mass killing.

Following the early work of the Clinton administration's policy initiative on genocide early warning and prevention, Professor Barbara Harff worked with the US State Failure Task Force to construct and test models of the antecedents of genocide and political mass murder and her results were published in 2003 ('Assessing risks of genocide and political mass murder since 1955', *American Political Science Review*, vol. 97, February 2003). Her optimal model identifies six preconditions that make it possible to distinguish, with 74 per cent accuracy, between internal wars and regime collapses in the period 1955–97 that did, and those that did not, lead to genocide and political mass murder (politicide). The six preconditions are: political upheaval; previous genocides or politicides; exclusionary ideology of the ruling elite; autocratic nature of the regime; minority character of the ruling elite; and low trade openness.

Minority Rights Group International (MRG) has drawn on these research findings to construct the Peoples under Threat table, although responsibility for the final table is exclusively our own. Peoples under Threat is specifically designed to identify the risk of genocide, mass killing or other systematic violent repression, unlike most other early warning tools, which focus on violent conflict as such. Its primary application is civilian protection.

Indicators of conflict are included in the table's construction, however, as most, although not all, episodes of mass ethnic or religious killing occur during armed conflicts. War provides the state of emergency, domestic mobilization and justification, international cover and, in some cases, the military and logistic capacity that enable massacres to be carried out. Some massacres, however, occur in peacetime, or may accompany armed conflict from its inception, presenting a problem to risk models that focus exclusively on current conflicts. In addition, severe and even violent repression of minorities may occur for years before the onset of armed conflict provides the catalyst for larger-scale killing.

The statistical indicators used all relate to the state. The state is the basic unit of inquiry, rather than particular ethnic or religious groups at risk, as governments or militias connected to the government are responsible for most cases of genocidal violence. Formally, the state will reserve to itself the monopoly over the means of violence, so that where non-state actors are responsible for widespread or continued killing, it usually occurs either with the complicity of the state or in a 'failed state' situation where the rule of law has disintegrated. Certain characteristics at the level of the state will greatly increase the likelihood of atrocity, including habituation to illegal violence among the armed forces or police, prevailing impunity for human rights violations, official tolerance or encouragement of hate speech against particular groups and, in extreme cases, prior experience of mass killing. Egregious episodes of mass killing targeted principally at one group have also seen other groups deliberately decimated or destroyed.

However, some groups may experience higher levels of discrimination and be at greater risk than others in any given state. MRG has identified those groups in each state which we believe to be under most threat. (This does not mean that other groups or indeed the general population may not also be at some risk.) It should be noted that although these groups are most often minorities, in some cases ethnic or religious majorities will also be at risk and in relevant cases are therefore also listed in the table. In some cases, for example in Iraq, all the groups in the country are at risk of ethnic or sectarian killing.

One indicator that has been tested and discarded by a number of studies is the general level of ethnic or cultural diversity in a society. Krain did not find any correlation between 'ethnic fractionalization' and the onset of genocide or political mass killing. Similarly, neither of the patterns of ethnic diversity tested by Harff had any effect on the likelihood of mass killing (although she did find the minority character of the ruling elite to be significant). These findings are supported by research on the relationship between diversity and conflict.

The overall measure is based on a basket of ten indicators. These include indicators of democracy or good governance from the World Bank, conflict indicators from the Center for Systemic Peace and other leading global conflict research institutes, indicators of group division or elite factionalization from the Fund for Peace and the Carnegie Endowment for International Peace, the State Failure Task Force data on prior genocides and politicides, and the country credit risk classification published by the Organization for Economic Cooperation and Development (as a proxy for trade openness). For citations and further information see the Reference section in this volume (pp. 161–7). For a fuller discussion of the methodology, see *State of the World's Minorities 2006.*

Based on current indicators from authoritative sources, Peoples under Threat seeks to identify those groups or peoples most under threat at the beginning of 2008.

An impending constitutional deadline for a referendum over the future status of Kirkuk has raised tension between communities in the city and in other disputed areas, and violence has increased. The most deadly suicide bombing attacks since the Iraq war began killed over 400 Yezidis in Sinjar in August, probably a calculated attempt to push the Kurdish-speaking Yezidis out of the area. It underscored just how dangerous the situation continues to be for minorities living in the disputed areas of Nineveh and Kirkuk adjoining Kurdistan. Major bomb attacks also hit the Kurdistan Regional Government and the use of Iraqi Kurdistan as a base by Turkish PKK rebels prompted serious invasion threats from Turkey. Iran, too, threatened further military action against Kurdish rebels based in Iraq.

In addition to the over 2 million people now believed internally displaced in Iraq, a further 2 million have fled the country, most of them for Syria or Jordan. Up to one-third of these are believed to come from Iraq's smaller minority communities, including Armenians, Chaldo-Assyrians, Faili Kurds, Mandaeans, Shabak, Turkomans and Yezidis.

Afghanistan, the other major theatre for US military operations, also continues to have a destabilizing influence on neighbouring countries. The use of bases across the border in Pakistan by al-Qaeda and Taliban fighters after 2001 made Pakistan a key ally of the US in the 'war on terror'. However, large-scale military operations by Pakistani forces in Waziristan and North-West Frontier Province (NWFP), including house demolitions and other violations against civilians, have had the effect of alienating the local Pashtun population. The Lal Masjid or Red Mosque in Islamabad, which had strong links to militants from Pakistan's tribal areas, was stormed by troops in July leading to the deaths of over 100. New military offensives were launched in North Waziristan in October and, after the declaration of a state of emergency, in NWFP in November. The year also saw continued repression of ethnic Baluchis, following the killing of a Baluchi leader in 2006.

In Afghanistan itself, NATO forces are still not able to guarantee security outside of the capital Kabul, particularly in the Pashtun south. In November, a bombing in Baghlan in northern Afghanistan killed six members of the Afghan parliament and some 80 others, Hazara, Tajiks and Uzbeks, raising fears of a new front opening up in the war. Growing instability in the north and the activities of criminal networks around heroin supply routes also threaten the security of Afghanistan's northern neighbours, including Uzbekistan, where repression targeted at religious groups continues amid rising tension over the future succession to President Karimov.

Sandwiched between the spreading conflicts in Iraq, Afghanistan and Pakistan lies the country of Iran. International coverage of Iran has focused overwhelmingly on the question of Iran's nuclear facilities and on Iranian support for insurgent groups in Iraq, but the developing domestic tensions are poorly reported. In addition to the low-intensity conflict in Iranian Kurdistan, the last year has seen high-profile bombings in south-eastern Iran blamed on armed rebels from the Baluchi minority. Iranian officials accused US and UK forces in Afghanistan of supporting the rebels, just as they claimed that US and UK forces in Iraq had supported violent protests by Arabs in the Iranian province of Khuzistan. Perhaps most significant is the growing repression of Iran's Azerbaijanis or Azeris, who make up some 25 per cent of the population. Major demonstrations in May 2006, sparked by the depiction of an Azeri as a cockroach in a cartoon in a state-run newspaper, turned violent and led to widespread detentions and the deaths of tens of Azeris.

Iran is the highest-ranked country in the Peoples under Threat table where there is currently no major armed conflict. If such a conflict were to erupt – precipitated, for example, by US air strikes at Iranian nuclear facilities or state institutions, or an increase in US support for rebel groups – the threat level for mass killing would become among the highest in the world. The consequences for civilian life of any major conflict could be devastating, and the spread of conflict would be extremely hard to contain.

In March 1945, President Roosevelt told the US Senate that the recent Yalta conference of the Allied Powers:

'… ought to spell the end of a system of unilateral action, the exclusive alliances, the spheres of influence, the balances of power, and all the other expedients that have been tried for centuries – and have always failed. We propose to substitute for all these, a universal organization in which all peace-loving nations will finally have a chance to join.'

The creation of the United Nations Organization in the post-war settlement had as its principal aim the outlawing of war, and the UN must take some credit for the fact that international wars between states have been comparatively rare since its establishment. However, the ongoing march of internal or civil conflicts, and the overwhelming preponderance of

civilian rather than combatant casualties in today's wars, present a challenge to the UN system of conflict prevention that was not anticipated in 1945 and for which the UN continues to be ill-equipped today.

It is perhaps in the Darfur crisis that this has been demonstrated most tragically, both with regards to the prevention of conflict and its containment. In a report published last year, MRG showed how, from as early as 2000, the warning signs in Darfur were clear: the escalation of violence against minorities, the depopulation of villages. But the UN ignored those warnings, including from its own staff on the ground, and the post of Special Rapporteur on Human Rights in Sudan was abolished in spring 2003, just as the violence sped out of control. Despite the UN World Summit in 2005 agreeing a 'responsibility to protect' populations against genocide, war crimes and crimes against humanity, the UN Security Council has repeatedly failed to authorize action sufficient to stop the Sudanese government continuing its campaign which to date has led to the deaths of at least 200,000 people and the displacement of over 2.4 million.

It is often remarked that the Darfur case illustrates the weaknesses of a multilateral approach when there is not sufficient consensus to apply genuine pressure on the state responsible for violating human rights. While this is undoubtedly so, it is once again dangerous to assume that it is only a question of political will. In most of the new generation of conflicts that extend from western Asia to Central Africa, the state not only fails to monopolize the means of violence, it also lacks the basic tools and skills to manage the claims of its diverse peoples. At a time when local conflicts over scarce resources are likely to intensify, those skills are more necessary than ever.

Resource conflicts and climate change

The phenomenon of 'resource conflicts' has been extensively described in the political science literature. A well-known study by Paul Collier for the World Bank, for example, suggests that a country that is otherwise typical but has primary commodity exports of around 25 per cent of GDP has a 33 per cent risk of conflict, but when exports are only 5 per cent of GDP the probability of conflict falls to 6 per cent. The correlation between armed conflict and a state's endowment with natural resources has also been linked by some commentators to the existence of a 'resource curse', where resource-rich countries exhibit stunted development. This is particularly the case in Africa, where struggles over the exploitation of resources have further led to the development of conflict economies, from diamonds in Sierra Leone, oil in Sudan and Nigeria, to minerals, timber and gas in the Democratic Republic of Congo.

The important role of natural resources in the creation and sustenance of conflict is not limited, however, to the case of resources for export. In each of the country situations listed above, and many other cases in every world region, the pivotal role of local resource conflicts over land, water and food security is increasingly being recognized.

In an article for the *Washington Post* in June, UN Secretary-General Ban Ki-moon claimed:

'Amid the diverse social and political causes, the Darfur conflict began as an ecological crisis, arising at least in part from climate change.... It is no accident that the violence in Darfur erupted during the drought. Until then, Arab nomadic herders had lived amicably with settled farmers.... But once the rains stopped, farmers fenced their land for fear it would be ruined by the passing herds. For the first time in memory, there was no longer enough food and water for all. Fighting broke out. By 2003, it evolved into the full-fledged tragedy we witness today.'

This account has been criticized for simplifying a complex and long-standing pattern of local conflicts between pastoralists and agriculturalists, and for downplaying the massive repression unleashed by the Sudanese government. However, the scale of desertification in northern Darfur is widely recognized, as is its impact on pushing pastoralist communities to move south in search of pasture, increasing tensions with settled communities. One could posit a growing pattern throughout east Africa and the Horn where local conflicts over changing land use spread and intensify when ethnicity or tribal identities are used as a mobilizing factor by local politicians or governments.

This year's edition of the *State of the World's Minorities* focuses on the impact of climate change, which is likely to prove a challenge to human security not just through changing our environment but also through precipitating violent conflict. And while climate change will affect us all, it is a particular threat to minority and indigenous communities because they frequently inhabit fragile environments, their land use is poorly protected, and they are vulnerable to displacement without reparation.

Preventing or containing the spread of violent conflict in many places around the world now depends on improving our understanding of the links between land use, food security and the protection of minorities and indigenous peoples. That this is also a matter of simple justice is reinforced by the new UN Declaration on the Rights of Indigenous Peoples, adopted by the UN General Assembly in September 2007 after over 10 years of negotiations. Article 8 of the Declaration establishes that 'States shall provide effective mechanisms for prevention of, and redress for … [a]ny action which has the aim or effect of dispossessing [indigenous people] of their lands, territories or resources …'

In a number of reports produced this year, MRG published the results of a major three-year programme of research on minority rights and the prevention of conflict. Recommendations on promoting the economic and political participation of minorities, on constitutional and electoral systems that strengthen cooperation between communities, on self-governance and combating discrimination, all aim to ensure that minorities and indigenous peoples feel they have a stake in the societies in which they live and to provide governments with effective tools for the management of diversity. The application of some of these tools to many of the country situations identified in the Peoples under Threat table could help to weaken or remove key factors contributing to the outbreak of violent conflict, including emerging disputes over natural resources.

For many years the high incidence of ethnic and religious factors in the entrenchment and proliferation of the world's conflicts has been noted with regret by the international community but also with a sense of powerlessness. According the protection of minorities and indigenous peoples a central place in conflict prevention initiatives is long overdue, to reduce the appalling toll of civilian casualties in today's wars but also to halt the spread of a new generation of conflicts that threatens to scar our globe for decades to come. ∎

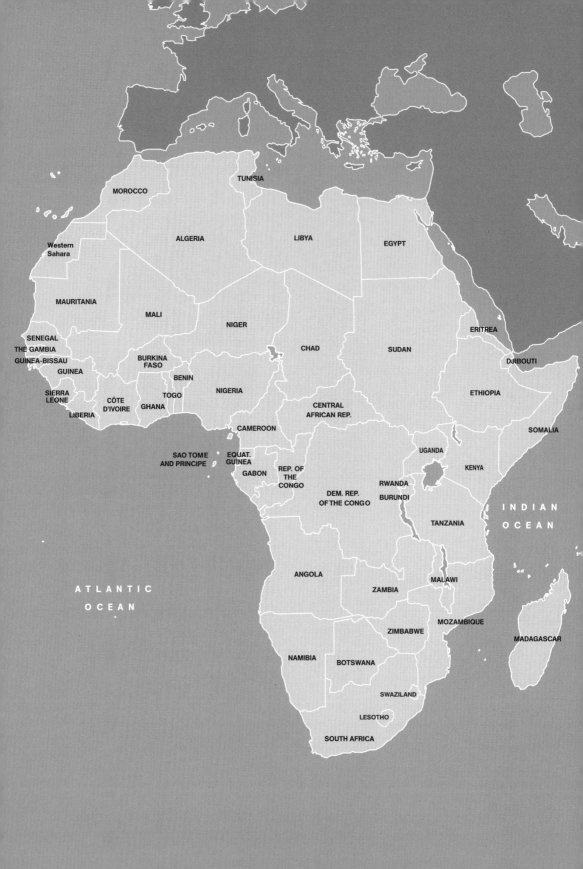

Africa

Ishbel Matheson

Africa is one of the continents hardest hit by climate change – and marginalized minorities are likely to be among the most vulnerable of all. According to data released in 2007 by the Intergovernmental Panel on Climate Change (IPCC), by 2020 between 75 million and 250 million people in Africa are expected to be suffering from increased water stress due to climate change. The IPCC also predicts that climatic developments make it likely that food production could halve by 2020, with the Sahel, arid but relatively densely populated, among the most exposed of regions (*Fourth Assessment Report*, October 2007). The resultant strain upon available resources would impact in particular upon the pre-existing tensions between farmers and transhumant pastoralists, with potentially severe consequences for minorities across the region, such as the Peul/Fulani, Mbororo and Tuareg and related groups. Similarly, the UNDP (United Nations Development Programme) *Human Development Report* for 2006 identifies drought-prone countries in Southern Africa – Angola, Malawi, Zambia and Zimbabwe as having the 'gravest food security challenges in the world'.

Some communities are already experiencing this, first-hand. In East Africa and the Horn of Africa, the Afar and the Somali in Ethiopia, and pastoralists like the Karamajong in Uganda, are already grappling with the reality of more frequent cycles of drought. Cross-border flare-ups between the cattle-herding tribes of the Horn of Africa, testify to the potential for conflict, as competition for scarce resources intensifies. In an October 2007 report, UNICEF reported that half of the total stock holding of pastoralists in the Horn of Africa had been wiped out, and that 'repeated bouts of drought have defeated pastoralists' capacities to recover their stock level'. UNICEF explicitly linked political marginalization of the pastoralists to the fact that governments and the international community fail to put in place services that would help mitigate the effects of drought (*Global Alert: Pastoralist Child*).

The freak rains which hit the continent, east to west in 2007, showed that the growing unpredictability of weather events is a further factor to which minority groups would be particularly exposed. The IPCC notes that low development levels, weak economies and poor governance records impact on the ability of states and communities to combat climate change. However, it did hold out the possibility that some nomadic groups, already

highly attuned to vagaries of the weather system, may in fact be better able to develop adaptive strategies than other communities (*Fourth Assessment Report*, October 2007).

Apart from the looming threat of climate change, conflict with an ethnic dimension, was, once again, the biggest immediate threat to minorities across the continent. In Ethiopia, the government launched an offensive against ethnic Somali rebels in the Ogaden region, after a rebel attack on an oil exploration site. The security forces' tactics – such as a food blockade and burning villages – attracted international criticism for indiscriminately affecting civilians. In Sudan, the unravelling of a key peace deal between Khartoum and the former Southern rebels, opened up the possibility of renewed warfare, while there were also new signs of restiveness in the north among the Nubian and Manassir peoples. The catastrophe in Darfur worsened, despite renewed efforts by the international community. Worryingly, the disruptive effects of this war are spreading, not just into neighbouring Chad and Central Africa Republic, but also within Sudan itself. In Somalia, clan-based warfare intensified, as the struggle between the supporters of the Islamic Courts Union (ICU) and the transitional government, backed by the Ethiopians continued. As predicted in *SWM 2007*, the fighting sparked a severe humanitarian crisis, with the United Nations (UN) estimating over 1,000 killed and 400,000 displaced in October 2007.

The difficulties of managing tourism development while still respecting the rights of minorities and indigenous peoples emerged as another powerful theme in 2007. For example, the plight of the Hadzabe hunter-gatherers close to the Serengeti plains in Tanzania is typical. According to reports in June 2007, the Tanzanian government struck a deal to lease the land, which was traditionally occupied by the Hadzabe, to a safari company from the United Arab Emirates. Although the deal supposedly included the development of roads and education facilities, the Hadzabe – who number around 1,500 – were not consulted on it, and were reportedly opposed to it. Following a campaign by indigenous activists, Survival International reported in November 2007 that the safari company had withdrawn from the project. However, the pattern of ignoring the rights of minorities when considering tourism issues was also evident in Botswana, Kenya and Uganda (see individual country profiles).

Country by country

Algeria

Parliamentary elections in May 2007 were only the third democratic poll to be held since 1992, when the army cancelled the first multi-party elections which were won by the fundamentalist FIS (Islamic Salvation Front) party. The consequences of the ensuing civil war, marked by extreme brutality, are still being felt today. The Salafist militants, re-launched in 2007 as a branch of al-Qaeda, have their roots in the armed Islamic opposition to the Algerian state. Al-Qaeda in the Islamic Maghreb has claimed responsibility for a number of attacks across North Africa, including a series of bombings in Algeria, leaving many dead. In January 2007, it targeted security forces in the minority Berber area of Kabylia in north-eastern Algeria. According to BBC News, seven bombs were detonated and at least six people were killed.

Observers said the low turnout in the parliamentary poll reflected the electorate's understanding that power was concentrated in the hands of the presidency not the parliament. For the Berber minority – which makes up approximately 25 per cent of the Algerian population – grievances about recognition of their distinct language and cultural rights remain. Berber political parties were divided about whether to contest the elections: the Rally for Culture and Democracy gained 19 seats, re-entering parliament after a boycott in 2002. However, the Social Forces Front decided once again not to contest the election. About half of the Berber-speaking population is concentrated in the mountainous areas east of Algiers – Kabylia – and this area and its language have been at the centre of most Berber issues in modern Algeria. In 2001, riots and demonstrations erupted in the region, due to widespread claims of repression and marginalization. Since then, the government has promised more economic assistance and eased some restrictions on the use of Tamazight – the Berber language. In its 2007 report on Algeria, the US State Department noted that:

'Access to print and broadcast media for Tamazight and Amazigh culture continued to grow. Tamazight programming also increased on the non-Berber language channels, as did advertisements in Tamazight on all television and radio channels. Beginning in the 2006–2007 scholastic year, the Tamazight language was officially taught in primary schools, starting in the fourth grade in 17 predominantly Berber provinces.'

However, this progress still falls short of Tamazight being recognized as an 'official' language – as demanded by Berber campaigners. Moreover, there are complaints that, outside Kabylia, Berbers' linguistic and cultural rights continue to be restricted.

Botswana

The efforts by Botswana's minorities for recognition of their rights continued in 2007. Despite being a multi-ethnic state, comprised of 45 tribes, Botswana's laws and constitution continue to discriminate in favour of those from the dominant Tswana-speaking group. Most of the laws of Botswana recognize and protect the rights of the Tswana-speaking groups with regards to ethnic identity (including language and culture), land and chieftaincy. However no such recognition or protection is given to the non-Tswana-speaking ethnic groups in Botswana. Indeed, following independence in 1966, the only languages allowed for public purposes or in teaching were Setswana and English.

A 2001 High Court ruling in a case brought by the Wayeyi tribe, found that the exclusion of the Wayeyi from the House of Chiefs – an influential body which advises parliament – was discriminatory and unjustified. However, despite the ruling, the government's action purporting to remedy this discrimination has been far from satisfactory. In 2005, the Botswana parliament passed a constitutional amendment, dealing with membership of the House of Chiefs. However, the campaign group Reteng concluded that this merely further entrenched the inequalities. It noted that when the present House of Chiefs was inaugurated on 1 February 2007, of the 45 tribes, 20 remained entirely unrepresented. In June 2007, the National Assembly proposed the Bogosi bill, which if enacted, would repeal the Chieftaincy Act. However, campaigners say the proposals fall far short of what is required and still preserve the disproportionate influence of the Tswana tribes in the House of Chiefs.

Reteng and Minority Rights Group International (MRG) have submitted a case, based on the Wayeyi ruling, to the African Commission on Human and Peoples' Rights, located in the Gambia, alleging violations of the African Charter on Human and

Peoples' Rights. These include violations of the right to participate freely in government (Article 13), the right to freely take part in the cultural life of a community (Article 17) and the right to equality (Article 19).

The treatment of the San hunter-gatherers in Botswana continued to raise concerns in 2007. The San scored a historic victory at the end of 2006, when the High Court in Botswana ruled that forcible evictions from their ancestral lands in the Central Kalahari Game Reserve in 2002 were illegal and unconstitutional, and that the ban on hunting was illegal. However, it became evident in 2007 that the Botswana government was intent on only allowing the narrowest interpretation of this ruling. It insists that the court's judgment only applied to those listed on the legal case papers, and there have been repeated arrests of San who have tried to hunt in the Reserve.

The court case followed progressive dispossession of the San of land which they have inhabited for thousands of years. The forces of modernization, economic imperatives (diamonds were discovered in the territory) and tourism have all been cited as reasons for the evictions of the San. Their subsequent existence in government resettlement camps, without access to the expanses of the Kalahari, has sounded the death-knell for their unique hunter-gatherer way of life.

Survival International reported in December 2007 that up to 150 people had managed to re-settle in the park despite the obstacles. But it is estimated that up to 1,000 more would like to go back. The non-governmental organization (NGO) said lack of adequate water supplies, lack of access to transport back to the reserve and undue pressure from government officials were preventing more people from returning (see also *Namibia*).

Burundi

Burundi's population is 85 per cent Hutu, approximately 14 per cent Tutsi and roughly 1 per cent Batwa. After the end of widespread hostilities in Burundi and the constitutional referendum and presidential election of 2005, the country has maintained a cautious path towards reconstruction and political stabilization during 2007, with considerable outside aid and diplomatic pressure. President Pierre Nkurunziza's majority Hutu government and legislature has been the main

political force since the 2005 polls – overturning the previous dominance by the Tutsi minority. The government is faced with the challenge of developing a genuinely pluralistic politics and functioning civil society after nearly 50 years of deepening ethnic violence. Despite a peace agreement between the government and the last remaining Hutu rebel front, the National Liberation Front (FNL), in September 2006, a minority break-away wing of the FNL under the leadership of Agathon Rwasa, was still in conflict with government forces in late 2007, staging hit-and-run raids in and around Bujumbura.

Unlike neighbouring Rwanda, Burundi does recognize the distinct ethnicity of the Batwa. There are estimated to be between 30,000 and 40,000 Batwa living in the country. The 2005 constitution set aside three seats in the National Assembly and three seats in the Senate for Twa. Nonetheless this group are still mostly landless and are among the poorest people in what is a very poor country. In testimonies gathered by MRG in Burundi in 2007, Batwa complained of many difficulties relating to land rights, either through lack of title, discriminatory practices relating to allocation on the part of the authorities or failure to recognize historic rights to land. According to the Forest Peoples Programme, land laws in Burundi blatantly discriminate against Batwa, as they base customary land rights on 'actual and visible occupation of the land', while the traditional hunter-gather lifestyle tends to not visibly impact on territory. The new Land Commission in Burundi is tasked with sorting out the complex land issues which have arisen since the end of the conflict, and the return of many refugees. The Commission has one Batwa member, and it is hoped that it will tackle the question of the land rights of indigenous peoples. Aside from land issues, Batwa also complained to MRG about discrimination in social services, especially in health and education. In particular, the difficulty of educating Batwa children beyond primary level was highlighted. A survey undertaken by UNIPROBA – an organization representing the Burundian Batwa – found just seven Batwa students in university education in 2006.

Central African Republic

The impact of the interlocking wars and rebellions in the central African region was felt in CAR. Rebels from Chad and Darfur continue to operate from northern CAR, while the government of General François Bozizé has accused Khartoum of allowing rebels from CAR to base themselves in Darfur. In an attempt to contain the spreading effects of the Darfur war, the United Nations approved the deployment of a 3,700 strong peacekeeping force mainly to Chad, but also to Central African Republic in September 2007. The troops are to be drawn from European Union (EU) nations – and the goal is to protect civilians from cross-border attacks. However, by late 2007 the EU force had run into difficulties – in particular due to the reluctance of states to contribute vital military hardware, such as helicopters, to the mission.

Attention also focused in 2007 on the home-grown rebellions within the CAR. In the past few years, two revolts have been under way in the north: one in the north-east and one in the north-west. An estimated 200,000 civilians have fled their homes during this time – with some 50,000 seeking sanctuary in Cameroon and Chad. Government forces confronting the rebellions have been accused of widespread human rights abuses, including summary executions. While the insurgencies have different dynamics, overall the political and economic marginalization of the north is the dominant factor. In the remote and underdeveloped north-east, the rebellion centres on the Gula ethnic group. In a 2007 report, Human Rights Watch (HRW) describes their grievances as, variously, discrimination against the Gula, and alleged embezzlements of community payments by government officials. After an offensive where the rebel Gula-dominated UFDR seized key towns, government security forces, supported by the French military, struck back. According to HRW, most of the Gula population fled for fear of retaliation by the government forces. However, a peace deal signed in April 2007 between the UFDR and the government has stabilized the situation. In December 2007, the UN noted that, while the situation remained 'fragile', it had been sufficiently good for some displaced civilians to return home.

The difficulties in the north-west, are driven partly by followers of the former president Ange-Félix Patassé (who hails from this region), who feel excluded from political patronage of the Bozizé regime. The unrest is also driven partly by sheer lawlessness, embodied by bandits known as *zaraguinas*, whose activities lead local communities

to seek protection from militias as well as fuelling discontent with the central government's inability to curb the criminal attacks. Cow-herding nomadic tribes, the Mbororo have particularly suffered in this prevailing atmosphere of lawlessness and rebellion across the north. Targeted for their wealth and livestock, many have fled to camps in southern Chad. In April 2007, Office of the UN High Commissioner for Refugees (UNHCR) announced the opening of a new refugee camp in Cameroon, following the flight of some 25,000 Mbororo from CAR. In a statement UNCHR said the Mbororo had been singled out 'relentlessly' by both bandits and rebels, and that 'a small number of those who managed to save some of their livestock continue to graze cattle inside Cameroon. But the others, having lost everything, are in an extremely precarious situation.' In November 2007, Amnesty International reported (*War Against Children in the Wild North*) on the pervasive practice of child abduction from Mbororo communities, for ransom. Some children have been abducted by *zaraguinas* more than 10 times. Girls are especially vulnerable; they may be held for months, and raped. Ransoms can be up to $10,000. Amnesty says that state security forces often fail to intervene, even when they are in a position to do so.

In the south of the country, the cultural survival of the forest-dwelling peoples of the CAR – the biggest group of which is the Aka – continues to be in question. UNESCO, which has recognized the unique polyphonic musical traditions of the Aka, warns that 'the scarcity of game resulting from deforestation, the rural exodus and the folklorization of their heritage for the tourist industry are the principal factors contributing to the gradual disappearance of many of their traditional customs, rituals and skills'. Illegal logging presents a huge problem for the Aka: even when logging is supposed to be state-controlled, and conservation measures are in place, there are difficulties. In a November 2007 report, the Forest Peoples Programme reports that in the Dzanga Protected Area Complex – where the Aka have some limited rights to hunt and pursue a traditional lifestyle – the younger generation is losing its forest knowledge, as development opportunities increase and the trend towards sedentarization takes hold. In all walks of life, the Aka still face deep-seated discrimination from other communities in the Central African Republic.

Songs, life in the forest and the struggle for acceptance

Matilde Ceravolo describes how the Aka Pygmies of Central African Republic came to learn about human rights.

'*So zo la, so zo la, zo kwe a'ke zo …*' – all around the Lobaye region, children going to school and women in front of their hearth, all sing a chirpy rhythm.

Aka Pygmies are renowned for being exceptional musicians. In their ancient oral traditions, ideas as well as stories have been diffused through easy-to-remember songs. This one means: 'This person here, and that one there, every person is a human being.'

That is not an obvious statement in the southern Central African Republic. Aka are normally considered as a bit less than human beings, something in between humans and monkeys. They are often regarded as private property, being 'owned' by the majority Bantu and used for hard farming tasks.

Once upon a time, when Aka were able to live on forest products, their relations with the Bantus were based on mutually advantageous trading arrangements. Aka would approach villages to exchange meat, fish, mushrooms and roots for semi-industrialized goods, such as cooking pots and matches. They would have a privileged relation with one specific Bantu family, but they were free to negotiate deals.

Since industrialized forest exploitation has begun, Aka have found it harder and harder to survive in the forest and have been forced to settle next to the villages, looking for seasonal jobs. Bantus have become their 'masters', deciding when to hire them, if and how much to pay. The traditional Pygmy values of living with no private property and their tradition of moving through the forests, with settled abodes, are seen by the Bantu as symptoms of under-civilization.

Targets of violence and discrimination

Misunderstandings between Aka and Bantus happen every day, and acts of violence are not uncommon.

Sanfami's daughter was beaten because she refused to work for a Bantu who had encountered her in the road. The baby she was carrying on her back, died as a consequence of the beating.

Aka men have been forced to work for leading citizens in the city of Bagandou, in Lobaye region. When human rights defenders approached, they were threatened with having one of the Aka killed in front of them.

Aka children at school are often victims of sneering from their schoolmates and are excluded from the class groups. At public health centres Aka are forced to allow all the other patients to be attended to before their turn comes.

Even the right to a nationality is denied to Aka. It is estimated that around 35,000 Aka live in the Central African Republic, while the official census of 2003 only registered 10,000 – the ones who were enrolled to vote at the presidential elections.

'Culturally unique'

Aka oral traditions have been declared as part of world heritage by UNESCO. Since then, the government has received funds to preserve their culture. Appreciable efforts have been made and the Ministry of Youth, Sports, Arts and Culture is working hard to improve the conditions of Aka Pygmies. However, the government tax that is charged for those visiting an Aka encampment, has not been used for the benefit of the communities.

The list of daily minority rights violations is long. Aka have been denied access to education: in the Lobaye region, only one Aka is known to have ever accessed secondary education, and this was under Emperor Bokassa, in the 1970s.

Learning about human rights

The Aka had never even heard about human rights until 2003, when the first project was funded by the European Commission and run by the Italian non-governmental organization (NGO) Cooperazione Internazionale (COOPI). The first steps of the awareness- raising campaigns were very basic: a drawing representing a child, a man and an antelope. And the question: what is the difference between each of them? What is

human? Are you human or animal? All that followed was developed from there, by the Aka themselves. Community leaders invented songs; they participated in public discussions; they manufactured objects to be exhibited in museums, contributing to the valorization of Aka culture. They created community-based organizations to promote human rights. They travelled to meet each other and to exchange lessons learned. They spoke on national radio broadcasts and answered questions at university conferences.

In October last year, at the official closure of the project, Germaine, a 30-year-old mother of two, gave a speech in front of journalists to all the national media. It was the first time in history that an Aka woman had talked in a press conference. She vibrantly asked for her children to have the right to go to school and for her to be considered a citizen like any other Central African.

The following day Antoine was received with a standing ovation at the National Assembly. He is one of the only three Aka to have been elected as village chief, after a long struggle. No Aka has ever held a higher administrative position.

This is the happy end of a first chapter. But the struggle of Aka Pygmies to have their rights recognized is just beginning.

Above: Aka leader. Germaine Dimanche (centre) and senior education and training adviser André Yakota talk with Matilde Ceravolo during a meeting with the Aka Human Rights Defence Group in Mbata. Photo by Guss Meijer/COOPI

Chad

The security situation in Chad deteriorated sharply, with continuing attacks by rebel groups in the east against the government of Idriss Déby. According to an IRIN report in December 2007, 90 per cent of the Chadian armed forces were tied up in the fighting in the east of the country. The apparent collapse of a 2006 agreement between a key rebel group, the United Front for Change (FUC) and the government at the end of 2007 placed further pressure on President Déby, who had already resisted a strong attempt to topple his government in April 2006.

A European Union (EU) peacekeeping force which was due to deploy by October 2007, was delayed until 2008, dogged by logistical difficulties. The UN-mandated mission is intended to protect civilians, refugees and aid workers from cross-border attacks, as the effects of Darfur conflict threaten to seriously destabilize Chad. The force will be approximately 3,700 strong – the majority of whom will be French. France, as the former colonial power, already has a strong military presence in Chad, however the UFDD rebel group in the east has already signalled its opposition to the peacekeeping force, claiming that the French are already using their military presence in Chad to support Déby. All the indications are that the EU force will deploy in a worsening security environment and will have a tough task fulfilling its mandate. There are an estimated 400,000 refugees and internally displaced people in the region.

Although the main crisis is presently in the east, Chad's inability to fashion a government inclusive of all sectors of society is a key factor in its instability. The peoples of the mainly Christian south make up approximately 45 per cent of the population but have been excluded from political power for over two decades. Under the former president Hissène Habré, who hailed from the north, an estimated 40,000 people were said to have been killed, many of them southerners (Human Rights Watch, 2005, *Chad: The Victims of Hissene Habre Still Awaiting Justice*). Habré attempted to wipe out the southern elite, and embarked on a scorched earth rural strategy in a region he viewed as secessionist. In 2006, the African Union mandated Senegal – the country where the ex-president has lived since he was ousted – to try Habré for his alleged crimes, including those relating to torture, murder of

political opponents and ethnic cleansing. In 2007, the UN Committee Against Torture criticized the slow progress being made to bring Habré to justice.

The south's sense of grievance has also been intensified by the discovery of oil in the region. There is discontent at extremely high levels of corruption in the Déby regime, and the inequitable distribution of the oil wealth, particularly to the south. In August 2007, Agence-France Presse reported that Ngarlejy Yoronger, the leader of the southern opposition party, the Front des Forces d'Action pour la République (FAR), refused to sign an agreement for improved electoral organization in the run-up to the 2009 election. He denounced the proposals as being worthless while the country was in the grip of a rebellion, and called instead for an inclusive dialogue with all sections of society.

The conflict in the east of the country has several different dimensions, all overlapping. There is an internal dimension, related to the autocratic nature of Déby's regime, as well as personal and sub-tribe rivalries. This has driven members of the president's own family, and his own Zaghawa tribe to take up arms. One of the main rebel groups, the RFC, for example, is led by the president's uncle. Another important factor is ethnic tensions, which spread across borders and run back decades, if not longer. In the simplest terms, the Sudanese government accuses the Chadian authorities of offering support to the Darfur rebels – particularly those from the Zaghawa ethnic group – to fight against Khartoum. Although a minority in Chad (estimated at 1–2 per cent of the population), the Zaghawa form the political elite in the country. By contrast, in Sudan, the Zaghawa are a marginalized group, excluded from political power by the Arab elite concentrated in Khartoum. Chadian Zaghawa have provided vital support, including funds and weaponry, to their Darfur kinsmen, in their struggle against the central government.

On the other side, Déby has accused Khartoum of allowing Chadian rebels to use Darfur as an operational base. In the Chadian context, this fact has special significance – as both Déby and his predecessor Habré launched their successful coups from rear bases in Darfur. There are several rebel groups ranged against Déby. One of the most important has been the FUC – fighters hailing from the Tama ethnic group, which has had a long-standing rivalry with the Zaghawa. This group – led by Mahamet Nour Abdelkarim – almost toppled

Déby in 2006. But a Libyan-brokered peace deal saw Nour appointed defence minister, and a promise to integrate FUC into the main armed forces. However, by late 2007, this deal had unravelled, with ex-FUC fighters taking up arms again and Nour seeking refuge in the Libyan embassy in N'jamena. The breakdown in the FUC agreement coincided with the collapse of another Libyan-backed peace initiative between the Chad government and four rebel groups: the UFDD, CNT, RFC and UFDD-Fondamental. This lasted just a month. By late 2007, these groups were reported to have embarked on a fresh offensive against the government, with correspondents reporting the fiercest fighting in the east for months.

The turmoil in the east has also become further complicated by the involvement of the Sudanese government-backed Janjaweed militia. Amnesty International (*Sowing the Seeds of Darfur,* June 2006) has documented the cross-border attacks from this Arab militia targeting 'African' tribes along the border. The causes of these attacks are partly criminal – theft of cattle and assets, and partly strategic. As Amnesty notes, the militia attacks communities that are left unguarded when the Chadian army is otherwise engaged with the rebels. The goal is to spread mayhem and insecurity, and thereby increase pressure on Déby. However, there are also disturbing racial overtones to the attacks, as it is 'African' tribes that are targeted. Amnesty reports victims being racially abused while being attacked, with comments from Janjaweed attackers such as 'This land is ours' – meaning it belongs to Arabs. The export of the racially motivated warfare, which is a defining feature of the Darfur conflict and which has led to accusations of genocide, is an extremely worrying dimension to the growing disorder and insecurity in the east.

Congo-Brazzaville (Republic of Congo)

One of the legacies of Congo's violent modern history is a tension between the increasingly personalized government of President Denis Sassou Nguesso and the Lari ethno-linguistic group of the Pool region, around the capital Brazzaville. This tension, which has taken an increasingly ethnic character since Congo's two civil wars after 1993, is largely modern in nature, and shows how identity boundaries can harden as a direct consequence of the struggle for political and economic power.

While the first round of violence, after the defeat of the previous single-party military ruler Sassou at the polls in 1992, was largely dominated by political and military allegiance (with much of the army loyal to Sassou), a resurgence of conflict from 1997 saw three major political figures – Sassou, head of state Pascal Lissouba and Lari figurehead Bernard Kolelas – recruit militias on consciously ethnicist grounds, often from villages away from the major centres in one of francophone Africa's most urbanized societies. The result has been the hardening of ethnic prejudices between Sassou's north-central Mbochi ethnic group, which dominates government, and the southern Lari. Matters have been complicated by the absence of effective political leadership among the Lari: an ageing Kolelas has compromised with Sassou, apparently for the sake of his immediate family, and has lost much credibility with his own previously loyal Lari followers.

In addition, recent years have seen an upswing in what some specialists refer to as 'Lari nostalgia' for the medieval/early modern Kingdom of Kongo, promoting further hostility among the Mbochi and related northern populations, themselves an overall minority. In recent years, this polarization has increasingly centred on the 'Beach affair', where approximately 350 Lari militiamen were forcibly repatriated from exile in Kinshasa and then extra-judicially executed, allegedly on orders from Sassou's presidential palace. The Beach affair has been the subject of repeated legal action in France and in Congo itself.

Within the Lari population in and around southern Brazzaville, tensions have remained high in recent months between the 'Nsiloulou' militias loyal to the neo-millenarian Pasteur Ntoumi, and 'Ninjas' still loyal to Kolelas. French and Congolese human rights campaigners are concerned that the continuing potential for conflict will be instrumentalized by Sassou as a means to further centralization of his control over the oil and infrastructure sectors.

Democratic Republic of Congo

In the year following the relatively peaceful election of Joseph Kabila as president, few of the DRC's underlying problems showed signs of being solved. In and around Kinshasa, the possibility of widespread violent social unrest remains ever-present, despite the efforts of the UN peacekeeping mission (MONUC) to bolster security infrastructures. But the worst of the continuing Congolese crisis is in the east.

The key factor remains the ongoing crises in the Kivu provinces, Katanga and Ituri. The upswing in violence seen in North Kivu in mid-2007 was the most recent episode in the continuing struggle for resources and local control between Congolese Tutsi (known as Banyamulenge) militias and the Hutu *interahamwe* of the Democratic Forces for the Liberation of Rwanda (FDLR), as well as independent raiding groups of often indeterminate allegiance who are looking for material resources rather than any strategic or political advantage. The renegade army officer General Laurent Nkunda, who has been under an international arrest warrant for war crimes since 2005, had been maintaining what he describes as the defence of the Banyamulenge. The Nkunda uprising began in earnest in December 2006, provoking immediate population flight estimated at 370,000 people, as the conflict rapidly became a four-cornered one, between Nkunda's National Congress for the People's Defence, FDLR bands, Congolese army units and Maï-Maï militias with little allegiance but to themselves. Attempts by the Congolese army to conquer Nkunda and his force (estimated at 6,000–10,000 strong) proved futile. In September 2007, an estimated further 170,000 civilians had fled fighting. Officials from the UN mission in Congo reported locating mass graves of unidentified civilians in areas previously occupied by units of Nkunda's Bravo Brigades. By late 2007, the rebel leader was calling for peace talks – something that Kabila had previously refused to consider, demanding instead that Nkunda integrate his force into the national army.

The Banyamulenge Tutsi issue is an old one in the DRC, dating back to the colonial era, with eastern Congolese Tutsis being marginalized under the former Congolese head of state, Mobutu Sese Seko. Although Banyamulenge were closely associated with his successor, Laurent Kabila, this relationship soured rapidly in the 1999–2001 period, which ended with Kabila's assassination by one of his own Swahili-speaking guards. This resulted in yet more popular anger in the capital Kinshasa, with Banyamulenge being aggressively stereotyped as 'non-Congolese' and an effective fifth column for neighbouring Rwanda –

whose ruling RPF come from the minority Tutsi ethnic group. Many Banyamulenge fled the capital at this time, fearing attack, and sought sanctuary back in the east.

The events in eastern Congo in 2007 are a continuance of the poisonous ethnic strife which led to the genocide of minority Tutsis and Hutu moderates in Rwanda in 1994. Beyond Nkunda's immediate circumstances, the long-term issue of the insecurity of the Banyamulenge minority in the DRC, and how they may best combat this, remains unresolved. The Banymulenge themselves are divided over the way to a solution. Most acknowledged Banyamulenge political thinkers are in favour of a negotiated political solution, but disapprove strongly of the lack of Banyamulenge representation at both parliament and senate level. In addition, prejudice against Banyamulenge interests remains entrenched in Kinshasa, including within the administration.

In Ituri, 2007 saw considerable progress in the demobilization, disarmament and reintegration of the six militias that had emerged along ethnic lines since 1999. Coordinated by the UN and the Congolese armed forces, the initiative achieved a major success with the adhesion to the process of the last of the main militias to have held out against it, the Lendu Nationalist Integrationist Front (FNI). Many of the FNI and other demobilized fighters were expected to join the armed forces. The Ituri conflict has always had a complex ethnic aspect to it, most obviously in the stoking up of mutual hatred between Hema and Lendu from 1999 onwards, the work of local warlords as well as Rwanda's and Uganda's interference in the region. However, like other such regional conflicts in DRC in the past decade, the violence has not merely been identitarian. As elsewhere, the control of resources has been at the centre of the conflict. On 18 October 2007, the International Criminal Court formally indicted Germain Katanga, one of the key military leaders of the FNI, for crimes against humanity, among other charges, after he was handed over by the Congolese authorities.

Among minority populations suffering particularly from the continuing conflict in the east are the Congolese Batwa/Bambuti. In South Kivu, continuing attacks by Rwandan rebel forces in the countryside outside Bukavu have had a grave effect on the Batwa/Bambuti as on other communities. Pillage, torture and killings are common, and there is a particularly high incidence of rape and extreme sexual violence. In North Kivu, some Batwa/Bambuti communities have been caught in the large waves of displacement caused by the ongoing fighting between forces loyal to Nkunda, Congolese Maï-Maï and the Congolese armed forces. Further north in Ituri, the situation in areas where Bambuti live was calmer during the course of 2006–7, although some parts of the district are threatened by the presence of hardcore FRPI fighters who have refused to join the demobilization programme. Throughout the region, the chronic proverty and marginalization experienced by Batwa/Bambuti communities is exacerbated by the security situation.

Control over forest resources continued to be of critical importance to the Batwa/Bambuti. In late 2007, a leaked report from a World Bank Inspection Panel said that the bank had backed the Congolese government in planning the extension of commercial logging in the DRC without consulting with the Batwa or considering the impact on their communities or the environment. Recently, a coalition of organizations based around forest peoples groups has also been lobbying at the UN against what they regard as a deficient government response to the plight of the forest peoples. Following the government's presentation in 2006 of its state party report to the UN Committee on the Elimination of Racial Discrimination (CERD), this grouping replied in January 2007, noting that forest peoples had been completely ignored in Kinshasa's submission. In its concluding observations issued in August 2007, CERD recommended that DRC take 'urgent and adequate measures' to protect the rights of the Batwa to land. It also urged that there be a moratorium on forest lands, that the ancestral lands of the Batwa be registered, and provision should be made for the forest rights of indigenous peoples in domestic legislation.

Egypt

Minorities' right to freedom of religion continued to give rise to concerns in 2007. The minority Baha'i, numbering approximately 2,000 at most, received a further setback in their attempts to be officially recognized when the Supreme Administrative Court reversed a lower court's decision earlier in the year to allow them to be officially registered for identity purposes. The result of this ruling was that Baha'is must continue to be registered as either Muslims, Jews or Christians. Refusal to do so entails the inability to obtain documentation ranging from birth certificates to other identification necessary to open bank accounts and send children to school. A government report in October 2006 argued that Baha'is must be 'identified, confronted and singled out so that they can be watched carefully, isolated and monitored in order to protect the rest of the population as well as Islam from their danger, influence and their teachings'.

Issues of religious freedom also arise in cases where individuals wish to convert to Christianity from Islam. Those who convert often do so quietly because of the harassment and intimidation from both the authorities, including the police, and religious groups. However, this approach was challenged in 2007, by the case of Mohammed Hegazy. According to reports, he undertook a court action to try to get his ID card changed to reflect his new Christian religion. His story was reported in national media, after which Mr Hegazy faced death threats and went into hiding. Mr Hegazy's case came amid a debate about apostasy, and its legitimate punishment. According to Associated Press reports, one of Egypt's most senior clerics, the Grand Mufti Ali Gomaa, issued guidance against the killing of apostates – a view which was rejected by other religious scholars in Egypt.

The minority Coptic Christians, estimated at 5–10 per cent of the overall population but concentrated more heavily in Cairo, Alexandria and the south, remained vulnerable through the year to attacks from Islamic extremists. In October 2007, two Copts were murdered at el-Kasheh, south of Cairo. Earlier in the year there were allegations of security force personnel destroying Coptic graves. There is currently internal debate among Copts over whether to support a possible presidential succession by Gamal Mubarak, regarded by some Copt leaders as their best guarantee of safety in the face of the Muslim Brotherhood.

Eritrea

The persecution of religious minorities in Eritrea remains a major concern. In its annual *International Religious Freedom* report 2007, the US State Department said that the Eritrean government's record on religious freedom had deteriorated even further. There are reportedly 1,900 prisoners held for their religious beliefs in this small African nation.

The country's population of 3.7 million is roughly half Christian and half Muslim. Since 1995, the government only officially recognizes four faiths – the Eritrean Orthodox Church (the biggest church in Eritrea with an estimated 1.7 million adherents), Islam, the Lutheran Church and the Roman Catholic Church. In May 2002, the government insisted that all unregistered groups stop operating until they had obtained official approval. According to research undertaken by the UK-based Royal Institute of International Affairs (RIIA) at Chatham House, the Baha'i faith, the Faith Mission Church, the Orthodox Presbyterian Church and Seventh Day Adventists did manage to register, but have not been allowed to operate publicly.

However, many evangelical churches have not been registered. According to RIIA, these have reportedly been growing rapidly in Eritrea – although exact membership figures are hard to come by – and their followers have been particularly targeted by the government. In September 2007, the BBC interviewed an Eritrean evangelical Christian who described the torture techniques which had been used on him – including being tied in a position known as 'the Helicopter' for 136 hours. Another victim reported that he was held for 12 months, forced to do manual labour and, on one occasion, 'suspended by his arms from a tree in the form of a crucifixion'.

The 'Open Doors' Christian charity reported that at least four Christians had died in 2007, following severe ill-treatment at the hands of the authorities. Jehovah's Witnesses are treated with particular harshness because their faith prohibits them from undertaking Eritrea's compulsory military service, in some cases being held without trial for up to 12 years.

In a rare success, the prominent gospel singer Helen Berhane was released in November 2006, after an international campaign led by Amnesty International. She had been held for two and a half years – most of the time in a metal shipping container, which served as a cell. In late 2007 she was granted asylum in Denmark.

Even followers of the officially recognized religions have not been immune from harassment and ill-treatment. The deposed Patriarch of the Eritrean Orthodox Church, Abune Antonios, has been under house arrest for over two years.

Ethiopia

Since a new constitution was established in 1995 following the overthrow of the oppressive Derg regime, the country has followed a unique system of ethnically based federalism. But the question of whether this structure actually helps minorities realize their rights, or whether it has been subverted by the present government to consolidate its hold on power, is now of urgent concern to minority rights activists.

The crackdown against opponents of the regime following the elections in 2005, the 2006 invasion of Somalia and its subsequent fall-out, as well as the 2007 heavy-handed security action in the Ogaden, have set the scene for an increasingly repressive and intolerant atmosphere.

Two major assessments of the Ethiopian government's recent record came in 2007 – one from the UN committee which monitors the implementation of the International Convention on the Elimination of all forms of Racial Discrimination (ICERD) and the other from the UN's Independent Expert on Minority Issues.

CERD's report – issued without the cooperation of the Ethiopian government – gave an extremely critical assessment of the country's record, noting that, among other things, it was 'alarmed' at information that military and police forces have been 'systematically targeting' certain ethnic groups, such as the Anuak and the Oromo.

It had – it said – received information about 'summary executions, rape of women and girls, arbitrary detention, torture, humiliations and destruction of property and crops of members of those communities'.

Other concerns expressed by CERD included the lack of information on minority representation in local and national government, in the judiciary and security services, and the establishment of national parks without the participation or informed consent of the indigenous peoples.

The latter point followed criticism of the transfer of the Omo National Park in south-west Ethiopia, from government to private control. Indigenous peoples' organizations – including Survival International – complained that the deal had gone through without prior consultation with the pastoralist tribes in the area, and that the government had obtained 'consent' of the communities to the boundary demarcation of the park by asking them to sign documents with a thumb-print.

In February 2007, the Independent Expert on Minority Issues, Gay McDougall, published her report on Ethiopia, following a country visit. Among her findings were that some smaller minority communities were considered to be on the verge of disappearing, due to 'factors including resettlement, displacement, conflict, assimilation, cultural dilution, environmental factors and loss of land'. She noted that, 'An unknown number of minority communities are believed to have already disappeared completely.'

While praising certain aspects of government policy – such as the re-establishment of local languages in schools and local administrations – she also found much that was of concern. She reported a perception that the political system was biased in favour of ethnic parties created by the ruling faction, rather than genuinely representative movements.

In a visit to the Gambella, where an estimated 424 people were killed by Ethiopian security forces and other groups in 2003, McDougall found many Anuak still being held in prison without trial. She also highlighted the case of the Karayu pastoralists, who had been displaced from their traditional land and water sources in Oromia because of the establishment of a national park, and industries, in the area.

Among her key recommendations were that the government take steps to depoliticize ethnicity, and promote the policy of inclusion, and that urgent steps be taken to protect the existence of some small minority groups. Moreover, she also called for an inclusive national conference to examine the federalist system.

The Independent Expert's report was roundly rejected by the Ethiopian government in its response to the Human Rights Commission, which said it was 'littered with information based on hearsay and unfounded allegations'. Meanwhile, the unfolding crisis in the southern Ogaden region left the impression that the Independent Expert's recommendations for political inclusiveness had gone unheeded.

In September 2007, a public plea by the international aid agencies, the International Federation of the Red Cross and Médicins sans Frontières, galvanized world attention on the security crackdown in the desert Ogaden region. Bordering Somalia in the south-east, the biggest group in the region is ethnic Somali.

In April 2007, a sputtering rebellion by the Ogaden National Liberation Front (ONLF) flared into life again. Rebels attacked an oil installation killing 74, including some Chinese workers. Security forces responded by blockading areas suspected to be rebel strongholds, denying international aid agencies access to supply humanitarian relief.

Food prices soared, livestock prices halved. Many people were forced to flee their homes – amid witness testimony that the government was burning villages. Worryingly, the Ethiopian army was said to be targeting certain sub-clans as supporters of the ONLF, and to be acting against them indiscriminately. As a result, hundreds of thousands were left dependent on food aid. There were also reports of abuses by ONLF – including punishments for civilians who failed to provide food or shelter.

The crisis in the Ogaden is intrinsically linked in to the wider upheaval in the Horn of Africa region, the epicentre of which is Somalia. Although the existence of the ONLF precedes the emergence of the Islamic Courts Union (ICU) in Somalia, strategic links between the ONLF and the ICU have been reported, while the Ethiopian government's bitter foe – the government of Isaias Afewerki in Eritrea – is widely believed to be actively supporting the ONLF.

Nevertheless, the Horn of Africa Group based at the Royal Institute for International Affairs, said the government's response was disproportionate and counter-productive. Its report, *Conflict in the Ogaden and its Regional Dimensions* (September 2007) concluded: 'Ethiopian action is leading to a revival of Somali national sentiment and a sense of common destiny that cuts across the clan divide.'

Kenya

The fall-out from the late 2007 elections plunged Kenya into chaos. Amid widespread allegations of rigging, President Kibaki and his Party of National Unity claimed victory in the closely fought elections – an outcome vehemently disputed by the opposition Orange Democratic Movement. The tribal fault-lines in Kenyan society were exposed when competing political interests overlapped with ethnic differences. President Kibaki and many of his close associates are Kikuyu, while his main rival Raila Odinga is a Luo. The Luos – who make up 14 per cent of the Kenyan population – have long seen themselves as being denied the leadership of the country. Kikuyus – who make up 20 per cent of the population – have dominated the country politically and economically since independence, and have traditionally been the target of widespread resentment on the part of the smaller tribes.

Alarmingly, post-election anger has mutated into the settling of old scores. In the Rift Valley, historic grievances against land allocations led to the mass targeting of Kikuyu farmers by the Kalenjin (around 11 per cent of the population), who regard the land in the Rift Valley as theirs. In western Kenya, the Kikuyu minority also found itself under attack; many fled, fearing for their lives. In a disturbing escalation of the violence, the Kikuyu criminal militia, *Mungiki*, struck back around the town of Naivasha in the Rift Valley, targeting Luo and tribes seen to support the opposition. By the end of January, hundreds had been killed in the violence, with tens of thousands displaced. Political leaders on both sides of the divide had no clear plan to pull Kenya back from the brink, despite high-level diplomatic efforts led by former UN Secretary-General Kofi Annan.

Earlier in 2007, control over Kenya's land resources was identified as one of the 'most pressing issues on the public agenda' by the UN Special Rapporteur for Indigenous Issues, Rodolfo Stavenhagen, in his February 2007 country report on Kenya. His assessment, based on a visit to Kenya undertaken at the end of the previous year, painted a bleak picture of the situation of Kenya's pastoralist, hunter-gatherer and forest tribes. Excluded from political and economic power, these peoples have seen their land seized, their resources plundered and their way of life become ever more untenable.

Since early 2007, tensions had also flared in the Mount Elgon region in western Kenya, as a long-standing dispute over land rights boiled over. After months of violence, an estimated 300 were dead, and 100,000 displaced in late 2007. The origins of the conflict lie in the displacement of the pastoralist Sabaot people from their traditional lands by the British colonial authorities, and subsequent botched attempts by the Kenyan government to resettle them.

According to the Kenya Land Alliance, the latest scheme was fraught with 'massive irregularities' and left 1,400 people 'homeless, landless, and with no means of livelihood'. Leaders of the indigenous Ogiek forest-dwelling tribe complained that their ancestral rights to live in Chepyuk forest had been ignored and called for the scheme to be nullified.

It was in this context that the Sabaot Lands Defence Force (SLDF) emerged. Although its origins, strength and precise motives remain unclear, the SLDF publicly states that it wants to reclaim lost territory, including its ancestral lands. By late 2007, it had carried out the burning of property and attacks in major towns such as Kitale, and driven tens of thousands of people from their homes. At the end of October 2007, in a series of gruesome attacks, six people were beheaded, reportedly by the SLDF. Many of the victims have been from rival Sabaot sub-clans, others were settlers from other tribes seen as 'incomers'.

In March 2007, the Ogiek issued a public plea for help, saying that 20 Ogiek had been killed in the violence and appealing to the international community for help. Humanitarian agencies say the conditions endured by the displaced are dire. Without a chance to harvest crops, displaced families face the prospect of malnutrition, and those who have sought refuge on the cooler, higher slopes of Mount Elgon are more susceptible to disease.

In August 2007, Kenya's draft National Land Policy was made public. This policy is an attempt to address the explosive issue of land ownership and land tenure, which has dogged the country since independence. As the fall-out from the election demonstrates, the colonial land policies, laws and administrative structure have given rise to entrenched corrupt practices, gross social and economic inequalities and, ultimately, conflict.

Potentially, this new draft policy – which was formulated after a wide-ranging consultative process – could redefine the relationship between the country's marginalized minorities and the state. Indeed, it includes a special section on minorities, pastoralist groups and coastal peoples. Some of the policy's provisions are: to draw up a legislative framework to secure the rights of minorities; to convert government-owned land on the coastal strip into community land; and, crucially, to recognize pastoralism as a legitimate land use and production system. The document has yet to be debated by the

Kenyan parliament. In view of the post-election crisis, however, it is unclear when this will happen. Previous experience suggests that the entrenched interests of the Kenyan business and political elite may find many of the proposals unpalatable, although it is now evident that, if Kenya is to overcome its current divisions, the settlement of historic land grievances will be an essential component of any road-map to recovery.

The political chaos is also a setback for minority rights campaigners, who had hoped that progress could be made on implementing the landmark *Il Chamus* decision in the Kenyan courts. This ruling,

delivered by the Constitutional Court in late 2006, found in favour of the Il Chamus community from Lake Baringo in the Rift Valley. This pastoralist tribe had complained that, under the current electoral arrangements, it was almost impossible to elect an MP from their group.

Activists believe the court verdict could help other minorities – such as the Boni, Endorois, Nubians and Tachoni – secure better political representation. Yobo Rutin, from the Centre for Minority Rights Development, says they pressed the Electoral Commission of Kenya and the government for the redrawing of electoral boundaries and the creation of special interest seats. But both measures got nowhere in advance of the hotly contested end-of-year poll.

Despite this disappointment, the Endorois, whose ancestral home is around Lake Bogoria in the Rift Valley, continued their fight to realize their rights. MRG has been working closely with this community, who were displaced from their traditional territory when the area was declared a wildlife sanctuary in 1973. Attempts to seek redress at a national level have failed, so the Endorois have taken their case to the African Commission on Human and Peoples' Rights. If successful, their case will have implications for many other minorities in similar situations across the continent.

Election season also focused attention on the Muslim minority in Kenya. Although there is no official figure, the total number of Muslims in Kenya is put at anything between 10 to 20 per cent of the population. This group has long-standing complaints about discriminatory treatment. Since 9/11 these have been aggravated by anti-terrorist activities, which have led to protests about arbitrary, unlawful detention and torture. Security sweeps in coastal cities such as Mombasa have often seemed counter-productive. The issues rose to the surface in 2007, partly because of the dislodging of the Islamic Courts Union in Somalia. The Kibaki government is widely believed to have 'rendered' suspected Islamic extremists back to Ethiopia. Amid considerable confusion, it was claimed that some of those handed over were of Kenyan nationality and therefore should have been tried under Kenyan law. In a bid to keep the Muslim vote on-side in a tight electoral race, President Kibaki appointed an official committee to investigate alleged discrimination against Kenyan Muslims by the government.

Mali/Niger

Unrest continues among the Tuareg populations of the Sahelian and Saharan north. The Tuareg – who represent approximately 5 per cent of Mali's 13.5 million population – have traditionally opposed the central government in the capital Bamako, complaining of political and economic marginalization. Frequent droughts in recent years have contributed to growing hardship among these pastoralist communities. Following a Tuareg-spearheaded revolt in 1990–96, a decade of uneasy peace has recently seen two major outbreaks of insurgency or less well-defined violence. In early 2006, a former rebel, Ibrahima Ag Bahanga, subsequently integrated into the Malian army, deserted his post accusing the government of neglecting the northern region around Kidal. This led to an Algerian-brokered agreement in July, providing for boosted development initiatives for the region. More recently, in August 2007, there was a further outbreak of violence led by men loyal to Ibrahima Ag Bahanga. They kidnapped at least two dozen army personnel near the north-eastern desert settlement of Tendjeret. Although this appears to have been a one-off series of events linked to the cross-border smuggling trade in the region, the United States has viewed northern Mali as an area vulnerable to terrorism in recent years and has conducted training exercises with Malian forces.

Across the border in Niger, there remains a state of high tension between the government and the Tuareg-led Niger Movement for Justice (MNJ), including firefights with government forces leading to several deaths. The MNJ has repeatedly declared that northern Niger is 'a war zone' and has attempted to target the region's uranium extraction industry, including an attack on installations at Imou-Araren in April and the kidnapping of a Chinese contractor in July. The MNJ has also accused the uranium sector, spearheaded by the French conglomerate Areva, of long-term neglect of the environment and of the safety and interest of local, largely Tuareg, populations. In both countries, there is resentment towards Tuaregs from sedentary and southern populations. The marginalization of the Tuaregs is likely to be aggravated by the continuing desertification of the Sahel, a process likely to continue as global warming begins to bite. In 2007 Oxfam warned that changed rainfall patterns in Niger are contributing to worsening desertification, which, for indigenous people like the Tuaregs, means massive losses in livestock and food insecurity.

Mauritania

A new president was elected in Mauritania, in a historic poll in March 2007, signalling the return to democratic rule. Up until 2005, the country had been ruled by the strong-man Maaouiya Ould Taya for quarter of a century. The new president, Sidi Ould Sheikh Abdallahi, was a former cabinet minister under Taya. However, he quickly indicated his intention to break with the past, especially over two issues: black Mauritanian refugees living in camps in Senegal and Mali, and slavery.

An estimated 70,000 black Mauritanians were driven from the country in 1989, in what ostensibly started as a border dispute about grazing rights. However, the expulsions were widely seen as a part of a racially motivated campaign against Mauritania's black citizens, based mainly in the south. According to Human Rights Watch (HRW), tensions between the black southerners and the Arab and Berber northerners date back to before independence. In colonial days, the more settled lifestyles of the black minority (who make up roughly one-third of the population) allowed them to do better educationally, and to dominate the civil service. However, after independence, the Arab and Berber northerners took control, purged the southerners from positions of influence and sought to Arabize the country. Since 1989, some black Mauritanians have drifted back home, but others have languished in poor conditions in refugee camps over the border in Senegal and Mali, and were regarded as an encumbrance by these countries' governments. However, on 12 November 2007, following the election of the new government, Mauritania and Senegal signed a deal which could allow the repatriation of 12,000 refugees, administered under the auspices of the Office of the UN High Commissioner for Refugees (UNHCR). The agreement seemed to mark the end of Africa's most protracted refugee crisis – but there will also be difficulties ahead, especially where the return of land and property is concerned.

New legislation criminalizing slavery in Mauritania was swiftly passed by the new parliament. Although slavery had been banned in Mauritania for over 20 years, there had been no criminal penalties for those flouting the ban. SOS Slavery estimates that there could be as many as 600,000 slaves in Mauritania. It is a deeply engrained practice, dating back hundreds of years,

Human Development Indicators by main language groups

	Life expectancy at birth (years) 2001	Literacy rate, +15 years (%) 2001	Gross enrolment ratio, 6–24 years (%) 2001	Annual average adjusted per capita income (N$) 2003/2004
Namibia	49	84	66	10,358
Khoisan	52	47	34	3,263
Rukavango	43	87	61	4,137
Caprivian languages	43	91	60	7,728
Nama/Damara	52	87	57	6,366
Oshiwambo	48	94	71	7,218
Otjiherero	58	86	59	11,478
Setswana	67	92	65	12,793
Afrikaans	62	99	66	28,684
English	63	100	67	66,898
German	79	100	79	87,649

Source: UNDP (2007): Trends In Human Development and Poverty in Namibia

to when Arab and Berber tribes launched slave raids against the African population. Those enslaved were converted to Islam and have been treated as inheritable property. While the new law has been welcomed by campaigners, it has also been pointed out that, as with previous attempts to introduce tougher punishments, much will depend on the authorities' willingness to enforce the law, if the practice is to be eradicated.

Namibia

The land rights of the San came under scrutiny in Namibia in 2007 in a highly critical report compiled by the Legal Assistance Centre (LAC), based in Windhoek.

There are estimated to be about 30,000 San in Namibia, belonging to the Hai//om, Ju/hoansi and Khwe sub-groups – and, since colonial times, they have been pushed off their traditional lands without adequate compensation. The LAC pointed out that the government land policy unveiled in 1998 had prioritized the needs of the San, but thus far had failed to deliver. The Hai//om in particular complained that the 2007 centenary celebrations to mark the establishment of Namibia's premier Etosha National Park, ignored the bitter experience of their people. Now thought to number 9,000, the Hai//om had been expelled from the reserve in the

1960s. They are currently the only San community without any communal lands.

A report from the United Nations Development Programme (UNDP), dramatically illustrated that the San people had borne the brunt of Namibia's worsening poverty and the HIV/Aids epidemic. Not only did the San (identified as Khoisan speakers in the table above), have the lowest incomes as a group, but their life expectancy has also dropped more sharply than that of any of the other groups surveyed. Namibia has one of the worst rates of HIV/Aids infection in the world. The study revealed that, in terms of income disparity, the country also ranked as one of the worst in the world. And the poverty experienced by the San community was comparable to that in the world's most deprived countries.

The deep-seated prejudice faced by the San in Namibia was highlighted by complaints over the treatment of San rape victims. A traditional leader, Michael Isung Simana, in the Omaheke region in eastern Namibia, reportedly told the *New Era* newspaper in October 2007 about the high incidence of rape of San women by members of other communities. He attributed this to 'persistent negative stereotypes, which place a lower value on the dignity of San women, than other women'. Simana also accused the police of not treating the rape of San women seriously enough, and of failing to vigorously investigate allegations or gather adequate forensic evidence (see also *Botswana*).

Nigeria

In April 2007, Africa's most populous nation held general elections, widely denounced as both fraudulent and incompetent. Even so, the outcome was largely accepted by the electorate. The winner of the presidential race, Umaru Yar'Adua – the chosen successor of the outgoing Olusegun Obasanjo – has a tough task ahead of him, managing this religious and ethnically diverse giant, whose population includes an estimated 250 ethnic groups.

Obasanjo's tenure was scarred by inter-communal fighting at the cost of thousands of lives. The entrenched nature of the conflicts in Nigeria – as well as the inability of the authorities to provide lasting solutions – was illustrated by the resurgence of fighting between the Tiv and Kuteb communities in Benue state and Taraba states in Central Nigeria. Hundreds were reported displaced, and dozens killed. The dispute over land rights of the various communities in the area has been simmering for years, with violence peaking in 2001, when hundreds died. Many were killed by the army in reprisal attacks against the Tiv community, after Tiv militants killed 19 soldiers who had been deployed in the area to quell the fighting. In November 2007, in a highly unusual move, the army issued a formal apology to the Tiv community. Condemned by some as inadequate because it was not tied to compensation for the victims' families, it was nevertheless welcomed by others as a sign that the Nigerian army was at last taking human rights issues seriously.

When he took power, President Yar'Adua identified the crisis in the Niger Delta as one of his top priorities. In November 2007 he unveiled a 'master plan' to develop the region. According to IRIN, this involves doubling the budget of the Niger Delta Development Commission (NDDC) in 2008. The NDDC's chairman then proclaimed that the Niger Delta would be 'Africa's most prosperous, peaceful and pleasant region by 2020'. It will be hard to match the rhetoric with the reality because of the worsening problems in the region.

The Niger Delta – a lush region of mangrove swamps, rainforest and swampland – is home to 6 million people including the Andoni, Dioubu, Etche, Ijaw, Kalibari, Nemba (Brass), Nembe, Ogoni

and Okrika minority groups. It is the site of rich oil and natural gas reserves both offshore and on land. But ethnic groups have protested about the environmental degradation and about the failure of the central government and the international petroleum companies to share the oil wealth with local communities. Little money goes into schools or hospitals. Public services are in a pitiable condition.

In recent years, disaffection has given way to militancy. Kidnappings of local and international oil workers have risen steadily, with the militias even resorting to the kidnapping of children. The situation is complicated by the links that the militias are alleged to have with powerful criminal and political networks. The gangs are known to be actively engaged in oil 'bunkering' – stealing oil from pipelines and using the proceeds to buy arms. Recently, there have been concerns that the oil giants may be further aggravating the problem by paying off the militants to 'protect' their facilities. The grip of the militants on the area was illustrated in August 2007, when fighting rocked Port Harcourt – Nigeria's main oil city. There were running battles in the street after government troops tried to arrest a prominent Delta militia leader. Criminality is alleged on the side of the military too, with accusations that local military officials are involved in selling oil to Eastern Europe in exchange for weapons.

In this context, the new president appointed Goodluck Jonathan – an Ijaw – as his deputy. Jonathan has already been targeted twice for assassination. The government, meanwhile, released the detained leader of Niger Delta People's Volunteer Force, Mujahid Dokubo-Asari, and the vice-president embarked upon a series of meetings with leaders of the different communities in the Delta. The main militant group in the Niger Delta, the Movement for the Emancipation of the Niger Delta (MEND), which claims to represent the interests of the Ijaw community, called a ceasefire which held for a few months from June. But by the end of the year the group had resumed attacks.

International Crisis Group (ICG) in May 2007 said that the failure of the electoral process has deepened the separatist sentiment in the south-east. In a year that marked the fortieth anniversary of the outbreak of the Biafran war, ICG said that, perhaps more than in any other region, the poll in the Ibo heartland was 'poorly conducted and mindlessly rigged', boosting the position of the separatist group,

Movement for the Actualization of the Sovereign State of Biafra (MASSOB), that Ibos would never 'realize their political aspirations with the Nigerian federation'. However, there was a question-mark over the MASSOB's tactics, after a 'sit-at-home-strike' failed to mobilize widespread support, showing that many Ibos did not want to publicly associate themselves with the separatist cause.

The 1960s Ibo separatist leader, the now-elderly Chukwuemeka Odumegwu Ojukwu, contested the 2007 presidential elections, coming sixth. He later told the BBC that the Ibo had more reason than ever to seek independence, basing his comments on the widespread electoral irregularities. Throughout 2007, there were protests from Ibo associations that Chief Ralf Uwazuruike, leader of MASSOB, remained in jail – although other separatist or rebel leaders had been released. Uwazuruike and other alleged MASSOB supporters were arrested in 2005 and charged with treason. But at the end of October 2007 Uwazuruike was released from detention. His message of independence for Biafra – however – remained the same. IRIN reported him saying: 'All we want is our Biafra. We want to secede.'

Rwanda

The Batwa community in Rwanda received a set-back in 2007. Following a long-running dispute with the government, the main Batwa organization, the Community of Indigenous People of Rwanda (CAURWA), was forced to change its name as the government refused to renew its charity licence until it had dropped the word 'indigenous' from its title.

Since the 1994 genocide, when the ruling elite of the majority Hutu group stoked up murderous hatred against minority Tutsis, ethnicity has been a difficult and sensitive area in Rwanda. The Rwandan government has prohibited identification along ethnic lines. Setting the over-riding goal as reconciliation, an official from the Ministry of Justice told IRIN in 2006 that 'ethnic divisions have only caused conflicts between the peoples of the country'.

However, for the marginalized Batwa community – historically discriminated against by both Hutus and Tutsis – recognition of its distinct identity has been extremely important. Without it, it will be extremely hard to tackle the multiple forms of discrimination this small group – estimated at 33,000 – faces, or to maintain what remains of their rich and distinctive cultural traditions. Batwa too

suffered in the genocide – it is estimated that a third of their community was wiped out.

However, even before that, the Batwa had seen their ancestral forests cleared. Some were able to survive but many had become landless beggars, whose traditional forests were taken over for agriculture, commercial forestry plantations and wildlife conservation areas. When it comes to education, health and other social services, Batwa fare worse than either Hutus or Tutsis. As the NGO Forest Peoples Programme notes in a 2006 submission to the Human Rights Committee, the protection of many of the Batwa's human rights is recognized neither 'by law [n]or in fact'.

When the African Peer Review Panel looked at the situation in Rwanda, its 2005 report concluded that the Rwandan authorities appear to be adopting a policy of assimilation. This was vehemently denied by Kigali. In its 2007 report to the African Commission, Rwanda once again resisted the use of the term 'indigenous' saying 'Rwanda is not a country where native populations can be identified in the Western meaning of the term', noting instead that, as the national programme against poverty was targeted at the poorest, then communities that have been 'historically marginalized' would be the first to benefit.

Somalia

The brutal bout of warfare which followed last year's invasion by Ethiopia, and the subsequent ouster of the Islamic Courts Union, means that, for the second year in a row, Somalia tops MRG's Peoples under Threat (PUT) table. PUT is a predictive tool, forecasting the places in the world where civilian protection will be worst in 2008, and where people are most at risk of mass murder, genocide or other extreme forms of violence. This means that, however bad 2007 was, 2008 in Somalia is likely to be worse.

Already the situation is catastrophic. In November 2007, UNHCR announced that the total number of people displaced has been a 'staggering' 1 million. Human rights groups complained that all sides were responsible for indiscriminate attacks on civilians, mass arrests and looting. Although Somalia has experienced over a decade of anarchy since the fall of dictator Siad Barre, the current fighting is particularly perilous because of the internationalization of the conflict. The involvement of external actors – both regional governments, like Eritrea and Ethiopia, and the US – has meant that the ramifications of this warfare are spreading beyond Somalia. This has potentially catastrophic implications for civilians in the region, but specifically for minorities – both inside and outside Somalia's borders. The conflict in Somalia has already been linked to a 2007 upsurge of fighting in the Ethiopian Ogaden region, with ethnic Somali civilians bearing the brunt of the violence. Sensitivities over discriminatory treatment of Muslims in Kenya have been exacerbated by allegations that the Kenyan government 'rendered' some Kenyans suspected of involvement in the Islamic Courts Union to Ethiopia, instead of trying them in their home country.

Because of the fighting, it is extremely difficult to obtain up-to-date information about the fate of Somalia's small, vulnerable minorities: at the best of times, information about these groups is difficult to come by. But if past patterns of violence are repeated, Somali minority communities will suffer greatly. According to Amnesty International, the Somali minorities comprise principally the 'African' Bantu/Jarir, who are mostly landless labourers; the Benadiri/Rer Hamar urban traders of Middle Eastern origin; and the smaller, dispersed Gaboye caste-based minorities, who are generally employed as metal-workers, leather-workers, hairdressers, herbalists and others. There are other smaller minorities, such as the Ashraf and Shikhal Muslim religious communities, Bajuni fishing people and remote hunter-gatherer groups. What these groups have in common is their vulnerability, as they fall outside Somalia's clan-based structure. They do not benefit from the protections of war-lords and militias. But they are also vulnerable to increased risk of rape, attack, abduction and having their property seized by criminals in an increased atmosphere of lawlessness. Equally, when some semblance of calm does return, they have little chance of gaining compensation for their losses, again because they fall outside the clan structure.

An Amnesty International Report in 2005 stated that the majority of over 300,000 internally displaced persons in several parts of Somalia are members of minority groups. It said: 'They subsist in mainly unregulated settlements in abject conditions, with international relief assistance reportedly often diverted and stolen by members of local clans.' The same report also noted that the international agencies involved in relief distribution were poorly informed about the special risks faced by minorities during times of insecurity.

Sudan

In Sudan in 2007 the position of minorities worsened. In a country which is home to more than 56 ethnic communities, and over 600 sub-ethnic groups, the relations between different minorities are extremely complex. However, the primary difficulty is that of governance. Successive governments in Khartoum, including the current one, have pursued a policy of disenfranchising minorities, while concentrating the economic and political power in the hands of narrow elite based in the capital. Marginalization has, in turn, fuelled conflict – historically in the south, among the peoples of mainly Christian and animist traditions, more recently in Darfur in the west and Beja in the east. And in 2007 new flashpoints emerged in Kordofan, in the heart of the country, and in the north among the Nubian and Manassir peoples.

The Comprehensive Peace Agreement

The biggest body-blow to the prospect of a new, more inclusive Sudan in 2007 was the prospect of the unravelling of the Comprehensive Peace Agreement (CPA). This keynote agreement, signed in 2005, brought an end to the war between the rebels of the South and the Islamic government in the North. Although not perfect, the CPA contains provisions of critical importance to minorities, including (1) a national census, which would have helped accurately determine the ethnic composition of the country, (2) national elections by 2009, which may have increased the political representation of minorities and (3) a referendum on self-determination for the South by 2011.

All of these were thrown into doubt when the former rebel movement, the Sudanese People's Liberation Movement (SPLM) announced it was withdrawing from the Government of National Unity (GoNU) in October 2007. It accused the government of reneging on key provisions in the CPA – including the re-deployment of troops, and the demarcation of North/South border, and status of the oil-rich territory of Abyei. Although the SPLM later rejoined the GoNU, the incident exposed the fragility of the CPA. If it does eventually collapse, then analysts predict catastrophic consequences – not only would there be the outbreak of a new, more deadly phase of the North–South war, but also the prospects of settling Darfur would recede even further.

Darfur

The conflict in Darfur is roughly said to pit 'African' farmers (the Fur, Masalit, Zaghawa and other, smaller ethnic groups) against 'Arab' nomads. This has always been an overly simplistic explanation, but in 2007 the picture in Darfur darkened even further, as allegiances started to fracture and shift.

At the start of the fighting in 2003, there were two main rebel groups. Now, there are over a dozen – some sponsored by regional governments, such as Chad, Eritrea and Libya. The fracturing of the rebels is partly a consequence of the ill-conceived Darfur Peace Agreement (DPA), signed by one rebel group and the government in 2006. Struck under international pressure – in particular from the US and UK – the DPA actually intensified the fighting on the ground, as former rebel allies took up arms against each other, while the government continued its military campaign, under the guise of supporting the peace agreement.

Another key development was the splintering of unity among the Arab Janjaweed militia. In January 2007, various militia – once allies – turned on each other in an outbreak of fighting just outside Nyala in South Darfur. This led some Darfuris from Arab tribes to seek refuge in enormous aid camps for the first time, heightening tensions there immensely.

Aid workers in Darfur, have reported that these developments have hardened ethnic divisions as, in times of great uncertainty, people have sought protection from their tribal groups. Although the international peace effort was re-invigorated in 2007, there is no doubt that the task of securing a lasting deal is immeasurably more difficult now compared with two years ago. The UN Security Council finally authorized deployment of a 26,000-strong peacekeeping force – with most of the troops drawn from Africa – although how easy it will be to deploy, given Khartoum's previous history of prevarication and obstruction, remains to be seen.

Meanwhile, the intolerable situation on the ground in Darfur is marked by upsurges of unpredictable violence. In October 2007, 10 African Union troops were killed in the town of Haskanita in North Darfur – their assailants rumoured to be a splinter rebel groups. Within days of the attack, the government had responded by flattening the town, leaving only a few buildings standing, and driving out the town's inhabitants – numbering several thousand.

Kordofan, and the North and the East of Sudan

In August 2007 a Darfuri rebel group attacked the town of Wad Banda in the neighbouring province of Kordofan, killing around 40 people, most of them from the police. This crystallized fears that the Darfur war would begin to spread to other disaffected regions. As analysts noted, as in Darfur, the marginalized, neglected status of Kordofan, with high levels of unemployment, made it ripe territory for rebellion.

Similarly, in July 2007, the International Crisis Group reported the growing restiveness in the north among the Nubian and Manassir peoples over unpopular plans to build hydro-electric dams on their traditional lands. The dams would cause massive disruption of local communities, and some – particularly among the Nubians – fear that the projects have the covert aim of destroying their ancient traditions and cultures.

The *Los Angeles Times* reported from the area in 2007, saying a rebel group calling itself the Kush Liberation Front had been formed, after security forces had opened fire on a Nubian protest in the northern town of Sebu. One rebel leader reportedly identified the need to get rid of 'the Arabs' as a prerequisite to building a new Sudan.

Meanwhile the situation in the east of the country remains fragile. The Darfur uprising was followed in 2005 by a rebellion in the eastern region, when the Beja Congress joined up with a smaller Bedouin group, the Rashaida Free Lions, to form the 'Eastern Front'. The fighting there ended in October 2006, with the negotiation of a CPA-inspired power-sharing deal, but this has yet to be fully implemented. Until it is, the threat of another uprising remains

Uganda

Peace negotiations to end the long-running rebellion by the Lord's Resistance Army (LRA) continued, while security in the north improved through 2007. The 20-year civil war has devastated the lives – and livelihoods – of the Acholi people of the north. But by September 2007, in a tangible sign of progress, the first refugee camps began to close, as families finally began to return home. In October 2007, for the first time in 20 years, two commanders of the LRA flew into Entebbe to consult on the ongoing peace talks.

At the height of the insurgency, some 1.8 million people were living in camps in the north. While the peace process holds out the prospect of ending the marginalization of the Acholi, Oxfam reported in

Michael Kuskus is a pastoralist from the Karamoja province in north-eastern Uganda, and the head of the Karamoja Agro-Pastoral Development Programme. His community is already working out ways to adapt to climate change.

'Enormous environmental changes have occurred in Karamoja in the past few years. In my childhood, I remember there were lots of forests in Karamoja, and some areas were unreachable because of the thickness of forests. People lived in scattered groups. At no time was there starvation.

'Since 1979 rain patterns have been drastically altered and food production and livestock rearing has been greatly affected as a result. Erratic and shorter rains means that the ground remains dry and nothing can grow. Cattle die.

'When cattle die the economic livelihood of people is greatly weakened. This leads to cattle rustling and conflicts arise between groups.

'Since 2000 we have experienced drought twice. Last year the whole of Karamoja province did not have food. Coping strategies for our people means having to leave our homes and search in the cities and towns for jobs just to get food to survive.

'In 1998 we started to ask people to group together to provide them with loans. A good harvest in 1998 meant loans could be used to purchase food stock that could be stored to be used later in periods of drought.

'When food is plentiful, we encourage people to sell their livestock (prices of livestock are higher when food is plentiful) to purchase food stock and to save their money. This helps them diversify their resources, which is what we need in times of drought. People need to be able to make profits so that they can sustain themselves in the future.

'Climate change in the future is going to affect Karamoja very badly. It used to be that we had rain for six months and it was dry for six months. It is now eight months of drought and only four months with rain. And even this rain is spread out and not continuous.

'This kind of rain leads to soil erosion, as the ground does not absorb enough water. This makes grass and crops impossible to grow. We are worried that in the next few years the rains will reduce even further, to only one or two months a year.

'This is going to have a huge negative impact on us and affect our lifestyle drastically. More people will move away and our communities will be splintered, traditions lost.

'How much more of this will we be able to take?'

Interview by MRG's Samia Khan

September 2007 that many Acholi communities were concerned that the peace was fragile and would quickly unravel in the absence of a signed peace deal.

The plight of the country's pastoralist peoples was highlighted by the public row over the invasion of Uganda's flagship nature reserve, the Queen Elizabeth National Park, by the Basongora cattle-herders. There were reportedly several thousand Basongora with large herds of cattle in the park. They had crossed over the border from the Democratic Republic of Congo, after being driven out of the Virunga mountain range.

However, Uganda's wildlife authorities were anxious about damage done to the park

environment. The Basongora pointed out that their traditional pastures had been in the territory now protected as the Queen Elizabeth National Park, but they had been evicted upon its creation in 1954.

In September, wildlife officials once again tried to evict them. But after claims that excessive force was being used, the government eventually offered the Basongora alternative land outside the park. However this settlement has also proved problematic: there were reports of the forcible removal of small-scale farmers to make way for the Basongora.

The biggest crisis to hit Uganda in 2007 was flooding. Heavy rainfall – the worst in three decades

– left large parts of the country inundated. The Karamoja region in north-eastern Uganda – home of the Karamajong pastoralists – was one of the worst-affected places. In September it was reported that the area had been totally cut off from food supplies. Michael Kuskus of the Karamoja Agro-Pastoral Development Programme complained of sharp rises in food prices and hoarding by unscrupulous traders. This region is already the poorest and most underdeveloped in the country, and, following the floods, there were fears of widespread hunger and the outbreak of epidemics.

The hardship endured by the Karamajong has intensified in recent years. Like other cattle-herders in the East African region, they have been at the sharp end of climate change. More frequent cycles of drought have led to greater competition for scarce resources; cattle-raiding has accelerated and this has been accompanied by an upsurge of violence. The ready availability of small arms in the region has led to deadly conflict, which has caused hundreds of deaths over the past few years.

In an attempt to curb the violence, the Ugandan government embarked upon a forced disarmament programme in Karamoja. But the way in which the policy has been carried out has attracted fierce criticism. In a stinging report issued in 2006, and followed up in April 2007, the UN Office of the High Commissioner for Human Rights (OHCHR) documented grave human rights violations carried out by the national army, the Ugandan People's Defence Forces. These included extra-judicial killings of civilians, torture, inhuman and degrading treatment, the rape of a woman, and the widespread destruction of homesteads.

By November 2007, OHCHR noted that there had been a marked improvement in the security and human rights situation – following increased efforts to seek the cooperation of Karamajong communities, and better training of the military in human rights standards. But OHCHR continued to call for those who had been responsible for the abuses to be brought to account, and condemned the culture of impunity in the armed forces when extra-judicial killings and torture occur.

Western Sahara
Attempts were made to break the deadlock over Western Sahara in 2007. In June 2007, the two sides – the Moroccan government and the Algerian-based Polisario Front – held talks under the auspices of the UN in New York for the first time in ten years. This followed a UN Security Council resolution 1754 in April, which called for the two parties to hold unconditional talks to achieve 'a mutually-acceptable political solution providing for the self-determination of the people of Western Sahara'. It remains unclear whether the 2007 contacts have yielded anything positive, although more discussions are scheduled for 2008. However, in December 2007 the Polisario Front held a party conference in Tifariti, which is located near a so-called 'defence wall' erected by Rabat in the 1980s to repel rebel attacks. The Polisario Front regards it a 'liberated area'. It is only the second time that the Polisario have held a conference in the buffer zone, and Morocco protested to the UN Secretary-General that the move was a violation of the 1991 UN-brokered ceasefire. The dispute may yet sour any prospects for forthcoming discussions.

The Saharawis – of mixed Berber, Arab and black African descent – have long insisted on their right to nationhood. Their struggle dates back to colonial days when they rose up against the European regional powers of Spain and France. Morocco annexed the territory in 1975 – and its attempt to impose control over Western Sahara has been marked by widespread human rights abuses against the Saharawi people, including 'disappearances' and torture. The UN mission has been overseeing a ceasefire in the region since 1991, but with Morocco refusing to allow a referendum on the self-determination issue, and the Polisario Front insisting on one, progress has been non-existent. There are roughly 165,000 Saharawis in refugee camps in Algeria. Many of them have spent over three decades there.

Zimbabwe
In 2007, the Zimbabwean crisis continued to accelerate, with grave implications for its citizens and for the region. In a September 2007 report, International Crisis Group reported 3,000 Zimbabweans per day crossing into South Africa, as well as other Southern African countries. High levels of violence continued – targets were political, economic and social. They ranged from teachers, students, street vendors and journalists to villagers trying to sell grain, human rights activists and opposition politicians.

As the Zimbabwe Human Rights NGO Forum details, human rights abuses range from torture to violations of freedom of expression, movement and association, disappearances, unlawful arrest and unlawful detention. The economy continues to be in freefall. According to the BBC in November 2007, the country's chief statistician indicated that the inflation rate was incalculable, but official reports in February 2008 put it at near 100,000 per cent.

South African-led quiet diplomacy continued to try to build fences between the main opposition MDC and the Zimbabwe government. By the end of the year this approach had not yielded significant benefits. President Mugabe continues to enjoy strong support from leaders of regional governments, unwilling to criticize the liberation-era leader, despite spreading effects of the country's implosion.

In this atmosphere of crisis, there is a strong risk that existing ethnic and racial tensions could be even more gravely inflamed – especially with presidential and parliamentary elections slated for 2008. This is reflected in the MRG's Peoples under Threat table (see pp. 161–7), where Zimbabwe is one of the fastest risers. Although, as indicated above, the Zimbabwe regime attacks a wide range of targets, two minorities are particularly at risk: the Ndebele and the Europeans. The former particularly because there has been a previous episode of mass killing, targeted at this community.

The Ndebele's heartland is the south-western territory of Matabele-land. In the years, immediately before and post-independence, divisions between the majority Shona and the minority Ndebele were evident. The main resistance movements opposing the racist regime of Ian Smith were the Ndebele's ZAPU, led by Joshua Nkomo, and the Shona's ZANU, led by Robert Mugabe. After independence, the Shona-dominated ZANU won the country's first free elections. Mugabe then moved to crush opposition among the Ndebele, embarking upon the 'Gukurahundi' pogrom. The killings, which continued from 1983 to 1987, resulted in an estimated 10,000–20,000 deaths.

Nevertheless, discrimination against the Ndebele continued. The Minorities at Risk (MAR) project notes that: 'There is massive unemployment and general social destitution in the area. Furthermore, although there are no restrictions to high office, civil servants in Matabeleland are disproportionately

Shona, and do not even speak Ndebele' (see www.cidcm.umd.edu/mar). These issues have become particularly acute since the emergence of the opposition Movement for Democratic Change (MDC); Matabele-land is an opposition stronghold. MAR reports that in 2002, prior to the elections, ZANU-PF allegedly threatened the Ndebele with starvation, and a document surfaced which allegedly contained a plan to exterminate the Ndebele. In the heightened tensions in the run-up to the spring 2008 elections, similar incidents may yet occur.

The leadership of the MDC – now split – has been Shona, in the shape of veteran leader, Morgan Tsvangirai and now the breakaway leader, Arthur Mutambara. But there has always been a strong contingent of Ndebele in the senior ranks of the MDC. The 2006 split within the MDC further emphasized the opposition's ethnic dimensions, with the Ndebele led by Secretary-General Welshman Ncube generally siding with the Mutambara faction.

Historically, Europeans owned half the arable land in country, and the large commercial farms supplied 80 per cent of the national agricultural product (Minorities at Risk project, 2000). However, when the Mugabe government embarked on its forcible land seizures policy, ostensibly to redistribute it to landless black Zimbabweans, this group came severely under attack. Many fled the country – those who remain are still extremely vulnerable. The white population of Zimbabwe is vastly reduced as farmers have fled to destinations including South Africa, the UK and Australia. Of some 4,000 white farmers in the 1990s, only around 400 remained in 2007, and the government announced that their farms would be taken in August 2007. Many whites have lost everything they owned. In addition to farmers, white civil servants who worked for the independent Zimbabwean state have been abandoned by their government and left impoverished. Much of the land seized has gone to individuals connected to the Mugabe elite, rather than to the landless. ■

Americas

Maurice Bryan

Overview

In 2007, the minority populations of the Americas continued to face significant human rights challenges. Many of these had their genesis in the socio-economic patterns established from the very beginning of colonial-era expansion.

Although this highly diverse region contains large populations of mixed ethnicity – including immigrants from Europe, Asian-Pacific and Middle Eastern countries – the most disadvantaged and vulnerable in 2007 continued to be those of African and indigenous origin.

Among these vulnerable groups the principal issues remain territorial dispossession, socio-economic marginalization and various forms of discrimination. In 2007 this continued to result in limited access to political and other decision-making processes, inadequate basic services and restricted opportunities for self-determination.

Biofuels

Throughout 2007, mineral resource extraction and monoculture plantation development remained the main causes of dispossession of indigenous and minority population territories. Oil palm and genetically modified soybean plantations geared to biofuel production are expanding at the expense of primary forests and the areas traditionally inhabited by these communities.

Dispossession and environmental devastation is making traditional rural lifestyles increasingly impossible. This is forcing indigenous and other minority populations off their ancestral lands to live in impoverished urban neighbourhoods in Argentina, Brazil, Colombia, Ecuador and Mexico.

Ironically, these socially and environmentally problematic agro-fuel initiatives are directly related to larger global efforts to combat environmental change through use of renewable resources.

Many regional governments now regard biofuel as the next major economic bonanza. During 2007 the government of Argentina declared its intention to convert the country into a global leader in renewable energy, and is offering investment incentives. Biofuel cultivation is expanding significantly, especially in the country's north-eastern province of Chaco, and is already causing displacement of indigenous communities.

In Colombia, oil palm plantations for biofuel are now spreading through historically Afro-Colombian

Pacific coast lowlands, sometimes prompting violent dispossession and dislocation. Furthermore, over the next decade the Colombian government proposes a seven-fold increase in cultivation of biofuel.

Monoculture oil palm expansion is also affecting Afro-descendant and indigenous populations in Ecuador; particularly in the biologically diverse Cayapas-Mataje Ecological Reserve in Esmeraldas. Local activists report oil palm companies are increasingly moving into the northern coastal province of Esmeraldas, which is a traditional Afro-Ecuadorian zone. This is having a direct social and environmental impact on Afro-descendant and indigenous Awá and Chachi villages, including land appropriation.

Biofuel investor confidence was boosted by the five-nation tour of Latin America by the US president in March 2007, aimed at pushing through ethanol accords. Investors, experts and producers also held the First Biofuels Congress of the Americas in Buenos Aires, Argentina with former US Vice-President and 2007 Nobel laureate Al Gore as the keynote speaker. In addition Mexico, Colombia and Brazil also organized biofuel seminars during 2007.

In addition to agro-fuel activity, significant deforestation on disputed indigenous lands has also continued for cattle ranching and for lumber extraction in Brazil, Honduras and Nicaragua.

Mining

Another area of concern for minority and indigenous populations is the mining sector. Open-cast gold mining continues to affect indigenous populations and seriously threatens their traditional Amazon rainforest environments and Yucatan villages.

While increased enforcement of indigenous land tenure and land-use laws in Brazil has checked once rampant *garimpeiro* or artisanal mining, this has merely shifted the problem. Brazil's *garimpeiros* have now relocated across the very porous under-monitored northern frontier into the Amazon regions of neighbouring Venezuela, Guyana, Suriname and French Guiana.

Nickel and other metal mining is also causing evictions and environmental degradation in Guatemala and Ecuador, as well as in the Chiapas and Oaxaca areas of Mexico. In other instances coal and petroleum extraction is being initiated on

Colombia: oil palm hurts minorities and indigenous peoples

Aparicio Rios (seen here on far right) is an indigenous activist from Colombia's Nasa people and leader of the Cauca Indigenous Regional Council (CRIC). Here, he outlines the effects of oil palm production – seen as a more 'eco-friendly' fuel alternative – on marginalized communities.

'Both communities [indigenous and Afro-descendant] have suffered massive displacement from their communal lands [in the Choco in north-western Colombia].

'Paramilitary groups first terrorize and then displace communities in the area and then take over the land to cultivate oil palm. They are rich, well-armed and powerful and often in the pay of large landowners.

'It takes five years before you can even begin to make any money out of palm oil. An indigenous farmer cannot afford to wait that long and doesn't have the resources to be able to survive in the meantime. Only rich people can afford to grow palm oil.

'In May the government pushed a Rural Development Statute through Congress which says that protected indigenous reservations won't be allowed where there are Afro-Colombian communities in the Choco.

'Land for indigenous use is already depleted and the statute means that there is even less – the two communities are faced with a struggle for resources. The most serious thing about this law is that it rules that a piece of land belongs to the

person who has been in possession of it for five years, ignoring completely the previous owners who were displaced by paramilitary violence.

'The paramilitaries are using this as a way of grabbing more and more land for oil palm cultivation in the Choco and the government is encouraging them.

'The Embera people who live in that area are semi-nomadic. [Before] they would sow crops such as maize, rice, plantains, coconuts and papachina in one area until the land was worn out and then move on in their boats down river and begin cultivating another area.

'This level of mobility just cannot be sustained any more. Life was similar for Afro-Colombians and they have been even worse affected by the oil palm monoculture. They don't even have the level of community organization that indigenous people have to fight against this.

'The UN Special Rapporteur on Fundamental Freedoms of Indigenous People concluded on his last visit that 10 of Colombia's 92 indigenous groups were in danger of extinction and that 42 per cent of those groups may only contain between 50 and 2,000 people.

'This is a critical situation, practically the same as genocide.... We ask that the international community pressure the Colombian government to provide comprehensive protection for indigenous communities and live up to its promises of buying and setting aside land for indigenous reservations so that we can preserve our traditional way of life.'

Interview by MRG's Emma Eastwood
Photo: CRIC

disputed lands in Venezuela. Among the hazards are oil spills, erosion, run-off of dangerous materials (mercury and arsenic) and social degradation caused by irreconcilable external influences.

Environmental refugees
A significant consequence of these activities during 2007 was the rising internal displacement rate of indigenous and Afro-descendant populations in Argentina, Colombia, Guatemala and Mexico. This continues to provoke rural-to-urban and cross-border migration in search of sanctuary from conflict and dispossession, or to find alternative means of livelihood.

Low social sector investment in the impoverished areas where the migrants eventually settle means continued limited access to basic education and health services, and migrants' futures remain uncertain.

All too often in 2007 forced dispossession and emigration of vulnerable groups in countries like Colombia and Guatemala was prompted by acts of violence. This was perpetrated largely by paramilitaries and national army units, who routinely ignore the rule of law and the rights of indigenous and minority populations.

Almost all major rights violations during 2007 were related to the historical non-recognition of the sovereignty of indigenous and minority peoples over their communally held lands and natural resources. During 2007, in Argentina, Brazil, Colombia, Ecuador, Guatemala and Honduras, ancestrally inhabited lands continued to be ceded to local elites and multinational concessionaries without any prior consultation, prompting protests.

Regional rights defenders
During 2007 Amnesty International and local non-governmental organizations (NGOs) across the Americas continued to express concern over the rise in threats against indigenous and minority rights defenders. As in the past, rights defenders in 2007 have stepped in demanding justice and protection thus becoming special targets for death threats, harassment, violence and politically motivated criminal charges. In many instances the judiciary was also compromised either in permitting incarceration without due process, condoning impunity, or sanctioning unwarranted searches of premises of particularly effective rights defenders and their families.

New legislation and policy changes
On 13 September 2007 the UN General Assembly finally adopted the UN Declaration on the Rights of Indigenous People (IP). There were 143 votes in favour and 11 abstentions. Only four member states voted against acceptance. These were Australia, Canada, New Zealand and the United States.

Although states would argue that it is not binding international law upon any country, nevertheless the Declaration does lay out the principles for governmental conduct. However, many activists contend that, given the long process of drafting, many of the final agreed provisions do, in fact, represent international customary law and, as such, must be adhered to by states.

The four dissenting member states were concerned that the Declaration gave indigenous peoples too much power over activities and operations occurring on their traditional territories. They agued that articles related to lands and resources, intellectual property, redress, restitution, and prior and informed consent implied that indigenous peoples were being granted the right of veto over national laws, administrative measures and national resource management; rights others did not have.

Nevertheless the adoption of the UN General Assembly Declaration after nearly 25 years of contentious negotiations was an especially important political triumph for the indigenous groups of the Americas. From the very beginning they argued that, as the beneficiaries of the Declaration, they should have control over wording. On the other hand, governments maintained that while indigenous views were acceptable, only governments have decision-making authority at the UN.

Meanwhile at the regional inter-state level, measures to guarantee indigenous rights continued in 2007 with the lengthy process of drafting the Declaration on the Rights of Indigenous Peoples for the Americas. The 10th Meeting of the Organization of American States Working Group was held in La Paz Bolivia on 23–27 April 2007.

The process has not been without dissent. At the beginning of the La Paz reunion the United States made clear its general reservation to all of the text under discussion. The US indicated it would not join in any text that might be approved or otherwise appear in the draft from that 10th session.

Drafting process

The UN Declaration was the result of decades of activism. The first indigenous organizations to begin lobbying for a major change to protect indigenous rights were the International Indian Treaty Council, spearheaded by the US-based American Indian Movement, and the World Council of Indigenous People (WCIP), supported by Canada's Assembly of First Nations.

In the late 1970s they criticized earlier UN initiatives and called for a new approach based on cultural and territorial rights. The UN responded with a series of studies and data gathering. This led not only to the drafting of a General Assembly Declaration but also to the adoption of the very influential International Labour Organization's Indigenous and Tribal Peoples Convention 1989 (ILO Convention No. 169).

The drafting of the text of the UN IP Declaration, which began in 1983, was an unprecedented consultative exercise. The Commission on Human Rights Working Group consisted of indigenous representatives, government delegations and experts who met regularly over two decades to review text and prepare the final draft. More than 100 indigenous organizations participated. Many thousands of indigenous representatives were able to contribute their proposals.

Moreover, even before the final UN General Assembly Declaration vote in September 2007, significant prior state ratification of ILO No. 169 during the 1990s had already enabled some indigenous populations to acquire large communal land titles and defend cultural and other rights in the Americas.

ILO No. 169 had also enabled Afro-descendant groups in Brazil, Colombia, Ecuador, Honduras and Nicaragua to be recognized by their governments as 'pre-state formation peoples', thereby guaranteeing their ethnic rights and gaining communal title to ancestrally occupied lands.

Moreover, the need for data gathering, especially during the 1970s and 1980s, prompted many governments and NGOs to allocate resources to support research, training, travel and the strengthening of indigenous organizations. These activities had a notable multiplier effect in the Americas – particularly in the emergence of new organizations that incorporated indigenous identity and defence of culture with traditional class concerns.

Willingness to organize and advocate rights

It could be argued that these steps towards greater inclusion have helped reinforce the confidence and readiness of indigenous groups in the Americas to assert their indigenous identity and campaign for change. This in turn has helped shape recent key election victories by pro-indigenous and minority candidates in Bolivia, Brazil, Ecuador and Venezuela, and increased calls for national constitutional reform.

Moreover, from Alaska to Argentina, formerly acquiescent indigenous groups like the Mapuche in Chile's southern region and the Guarani in Brazil are now increasingly vocal about claiming ancestral lands which government and private industry are still seeking to appropriate and exploit in 2007.

In Argentina for example, after generations of silence, on 24–25 June 2007, indigenous representatives held the very historical first ever National Meeting of Indigenous Nations and Peoples of Argentina. They aimed to unite in their efforts and to demand an end to centuries of discrimination, dispossession and unequal treatment.

Also, on 11–14 October 2007, over 1,500 delegates representing at least 67 indigenous nations from Canada, Mexico, Central and South America and the USA met at an intercontinental gathering in Sonora, Mexico, to consider similar themes. The intercontinental congress, held on indigenous Yaqui territory in Vicam, focused on strengthening socio-economic, political and cultural ties to better defend and reconstruct indigenous societies, and to guarantee indigenous rights at all levels, including the global level.

According to the final communiqué, of particular significance was an agreement to initiate international efforts to halt the 2010 Winter Olympics Games in Vancouver, British Columbia, Canada. Canadian indigenous delegates argue that the upcoming Games are destructive to the environment and have already disrupted indigenous hunting and fishing grounds and destroyed sacred sites. They also maintained that the event posed a long-term threat to indigenous identity, health, culture, livelihoods and future generations, and called for an intercontinental protest movement and boycott.

Country by country

Argentina

The UN General Assembly IP Declaration ultimately may be largely symbolic since in Argentina, for instance, indigenous claimed land continued to be sold on a massive scale to multinational companies in 2007, particularly for petroleum, open-cast mining and genetically modified soy industries. The result is that Argentina's indigenous peoples continue to be evicted from ancestral lands to make way for these enterprises.

Furthermore, the victory of Argentina's former first lady, Cristina Fernandez de Kirchner, in the country's 26 October 2007 presidential election, points to a continuation of existing national policies.

Argentina is now the third largest soybean producer in the world after the United States and Brazil. It is the world's second largest producer of genetically modified soy and plans to increase production.

Argentina's indigenous communities mainly live in the forested north-eastern province of Chaco. A large percentage of Chaco's public land and jungles have already been cleared to grow genetically modified soy. Out of some 3.9 million hectares of Chaco public land, which should have been granted to indigenous groups, only 660,000 hectares remain. The rest has been distributed to individual entrepreneurs and companies. Seven per cent of all private land title owners in Chaco now lay claim to 70 per cent of land. Companies in 2007 deployed private security guards who are prepared to shoot at supposed intruders entering the former primary forestlands.

As genetically modified cultivation for biofuel spreads, indigenous and other small-scale peasant farmers are being forced from their land by aerial chemical spraying, topsoil erosion and pollution. The application of massive amounts of pesticides and fertilizers needed to grow genetically modified soybeans on otherwise low-fertility forest soil makes it impossible for communities to remain for health reasons.

In March 2007, seven small-scale farmers were arrested for resisting eviction from lands slated to be cleared for soy production in the northern province of Santiago del Estero, whose provincial government co-sponsored the Buenos Aires Biofuels Congress.

Patagonia land sales

As in the north-east, the continuing sale of land in the southern Argentine region of Patagonia is also affecting indigenous populations.

Indigenous Mapuche who took part in the 2002 land dispute against the Italian textile group Benetton, returned in February 2007 to occupy land belonging to the firm. They declared the need to reclaim their ancestral rights. Since 14 February 2007 over 30 Mapuche have occupied the Santa Rosa farm in the southern province of Chubut in Patagonia.

According to the Argentinean Constitution, indigenous Mapuche are the legitimate owners of the lands in Patagonia. Nevertheless, large parcels of Patagonia continue to be acquired by wealthy foreign buyers for personal use or tourism development. Well-heeled foreigners attracted by the scenic beauty of the barren windswept region have continued to purchase large land holdings ranging from 80,000 to 200,000 acres.

As reported by Gonzalo Sánchez, author of the recently published 2007 bestseller *La Patagonia Vendida* (*Patagonia: Sold*), Argentine officials are doing brisk business selling publicly owned land in Patagonia.

The UN-backed Tierramérica Network reported in 2007 that land titling continues to be at the root of the problem. The majority of the indigenous Mapuche living in Patagonia do not hold legal title to lands inhabited by their pre-colonial ancestors, and this is now regarded as 'publicly owned property'. As a result, indigenous land is frequently sold off to the highest bidder thus creating the underlying conditions for all the land ownership disputes in that region.

Bolivia

In Bolivia, indigenous issues and politics continued to intersect very strongly during 2007.

Besides being the first Bolivian president of indigenous descent, Evo Morales is the still-sitting long-time leader of the Six Federations coca growers' union. Morales is a declared opponent of the violent militarized eradication of the coca crop as advocated by the United States.

The coca leaf remains an integral part of traditional indigenous culture across the Andean region, with practical medicinal and religious uses dating back several thousand years. Besides being an excellent source of vitamins, it is widely brewed as a popular tea and traditionally chewed by Bolivian miners and farmers as a coffee-like stimulant and antidote to altitude sickness.

Natural coca leaf is still listed as an illegal drug in UN documents dating back to 1952. However, one of Morales' stated aims in taking office is the decriminalizing of natural coca production as a key step towards legalizing the traditional coca leaf and officially differentiating it from processed cocaine.

The year 2007 saw increased efforts to strengthen this policy, with continued restriction of individual cultivations to a legal limit of 1 *cato* (40 square metres). Nevertheless the US government maintains that liberalizing coca leaf production among indigenous peasants will only fuel the illicit market.

In 2007 Bolivian critics, including the president, continued to argue that both illegal cocaine consumption and the manufacture and export of the necessary precursor processing chemicals are centred in the United States and do not involve the indigenous population's rights to produce the leaf in peace.

Approximately 62 per cent of the Bolivian population self-identifies as indigenous, primarily from the Quechua and Aymara groups, with Guarani constituting 1 per cent. Around 70 per cent of Bolivia's indigenous population live in poverty or extreme poverty. The Inter-American Commission on Human Rights reported in November 2006 that this majority continues to exist with minimal basic services, little access to education and to be under-represented in government and politics.

Likewise, despite legal prohibitions against social and systemic discrimination, the small Afro-Bolivian minority in 2007 generally remained low on the socio-economic scale and faced severe social and economic disadvantages. The majority of the estimated 35,000 self-identified Afro-Bolivian population lives in the Yungas region of the Department of La Paz.

In parts of the La Paz Yungas where coca-leaf cultivation was previously illegal, communities have accepted the *cato* programme and agreed to eliminate non-sanctioned coca cultivation. However, in other sections of Yungas, where coca growing has long been traditional and legal, farmers have resisted reductions but agreed to establish 'coca free zones' where new planting is prohibited.

A conflict that erupted between Bolivian forces and coca growers during late September 2006 in the Department of Cochabamba caused critics in 2007 to strongly advocate the need for more dialogue and negotiated solutions between officials and coca growers.

A joint police–army coca eradication task force was reportedly attacked by nearly 200 armed coca growers (*cocaleros*) in Cochabamba's very remote Carrasco national park, resulting in the deaths of two young *cocaleros*, hostage-taking, and police and civilian injuries.

As a result, monitoring groups like the Andean Information Network during 2007 increasingly called for coca-control methods that would respect growers' human rights, instead of harsh military intervention designed essentially to meet US eradication targets.

Debt bondage

There were also special issues involving indigenous workers from the Altiplano region who remained at risk of being trafficked for agricultural work and other reasons.

Besides being a major producer of sugar, according to World Bank data since 2003 Bolivia has also been a major exporter of Brazil nuts, providing 73 per cent of the world supply. In 2007 the seasonal harvesting of sugar cane and Brazil nuts continued to be the main cause of debt bondage style forced labour for over 20,000 indigenous people in the eastern lowland departments of Beni, Santa Cruz, Tarija and Pando.

According to ILO researchers, sugar producers hire subcontractors who travel to the heavily populated western Bolivian highlands and lure potential indigenous agricultural workers by offering cash advances prior to Christmas, New Year and Carnival celebrations. The debt, which is linked to future salaries, is then used to obtain and retain labour.

The mostly Quechua workers bring along their families and are obligated to the labour contractor throughout the sugar and Brazil nut harvest season. They are denied the option of returning the cash, or switching to better-paying employers. Contractors maintain indebtedness by charging hugely inflated prices for basic goods at shops on the often-isolated harvesting sites.

According to Anti-Slavery International, up to 7,000 indigenous children, some as young as 9 years old, share the debt bondage along with their parents. In instances such as parental demise the debt is sometimes transferred to the next generation.

Besides sugarcane and Brazil nut plantation work, indigenous children are also trafficked for *criado* service. This involves 10–12-year-old male and female children who are indentured to middle- and upper-class families in areas like Santa Cruz and Pando. They perform domestic work supposedly in exchange for education, room and board. However, according to UNICEF studies, in most cases the child's labour input is considered inadequate for education costs so many do not attend school. As of 2007 there was still no official oversight of these practices.

Constitution debates

Indigenous issues have continued to surface strongly in the political arena. During 2007 the non-indigenous landowning minority in the wealthy Departments of Santa Cruz, Beni, Pando and Tarija, continued to largely oppose the indigenous-oriented Morales government, and remained adamant in their call for departmental autonomy. This represented a continuation of the deep polarization that began in August 2006 with the formation of the Constituent Assembly aimed at fundamentally rewriting the Bolivian Constitution to provide greater empowerment to the indigenous population.

However, constitution reform drafting, which began in August 2007, seemed to represent another major area of contention between the elite and the impoverished and marginalized indigenous majority – especially as it came on the heels of the earlier land reform programme of June 2006, which began to distribute state-owned and under-used land to peasants and indigenous people. By its own admission the government considers constitution reform and indigenous land ownership as key measures to address chronic social imbalance and to counter exploitative practices like debt bondage.

Besides fermenting strong political antagonisms, the proposal to reform the constitution to grant special indigenous autonomy, brought to the fore what some see as the historical racist and xenophobic underpinnings of the ethnic, cultural and geographical divide between eastern and western Bolivia.

In December 2006, members of indigenous NGOs, civilian groups and pro-secessionist elements in the eastern department of Santa Cruz clashed over local consultation for regional autonomy. The premises of the national governing party – Movement toward Socialism (MAS) – and offices of indigenous community centres were set on fire, and members of indigenous groups had their houses ransacked.

This tension continued throughout 2007, fuelled by growing internal migration of the indigenous population from the poor western highlands to the relatively less populated richer eastern lowland regions. Indigenous groups continued to use the Popular Participation Law to form municipalities and to protest at the government's failure to provide title to all claimed territories, despite the Agrarian Reform.

The mid-2006 decision of the Morales government to nationalize all hydrocarbon resources in Bolivia appeared to come in response to calls by indigenous supporters to end outside exploitation of the country's natural resources. However, in 2007 this continued to be a thorny issue among residents of gas-rich lowland areas like Santa Cruz and Beni. Like other efforts at systemic reform, it was viewed as more evidence of bad faith on the part of the more numerous indigenous population, who are seen as wanting to deprive the non-indigenous elite of their economic rights and long-held privileges.

At the end of 2007 indigenous groups were still awaiting signs of a meaningful long-term social change and more opportunities to improve the quality of their lives. However, the August 2007 revival of the ultra nationalist right-wing Bolivian Socialist Falange party after five dormant decades, and the disruptive November 2007 Constitution Assembly clashes between government supporters and opposition demonstrators in the city of Sucre, did not offer much hope for an easy or tranquil resolution of these issues.

Brazil

As in Bolivia, vulnerable groups in Brazil received increasing attention during 2007 as a result of internal policy developments, but change remained slow. Brazil has a population of approximately 188 million, of whom between 40 and 75 per cent or 65 and 120 million are of African descent.

Historical discrimination against Afro-descendants and indigenous minorities continued to be a major issue in 2007. Although the law prohibits racial discrimination, Brazilians of African and indigenous origin continued to be frequent victims of discrimination in a social climate that tends to downplay ethnicity while still displaying strong prejudices against dark skin colour.

The UN Office on Drugs and Crime (UNODC) in 2007 reported that Brazilian women continued to be among the primary victims of international sex trafficking to Europe. According to the Reference Centre on Children and Adolescents (CECRIA), the typical victims were dark-skinned women between 15 and 27 years of age.

The second term re-election of President 'Lula' da Silva in October 2006 was seen as a plus for minorities due to his commitment to social welfare reform. Da Silva won 77 per cent of the vote in his north-east birthplace, which is home to dark-skinned, poorer Brazilians who especially benefit from the government's 'Bolsa Familia' cash-transfer programme.

In 2007 Afro-Brazilians continued to earn less than 50 per cent of the national average income. They also suffered from the highest homicide, poverty and illiteracy rates in a country which the Organization for Ibero-American States (OEI) 'Map of Violence 2006' grades as having the third highest homicide rate in the world and ranks at number one out of 65 countries for death by firearms.

According to human rights NGOs and Amnesty International December 2006 reports, paramilitary-style militias, often composed of active and former police officers, continued to regularly invade and terrorize Rio shantytowns, which historically have large Afro-descendant populations. They also intimidated human rights activists attempting to investigate abuses.

Seriously under-represented in professional positions and in the middle and upper classes of society, in contrast Afro-Brazilians continued to have a significant presence in prisons. According to the Ministry of Justice, Afro-Brazilians in 2007 made up more than 56 per cent of the prison population, while the UN Special Rapporteur on the Judiciary noted (in 2005) that persons of African origin occupied less than 1 per cent of the senior posts in the judiciary and the Public Prosecutor's Office.

Nevertheless, racial discrimination continued to receive more recognition and remediation attempts from the 'Lula' government in 2007. A quota law still under consideration will institute a system of racial preferences for the civil service, private sector and universities. Currently, Afro-Brazilians represent only 16 per cent of the university population. During 2006–7 more than 30 universities voluntarily implemented a quota system.

Efforts to deal with the most vulnerable of the marginalized gathered momentum in mid-2007 as part of the government's Special Secretariat for Racial Equality Promotion Policy (SEPPIR). The agency introduced the Quilombolas Development Programme, which seeks to improve living conditions of communities that are among the most marginalized in Brazil. Initially it will benefit 525 *quilombo* settlements in 22 of Brazil's 26 states.

Like elsewhere in the Americas, *quilombos* were colonial-era 'maroon' settlements established by self-liberated Africans who fled to dense jungles or remote mountain regions to escape enslavement and created independent African-based communities.

According to SEPPIR there are 1,170 recognized *quilombo* heritage communities, but the real total could surpass 3,000. This would represent some 1.7 million people. The highest concentrations are in once inaccessible areas of Bahía (north-east), Pará (north), Mato Grosso (west), Goiás (central) and Minas Gerais (south-east). *Qilombos* also exist in major cities like Rio de Janeiro and São Paulo.

Government statistics reveal that 91 per cent of *quilombo* families in 2007 had monthly incomes of less than US $190, though the national minimum wage is US $204 a month. A 2006 Ministry of Social Development study shows the number of malnourished under-5 children in *quilombos* is 76 per cent higher than for the child population as a whole. Only 3.2 per cent of *quilombo* children have access to sanitation.

Quilombos have been recognized since the mid-1990s under Convention ILO No. 169 and the current programme includes granting collective land titles as well as improving roads and providing sanitation, water, education and health services.

Titling is viewed as all-important since some *quilombos* existed before major cities like Rio de Janeiro and São Paulo were established and eventually became absorbed as poor urban neighbourhoods.

Indigenous groups

According to official government figures Brazil's indigenous population numbers close to 460,000 and belong to 225 'nations'. In 2007 more than half continued to live in poverty in communities where traditional ways of life are increasingly threatened by land development, agricultural expansion and mining.

The National Foundation for Indigenous Peoples (FUNAI), a government agency, reports that Brazil's indigenous people continue to face disease and poor healthcare, loss of native culture and recurring incursions, especially in rainforest regions.

Since 1988 Brazil has set aside roughly 12.5 per cent of the country's total land area and 26.4 per cent of the Amazon basin for the indigenous population. However, there was continued evidence in 2007 of eroding government concern over indigenous land rights.

According to April 2007 articles in the *Christian Science Monitor* and *Scientific American*, veteran advocate for the protection of isolated indigenous groups, Sydney Possuelo is reported to have publicly criticized the director of FUNAI for suggesting that indigenous people in the Brazilian Amazon may have too much land.

This largely matches the attitude of Brazil's powerful elite, who seek even more Amazon deforestation and land enclosure for cattle and large-scale agriculture. Ranchers, land-grabbers, miners and loggers have already destroyed nearly one-fifth of the Brazilian rainforest. Brazil's National Institute of Space Research reported in October 2007 that the annual Amazon deforestation rate has fallen to the lowest on record, but more than 17 per cent of the original tree cover has already been eliminated and what remains continues to disappear.

Violent land wars between indigenous groups, ranchers, companies and farmers, increased in 2007, continuing to reflect what a local NGO, the Pastoral Land Commission, described as a 10-year high in indigenous murder rates. Killings were mostly related to land disputes. Rural activists were specially targeted.

In September 2007 the indigenous Yanomami of Brazil's Amazon rainforest increased protests against a draft mining law that may force them to expose their currently state-protected communal lands to international mining companies. Mining on indigenous lands in Brazil is currently prohibited, however the draft law once again allows mining of indigenous territories, with Yanomami lands likely to be the most affected.

According to the Instituto Socioambiental, the 'Lula' government has created 15 million hectares of environmental conservation areas in Amazonia, some of which had been demarcated for indigenous groups since 1992. Environmental monitors point out, however, that a large proportion has already been surveyed or explored by mining companies. This could mean a repeat of the cycle of deforestation and disease first suffered by Yanomami in the mid-1970s, during construction of Brazil's Northern Circumferential Highway, when nearly 20 per cent of the Yanomami died from lack of immunity to unfamiliar diseases.

Brazil biofuel

As a world leader in ethanol production, biofuels from agricultural crops are important in the country's long-term economic vision. Brazil's National Institute for Amazonian Research reports that local scientists have developed a new variety of soybean that is expected to flourish in rainforest climates like the Amazon.

Indigenous small farmers in Brazil are steadily being pushed off lands cleared for soy production, sometimes violently. This is also affecting Afro-descendant and indigenous 'nutcracker' women, who, as of August 2007, continued fighting to retain access to the babaçú palm tree; native to the Brazil forest.

The babaçú palm grows wild in the 18.5 million hectare forest area extending across four states between the Amazon and the semi-arid north-east of the country. The 20-meter-tall palm tree has multiple uses according to the United Nations University. Among them are cattle fodder, natural medicine, house construction, basketry and fuel. The flesh of the nut is eaten or made into oil for cooking, lubrication, as well as soaps and other cosmetics.

Babaçú gathering dates back to pre-Columbian times. It now represents a major income source for half a million mostly Afro-descendant and indigenous female Quebradeiras who gather and process the babaçú nut. However large-scale land appropriation is now making it increasingly difficult for women to access babaçú forests.

Since the 1980s, industrial farmers have been acquiring and enclosing vast parcels of primary land where the babaçú grows, and they now intend to clear-cut and burn the forest to breed cattle or grow soybeans for biofuel. They especially want to stop indigenous and Afro-descendant collectors from traversing the forested areas, even though the babaçú nut just falls to earth and otherwise remains unused. Deterrents include erecting barbed wire fences or hiring gunmen.

The Interstate Movement of Babaçú Coconut Breakers (MIQCB) has been trying to negotiate access with the local, regional and national governments, and discussing the laws for free access to the babaçú forests. They have also held the government accountable for illegal logging and forest destruction.

Some researchers see potential in the babaçú palm for biofuel, but industrialists lack interest because of supply logistics and difficulty in processing the nut. Nevertheless, NGO and university projects in 2007 continued trying to attract Afro-descendant and indigenous Quebradeiras women toward using babaçú for agro-fuel. Collectors can earn more selling the multi-use nut than from processed oil. They are also well aware of the effects of the soybean and sugarcane industries on independent farmers and remain uninterested in turning babaçú into a corporate biofuel activity.

Canada

Although Canada never ratified ILO No. 169 and voted against the 2007 UN General Assembly Declaration on Indigenous People, it greatly supported the drafting of both documents and provided a relatively progressive example of policy reform and reconciliation between government and indigenous nations. Moreover, its policy of multiculturalism also stood as a model of diversity. However, events during 2007 have called into question full national commitment regarding these issues.

The June 2006 arrest of a group of 12 men and five youths for planning terrorism renewed the focus on the country's Muslim minority. This continued into 2007 when several aspects of Canada's anti-terrorism policy came under renewed legal pressure. Anti-Muslim incidents occurred sporadically in various locations, including Montreal and Toronto.

Controversy also continued over Canada's policies of multiculturalism in education, law and social life, especially with respect to allowing the application of Sharia law in certain cases involving Muslim citizens.

Sharia

According to Statistics Canada estimates (2007), there are now between 750,000 and 1 million Canadian Muslims. Some Muslims argue that Canada's secular legal system makes it difficult to govern themselves by their own religious laws, for instance in matters related to marriage and divorce.

However, critics of Sharia law like the Muslim Canadian Congress cite the absence of a formal certification process for interpreters and the subjectivity of interpretation. They also question the motives of the pro-Sharia lobby and warn that implementing a parallel justice system would infringe on the rights of Canada's Muslim women.

Attempts to introduce Sharia law in Ontario to settle family disputes in a manner similar to Jewish and Catholic arbitration bodies were rejected in 2005 by the provincial government, which then moved to prohibit all religious-based tribunals. In Quebec, cabinet ministers also rejected the use of Sharia law in that province, claiming that it discriminates against women.

In May 2007, after several Canadian financial institutions indicated they were preparing Sharia-compliant mortgages and other financial products to serve the growing Muslim population, critics once again began voicing opposition to what they claim was another veiled attempt to introduce Sharia law into Canada.

Canada maintains relatively liberal immigration policies and Muslims now represent the fastest-growing part of the population. Given the international political climate. the debate has continued in 2007 over possible entry into Canada of immigrants involved in terrorist missions.

Terrorism and First Nations

Increased focus on terrorism also threatened the ability of Canada's 612 different First Nations to demand their rights and protest injustices.

Controversy arose in April 2007 following Canadian media reports that the indigenous Mohawk Warriors Society had been included in the Department of National Defence's counter-insurgency draft training manual along, with other groups labelled as international security risks.

Assembly of First Nations National Chief Phil Fontaine protested what he described as a move to criminalize the legitimate rights of Canada's indigenous people to obtain redress and demanded immediate removal of any reference to First Nations from the document, which seeks to associate aboriginal protest groups with large well-armed radical militia such as the Tamil Tigers, Hezbollah and Islamic Jihad.

Following the media attention, the Canadian government made a special effort to assure indigenous leaders that the references will not appear in the final version of the manual, which recommends the army use deception, ambushes and assassination against insurgency groups.

Social conditions

There were renewed efforts by Canada's First Nations to continue generating awareness of the socio-economic status of some First Nations communities in the country, as highlighted on the 29 June 2007 National Day of Action.

Indigenous areas continue to represent 92 of the bottom 100 communities in the country according to the Department of Indian Affairs and Northern Development. As in the rest of the region, this minority lags badly on practically every social indicator, including education, health and employment.

Aboriginal poverty, traditional land rights, control of resource extraction and tourism, and discrimination remain among the major issues. Protests and civil disturbances, including blockades, continued in some provinces – notably in Ontario, British Colombia and Manitoba – related to failure of the provincial governments to consult with native groups over sale and use of disputed treaty lands.

In April 2007 the Manitoba provincial government, along with First Nations leaders, signed the Wabanong Nakaygum Okimaw accord. It mandates each provincial First Nation to create its own lands development plan, including decisions on resource extraction, housing and any other development.

Signatories hope to create a UNESCO World Heritage site to preserve and promote one of the last intact parcels of primary boreal forest on the entire North America continent. Along with enabling environmental conservation, it is intended to enable aboriginal people to control and gain revenue from traditional lands.

Nevertheless indigenous groups argue that the Manitoba government is failing to fully uphold the agreement with regard to consultation, and is only selectively applying the accord.

Canada and the UN GA Declaration on the Rights of Indigenous People

Despite Canada's international lead in granting indigenous land titles, greater degrees of autonomy, self-government and control over resources, Canada's indigenous communities became very concerned in July 2007 when the country joined six other states in signing a letter to the UN calling for redrafting of key provisions of the General Assembly IP Declaration.

Canada's Assembly of First Nations (along with ecumenical groups, indigenous NGOs and human rights bodies like Amnesty International) immediately sent an open letter reminding the Conservative government that, by seeking to redraft the document, Canada was failing to honour its international obligations as an elected member of the Human Rights Council. Moreover it was reversing its own positions and arguing against content it had originally participated in drafting.

In September 2007 Canada was among only four countries that cast a negative vote in the General Assembly. Included in its range of concerns was that Article 28 related to providing redress for property taken without free, prior and informed consent, and could be interpreted as promoting the re-opening of settlements already reached between states and indigenous peoples.

There seem to have been no similar concern during 2007 about re-opening the debate over the territorial integrity and future status of the French minority within Canada. The Prime Minister had earlier revived status discussions over Quebec and declared that the predominantly French-speaking province should be recognized as a nation 'within a unified Canada'.

Mining

Like its powerful industrial neighbour to the south, actions in Canada also had an impact on the minorities in the rest of the Americas during 2007, especially in the mining sector.

Canada's mining corporations continued to be leaders of the global mining industry and have already been challenged over environmental practices and exploitation of indigenous lands at home. Canadian mining companies in 2007 accounted for over 40 per cent of global exploration budgets and nearly 3,200 concessions in more than 100 countries. Government figures indicate almost 60 per cent of the world's mining and exploration companies are listed on Canadian Stock Exchanges.

Canadian companies that boast of low-cost operations maintain several typical open-pit mines in the Americas in places like San Martín in the Siria valley of Honduras. Water-based sodium cyanide solution is used to separate the gold. Environmental experts argue that, besides considerable fresh water consumption, they generate highly toxic by-products, including heavy metals like mercury and arsenic that can contaminate potable water sources and affect nearby inhabitants. This occurred in the indigenous communities around San Martin.

Critics have therefore sought to link rights violations of indigenous communities in Bolivia, Ecuador, Guatemala, Guyana, Honduras, Peru and Suriname to the environmental devastation and violence allegedly perpetrated by Canadian mining corporations in the Americas.

As of December 2006, according to Guatemala's Ministry of Energy and Mines, there were 356 mining licences granted and an additional 250 concessions in process, covering more than 10 per cent of the country, which has a majority indigenous Maya population. Of these concessions, 80 per cent are owned by Canadian companies.

According to Rights Action, a US-based NGO that supports indigenous land reclamation efforts, protesters in the Q'eqchi' Mayan village of Chichipate, located atop a large deposit of nickel in Guatemala, have claimed Canadian mining company complicity in the forced removal of indigenous residents to begin mine construction. Environmentalists are also concerned about damage and pollution of water sources through use of water from nearby Lake Izabal to cool nickel-smelting furnaces at a rate of 200 litres per second.

The Ottawa-based NGO Mining Watch Canada (MWC) reports that Canadian mining companies already have 10 projects in development in Oaxaca Mexico, covering over 70,000 hectares of land, and in 2007 continued to consolidate larger land holdings. The impoverished (and militarized) neighbouring Mexican state of Chiapas has over 72 Canadian mining concessions, representing a total of 727,435 hectares. More than 55 per cent of these were conceded without any information-sharing or consultation with local indigenous communities.

In May 2007 busloads of people stood in front of the Canadian Embassy in San Salvador to protest the Canadian government's role in Central American mining, and specifically in the 29 mining projects currently active in El Salvador.

British and Canadian parliamentary representatives travelled to Honduras in August 2007 and spent four days listening to all sides in the mining debate. They offered significant support to civil society sectors seeking just and responsible mining laws, and environmental and local community protection.

One central theme was the need for Corporate Social Responsibility (CSR) legislation and the application of Canadian mining laws to Canadian companies operating in the Americas to ensure ethical conduct. This is especially important because extractive industries routinely take full advantage of the absence of adequate local laws and any frailty or corruption they may encounter in governments of the NAFTA area. The initiative includes appointing an independent ombudsman to verify compliance with standards.

Colombia

The country's 42-year-long internal armed conflict, continued relentlessly in 2007, although paramilitary demobilization is supposed to have been concluded during 2006. Serious human rights abuses remain at shockingly high levels, especially in rural areas that are traditional indigenous and Afro-descendant locations. All armed parties involved – government forces, two leftist insurgent groups (FARC and ELN) and innumerable 'renegade' paramilitary groups – continue to abuse human rights and breach international humanitarian law with apparent impunity.

Colombian politics in 2007 was rocked by a massive scandal resulting from revealed connections between high-ranking political leaders and paramilitary death-squads. Paramilitaries are accused of seizing mostly Afro-descendant and indigenous lands and intimidating or assassinating rights defenders.

According to prior agreement, more than 32,000 Colombian paramilitaries were supposed to have been demobilized and removed from the conflict by early 2007. However, reports of abuses by these armed non-state actors continued throughout 2007, with negative consequences for Afro-descendant and indigenous populations that have traditionally shared the same rural locations for several decades.

Victims of violence
According to the national census (2005) approximately 11 per cent of Colombian population is of admittedly African origin. In 2007 they

continued to face significant economic and social discrimination. The mostly rural Department of Choco, with the highest percentage of Afro-Colombian residents, continues to have the lowest per capita level of social investment and ranked last in all social indicators. Moreover it is now deeply embroiled in the ongoing conflict.

Having been spared most of the fighting in prior years, Afro-descendants in 2007 increasingly experienced some of the worst violence as paramilitaries and guerrillas struggle for control of territory and the loyalty or acquiescence of local populations.

Government figures indicate that Colombia has over 800,000 indigenous inhabitants belonging to approximately 80 distinct ethnic groups. They live on more than 50 million acres granted by the government, often located in resource-rich, strategic regions, which continue to be fought over by the various armed groups.

Many indigenous communities have acquired legal title to claimed lands under ILO No. 169, however illegal armed groups in 2007 continued to violently contest indigenous land ownership and acted to drive them off their holdings.

Rights defenders report that many indigenous groups are now in imminent danger of extinction, with the greatest risk coming from government soldiers and army-backed paramilitaries, who threaten, intimidate and accuse them of complicity with insurgents and drive them off their lands.

Afro-Colombian and indigenous communities were at particularly high risk of mass displacement during 2007 due to armed confrontations, forced recruitment and minefields.

In July 2007 the Ombudsman's Office reported that 600 members of the Awa indigenous community, who were returnees from earlier displacement in 2006, once again came under pressure due to minefields planted throughout their Magüí reservation. In July 2007 five community members – including two children – were killed by landmines, prompting another mass exodus into neighbouring rural areas and the urban zone of Ricaurte.

Also in July 2007 the UN Office of the Commissioner for Humanitarian Affairs (OCHA) was informed of an increase in the forced recruitment of Afro-Colombians in the Pacific Coast town of Olaya Herrera. This is part of a country-wide pattern whereby young people are forced to join the fighting forces. Students in some areas stopped attending classes during 2007 out of fear of paramilitary unit recruitment.

In July 2007 a coalition of national and international NGOs presented a formal report to the Inter-American Commission on Human Rights focusing on child recruitment and demobilization. An estimated 13,000 children comprising 25 per cent of all combatants in the Colombian conflict are under 18 years old.

Meanwhile the US government aid agency USAID in 2007 continued to fund projects in which the demobilized right-wing paramilitary members are given land to cultivate in an effort to resettle those who agree to be disarmed. Activists point out that this resettlement is usually at the expense of Afro-Colombians, since the lands are mostly located in historically Afro-Colombian areas.

The issue is further complicated by the increasing interest of wealthy Colombian investors in biofuels. In 2007 oil palm planters took advantage of the growing depopulation of the Afro-Colombian countryside to expand their holdings. They are accused of using armed guards and paramilitaries to drive reluctant people off the land as well as assassinating Afro-Colombian activists

In September 2006, paramilitary gunmen invaded the home of Juan de Dios García, an Afro-Colombian community leader in the city of Buenaventura. As a member of Proceso de Comunidades Negras (PCN) he had been trying to recover land inhabited by Afro-Colombians for five centuries.

Advocates for Colombia's 3.6 million internally displaced population continued to insist in 2007 that land taken over by paramilitaries should be returned to former owners – mostly poor and marginalized Afro-Colombians and indigenous people. García escaped but seven members of his family were killed by the gunmen who reportedly arrived in police and army vehicles.

State forces also acted against protesters on 15 and 16 May 2007 in Cauca and Nariño Departments. Security agents allegedly used excessive force during mass demonstrations that involved Afro-descendant and indigenous protesters. At least one demonstrator died.

In July 2007 over 2,200 people, including small farmers, Afro-Colombians and indigenous people, gathered in Bogotá to protest against the attacks. They reaffirmed that crimes committed by paramilitary groups were part of systematic, planned actions directly permitted by the state. Thereafter the National Coordinating Organization of Displaced Persons (CND) and the Yira Castro Legal Corporation, which function as rights defenders, began to receive threatening emails.

Inter-American Court of Human Rights
Rights defence has long been a high-risk occupation in Colombia. On 4 July 2007, the Inter-American Court of Human Rights condemned the Colombian state for the 1998 extra-judicial execution of the Nasa Yuwe indigenous community leader and rights defender Germán Escué, who fought against territorial dispossession.

The Court held the Colombian state responsible for arbitrary and abusive intervention in the home of Germán and his family, and for making them wait four years for the return of the remains. This had spiritual and moral repercussions since indigenous Nasa Yuwe culture considers interment a mandatory sacred act that ensures collective harmony and balance.

As reparation the Court required the Colombian government to very publicly acknowledge its responsibility. This involves prosecuting those responsible, establishing a Community Development Fund in German Escué's memory, providing his daughter with a full university scholarship, and specialized physical and mental healthcare for family members.

Ecuador
Along with Rafael Correa, who took office as president on 15 January 2007, four indigenous persons and one Afro-Ecuadorian managed to get elected to the 100-seat Congress. Correa has stated he will seek to establish a Bolivia-style Constituent Assembly of national indigenous leaders to rewrite the constitution to include empowerment for Ecuador's indigenous majority.

Despite growing political influence, in 2007 indigenous and Afro-descendant minorities in Ecuador continued to suffer discrimination at many levels of society. According to Ecuador's Ministry of Social Development, 70 per cent of the estimated 600,000 Afro-Ecuadorian citizens continued to suffer widespread poverty and very pervasive educational and societal discrimination in 2007. Despite the absence of official discrimination, there were still no special government efforts to address these problems in 2007.

The UN Special Human Rights Reporter on Indigenous People raised concerns at the lack of consultation on extractive projects in indigenous territories and the negative impact of resource extraction activities on the environment and indigenous living conditions.

Indigenous activists, environmentalists and rights defenders report frequent threats and violence against them by police, soldiers and private security forces, including the laying of unsubstantiated charges. This legal team representing indigenous communities suing a multinational oil company for pollution caused by drilling between 1964 to 1992 in Sucumbíos province has also been affected by such activities.

Much of Ecuador's wealth lies in the Amazon rainforest region, where some indigenous populations still live in voluntary isolation. According to the Ecuadorian NGO Acción Ecologica, of the 400,000 barrels of oil per day produced in Ecuador more than 32,000 barrels annually spill into the Amazon river systems, mostly in areas inhabited by indigenous groups like the Cofanes.

An estimated untapped 900 million barrel oil reserve has been identified in the heart of the biodiverse rainforest. In light of ecological concerns – including the future of indigenous populations – Ecuadorian officials have indicated to the UN that Ecuador would ban exploitation of huge oil reserves if compensated by the international community for its effort to save the Amazon region and its indigenous inhabitants from ecological collapse.

In September 2007 the Ecuadorian government for the fourth time ordered the suspension of all activities at the controversial Junin open-pit copper mining project located in the ecologically diverse Tropical Andes of Ecuador.

In light of the forthcoming Constituent Assembly to re-write the country's constitution, open-pit mining may be altogether barred in Ecuador, along with future large-scale mining projects.

Nicaragua
After years of chafing under limitations imposed by Nicaragua's Supreme Electoral Council (CSE), the country's largest indigenous social movement YATAMA chose to form a political alliance with its

former wartime adversaries the Sandinista Front for National Liberation (FSLN) to contest the December 2006 national elections.

The favourable outcome, which saw the return of the FSLN to power, was seen as an important development given the role the Frente (FSLN) had previously played in advancing the issue of autonomy for the North and South Atlantic coast regions (RAAS and RAAN).

The unprecedented action by YATAMA (Yapti Tasbaya Maraska Nani Asla Takanka or Organization of the Nations of the Mother Earth) – which historically has been Miskitu-led – was intended to ensure greater ethno-cultural inclusion. This implies enabling the indigenous Mayagna, Miskitu and Rama peoples, and Creole and Garifuna minority populations, to collectively address issues like enhancing socio-economic development and exercising more control over regional resources.

Given the multicultural history of Nicaragua's Caribbean coast and the mixed Afro-indigenous nature of the society, the issue of ethnicity has always been a fluid reality, often based more on self-definition and cultural preferences rather than fixed genetic boundaries.

YATAMA's decision to field candidates from other ethnic groups – such as their ultimately successful Creole woman representative – was therefore a significant step towards rebuilding strong intercultural understanding and avoiding conflict; especially given the tensions that had emerged in the post-civil war years, when Atlantic coast communities increasingly begun to divide along exclusionary ethno-political lines.

The winning candidates of the FSLN/YATAMA coalition, upon taking office in 2007, declared their intention to work together to increase participation of the region's ethnic groups at the national level, to develop the Atlantic regions and improve the overall functioning of the autonomy process.

They claimed that the former governing party (PLC) has never defended the region's multi-ethnic group interests, choosing instead to promote Hispanic cultural homogeneity that failed to protect minority languages or cultures.

The need for conflict avoidance in the region during 2008 is very important. On 4 September 2007 the Caribbean coast of Nicaragua was hit by Hurricane Felix, a category 5 storm with an average wind speed of 230 mph. The North Atlantic Autonomous Region (RAAN), which was the worst affected area, is mainly inhabited by the Miskitu indigenous group.

The Nicaragua army reported the destruction of over 19,000 houses affecting nearly 32,000 families; 102 people lost their lives and 90 per cent of the crops were destroyed, along with livestock and fishing equipment. Reconstruction was estimated to cost approximately US $50 million.

Peru

According to government figures, the Afro-descendant minority in Peru numbers about 2 million people out of a total population of about 23 million – 45 per cent of whom are indigenous.

The continuing marginalization and difficulty experienced by Afro-Peruvians was once again demonstrated in 2007. This was very evident following the 8.0 magnitude earthquake that hit Peru's southern coast in August 2007, killing more than 500 people, injuring over 1,000 and destroying some 34,000 homes.

One week after the disaster MRG expressed concern that crucial humanitarian relief was still not reaching the Afro-Peruvian population who made up the majority of the worst affected among the hundreds of thousands left homeless.

Peruvian Afro-descendants' rights advocate Jorge Ramirez Reyner of ASONEDH criticized the government for doing nothing to help the mostly rural Afro-Peruvian communities and for excluding them from the relief process, especially since all humanitarian aid was channelled through the government.

In keeping with the all-pervasive national climate of deep discrimination and prejudice, there were also charges that the Peruvian media chose to ignore the plight of the disaster-affected Afro-Peruvians – who had lost everything – and instead preferred to portray them as looters and thieves.

Additionally, critics pointed out that severely damaged road systems made it particularly difficult to deliver relief to the rural zones where most of the Afro-Peruvian communities are located. They charged that this was another indication of an ongoing pattern of infrastructural under-investment and official neglect that has characterized the relationship between successive Peruvian governments and the Afro-Peruvian population.

Unlike efforts in neighbouring countries, the Afro-Peruvian presence is still not adequately addressed by the country's statistical instruments, which means that Afro-Peruvian communities remain officially invisible as well as deprived.

United States

One consequence of the influence and reach of the United States as a global superpower in 2007 is that minority rights concerns within its own society have grown more varied. In addition to its historically derived indigenous and Afro-descendant minorities it must now also consider a range of other issues related to vulnerable ethnic and religious minorities.

In the context of counter-terrorism, the continued holding of hundreds of mainly Muslim detainees in offshore custody without charge or trial has served to maintain focus on the Islamic religious minority within the United States. In 2007 they continued to express misgivings at what they saw as unwarranted profiling and increasing xenophobic actions directed against their persons and assets.

Issues related to other minorities within the US also had a decidedly international dimension, especially with respect to the Americas. Spanish-speaking immigrants from Latin America and the Caribbean now represent one of the fastest growing minority groups in the United States. Since many of the immigrants – whether legal or undocumented – are of indigenous and Afro-descendant ancestry, the need for the continued migration of these marginalized groups to the United States in search of opportunity can be seen as another indication of the general low status of minorities in the Americas as a whole.

Native Americans

In 2007, the approximately 2.5 million Native Americans were increasingly urban and many reservations derived self-supporting revenues from gaming casinos and resource extraction. However, Native Americans as a whole still lagged behind in education and income, and were high up the unemployment and poverty indicators.

In 2007 they continued to seek redress for alienated lands and fractured cultures, and to claim right of ownership to significant parts of some states like New York, California and Nevada.

The Onondaga Indian Nation has gone to court claiming rightful ownership to a 2 million acre territory in New York State that runs from the Canadian border to Pennsylvania, and includes cities like Syracuse and Binghamton. One key indigenous aim is the environmental clean-up of hazardous waste from Lake Onondaga.

According to the US Justice Department, the Western Shoshone Indian Nation is also seeking to confirm title to more than 60 million acres of land comprising most of the state of Nevada and parts of California, Idaho and Utah. Prior attempts at settlement have failed and, despite a bill before Congress to provide $150 million in financial compensation, the Western Shoshone have refused to accept money and indicated that their land is not for sale.

African-Americans

African-Americans have made substantial gains, especially in the past decade, nevertheless, as in the rest of the region, this Afro-descendant population (36 million) continued to lag in all social indicators in 2007 and to seek an end to complex forms of social and economic discrimination that are mainly historically rooted.

At the end of 2007 questions were raised even about sustainability of the supposed gains and the difficulty of passing them on to the following generation. A study by the Pew Charitable Trusts released in November 2007 revealed an as yet unexplained downward economic trend among nearly half of the African-Americans surveyed.

According to the study, 45 per cent of the African-Americans whose parents were solidly middle income in 1968 fell to the poverty or near-poverty levels of income distribution in the next generation, ending up among the lowest fifth of the nation's earners. Only 16 per cent of Euro-Americans showed a similar downward trend.

Justice

Besides the fragile nature of middle-income life, for many African-Americans obtaining just and equal treatment under the law continued to be an issue. With the post-Hurricane Katrina resettlement of the mainly African-American victims still unresolved, the State of Louisiana in 2007 also experienced mass protests over unequal treatment of minorities in the justice system.

This took the form of the largest civil rights demonstration in the United States for more than two decades. On 20 September 2007 an estimated 50,000 mainly African-American protesters from across the country travelled to the small town of Jena Louisiana to petition the justice system to uphold the law with respect to the trial of juveniles.

Six teenagers faced years in adult prison for violent altercations that followed a silent protest vigil under a tree on the Jena High School lawn, where symbolic neo-segregationist nooses were found hanging.

Authorities directed the full force of the law upon the defendants. However Louisiana's Third Court of Appeals overturned the conviction on the grounds that one of the main defendants was improperly tried as an adult.

Participants saw their demonstration in national terms, indicating that the mistreatment of the so-called 'Jena 6' was just a local reflection of a nationwide historical pattern of unjust treatment by the judicial system, especially given the connections of the case to racism, xenophobia and so-called hate crimes.

With reports continuing to surface in the national media regarding symbolic noose hangings – including on the office door of an Ivy League professor and in the locker room of a Long Island police station – African-American protesters once more took to the streets. Thousands of demonstrators descended on the Justice Department building in Washington DC on 17 November 2007 to demand a federal crackdown on hate crimes and a stronger official response to continued public displays of racial antagonism. The demonstrators pointedly marched around the government building seven times in an apparent reference to the biblical story of the fall of Jericho.

African-American incarceration

Despite a strong rule-of-law tradition in the Unit ed States, minority defendants continued to complain of unequal prison sentences in 2007. There was also concern about unfair use of race during jury selection, which critics claim is designed to exclude African-American jurors.

Justice Department figures indicate that African-Americans account for less than 14 per cent of the national population, however they constitute nearly 44 per cent of the 2.2 million people in jail, with a large percentage being 18–24-year-olds.

According to a Washington-based think-tank, the Sentencing Project, some states, like Iowa, imprison blacks at more than 13 times the rate of whites, which has a socially devastating multiplier effect. Moreover, only 27 per cent of African-American inmates incarcerated nationally were there for violent crimes. Of all inmates locked up for minor drug offences, 62 per cent were African-American, having received mandatory five-year sentences.

According to the *Washington Post*, federal judges, law enforcement and civil rights groups have long criticized the stricter federal penalties for crack cocaine (primarily used by African-Americans), versus lighter penalties for the same amounts of powder cocaine, (more generally used by European-Americans) and deemed it a race-based double standard. The US Sentencing Commission, which sets incarceration guidelines, has come under increasing fire from civil rights organizations and prisoner advocacy groups to decrease these sentences by at least two years.

In November 2007 federal authorities announced reduced penalties for new cases, and a plan to retroactively reduce prison sentences. This could result in the unprecedented nationwide release of 19,500 mostly African-American inmates. The new proposal was immediately challenged by the Justice Department and further fuelled the debate about race and the justice system; especially since an earlier sentence-reduction initiative for crimes involving marijuana, LSD and OxyContin – which primarily involve whites – was made retroactive.

Political participation

Of great significance is that these events in 2007 were occurring at a time when a first-generation African-American senator Barack Obama – of partly Kenyan heritage – was demonstrating a significant ability to obtain the substantial financial and popular support needed to mount a credible US presidential election campaign. Also among Democratic Party contenders was New Mexico governor and former UN ambassador Bill Richardson, who is of Hispanic heritage.

Venezuela

In December 2006 elections the high-profile Venezuelan President Hugo Chávez won a third term with over 60 per cent of the vote. Chávez has openly declared his African and indigenous heritage and draws much of his support from the country's poor and marginalized, most of whom share the same roots.

No accurate count exists but Venezuela's indigenous population is estimated at between 600,000 and 700,000, representing 32 distinct peoples. Venezuela's 1999 Constitution codified indigenous rights to an unprecedented degree, including in the preamble. In 2007 challenges continued to come from conservative business organizations like FEDECAMARA that have denounced indigenous rights recognition specifically and the idea of multiculturalism in general.

Indigenous representatives have participated in the Chávez government from its inception. The Venezuelan National Indian Council (CONIVE) helped to draft the 1999 Constitution, which provides for indigenous representation in Congress. Noeli Pocaterra, an indigenous Wayu congresswoman, continues to hold the position of vice-president of Congress.

On the other hand, as of 2007, the Afro-Venezuelan population has still not experienced a similar degree of ethnic recognition. Apart from estimates that they make up 20 per cent of the national population, there is no data regarding actual Afro-Venezuelan demographics.

On 20 March 2007 thousands of urban and rural Afro-Venezuelans took to the streets of the capital Caracas, in a march for recognition. The Network of Afro-Venezuelan Organizations (ROAV) presented a proposal calling for a rewriting of the constitution to include text in the preamble related to the many sacrifices made by Africans and their descendants in gaining the country's independence.

They also requested the inclusion of a special chapter dedicated to Afro-Venezuelan communities, highlighting respect for their spiritual values, protection of ancestral lands and ecology, and inclusion in the educational curriculum of their cultural and historical contributions.

Moreover, in June 2007, with support from the Venezuelan Ministry of Culture and UNICEF, the Network of Afro-Venezuelan Organizations organized an international seminar to gather regional experiences on statistical inclusion of Afro-descendant populations, with the aim of eliminating Afro-Venezuelan invisibility in the next census (2010). ■

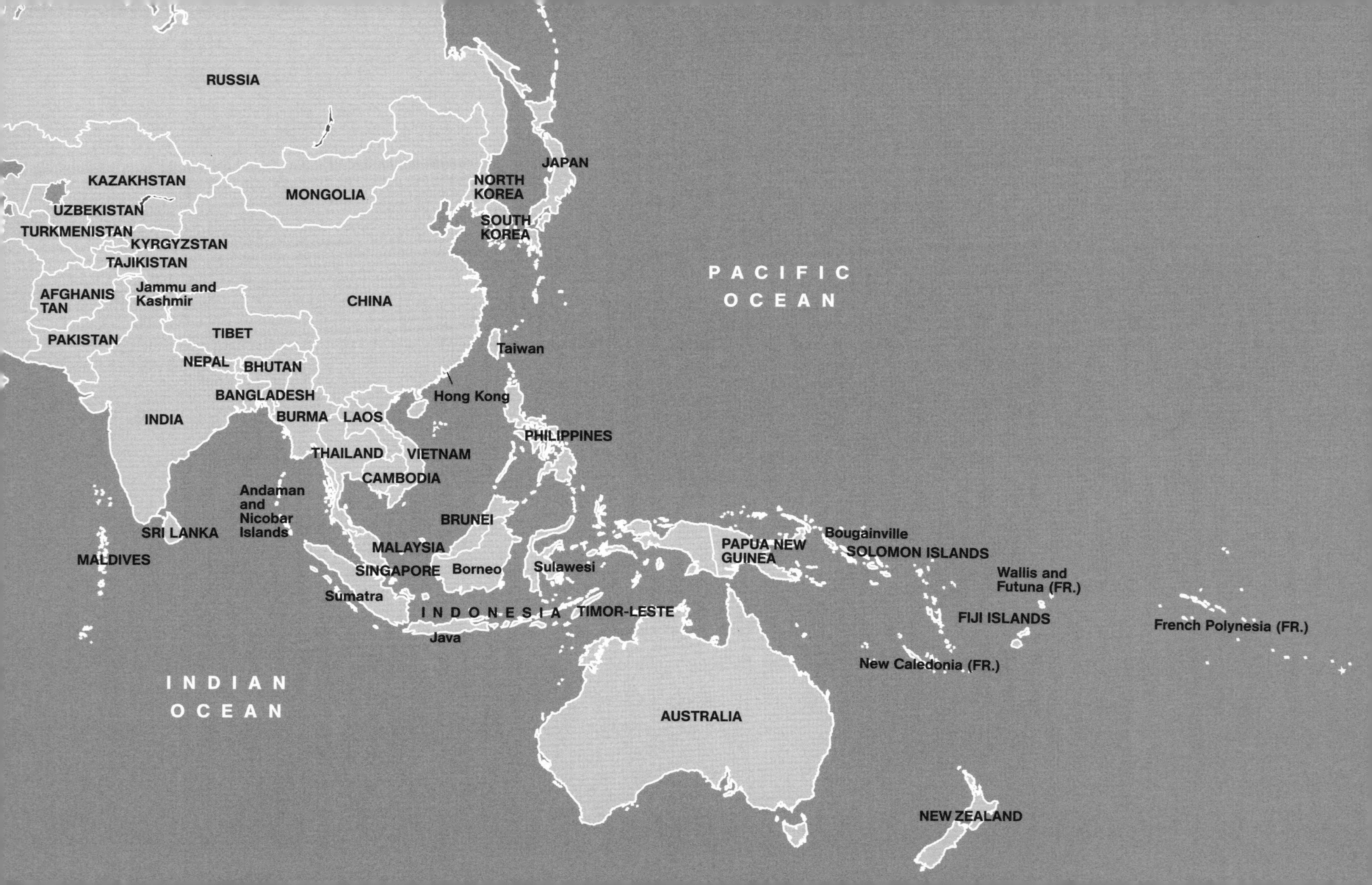
RUSSIA
KAZAKHSTAN
UZBEKISTAN
TURKMENISTAN
KYRGYZSTAN
TAJIKISTAN
AFGHANIS TAN
Jammu and Kashmir
PAKISTAN
MONGOLIA
CHINA
TIBET
NEPAL
BHUTAN
BANGLADESH
INDIA
BURMA
LAOS
THAILAND
VIETNAM
CAMBODIA
NORTH KOREA
SOUTH KOREA
JAPAN
Taiwan
Hong Kong
PHILIPPINES
PACIFIC OCEAN
Andaman and Nicobar Islands
SRI LANKA
MALDIVES
BRUNEI
MALAYSIA
SINGAPORE
Borneo
Sulawesi
Sumatra
INDONESIA
Java
TIMOR-LESTE
PAPUA NEW GUINEA
Bougainville
SOLOMON ISLANDS
Wallis and Futuna (FR.)
FIJI ISLANDS
New Caledonia (FR.)
French Polynesia (FR.)
AUSTRALIA
NEW ZEALAND
INDIAN OCEAN

Asia

Emma Eastwood and Farah Mihlar

Central Asia

A common factor seen across all of Muslim-majority Central Asian countries is the continuous human rights violations of religious minorities. Christians in particular appear to suffer persecution, and in some cases violence, across almost every state. Christian preachers have faced arrest, detention and deportation, and church activities in some countries have been made illegal.

However, as most of these countries support the Western 'war on terror', governments have also come down harshly on the rising trend of Islamic extremism/militancy. Uzbekistan and Kyrgyzstan have seen government-led crackdowns on Islamic groups which, in some instances, have made little distinction between radicals and moderates.

There also appears to be a strong tendency to emphasize national identity in some of the Central Asian countries. This nationalistic trend manifests in promoting national language and dress, as in the case of Turkmenistan. Such situations tend to marginalize ethnic minorities and put them in very disadvantageous positions, as also seen with the Uzbek community in Kazakhstan, Tajikistan and Kyrgyzstan. Conversely, in Uzbekistan dominance of the Uzbek language effectively bars many ethnic Tajiks from entry into higher education and public employment. Ethnic Russian emigration from the region is rife and the teaching of the Russian language is being phased out in Kazakhstan.

In terms of the security situation in the region, undoubtedly Afghanistan stands out as one of the most dangerous countries. Violence has increased in Afghanistan, putting ethnic and religious minorities under threat. Generally the human rights record of most Central Asian states remains poor, despite constitutional guarantees. Uzbekistan in particular will be remembered for the 2005 Andijan massacre, where government troops attacked innocent civilians during a political protest. Two years on the country has ignored international calls for an independent investigation and remains one of the region's main human rights violators.

Afghanistan

The year 2007 has reportedly been the most violent year in Afghanistan since the 2001 US-led invasion. Media reports quoted an internal UN mid-year review as saying that incidents of violence in 2007 were higher than the previous year, which, since the invasion, had so far been the country's most violent one. According to the UN report there were 525 security incidents every month during the first half of the year, up from an average of 425 incidents per month in 2006. These violent incidents range from attacks by the Taliban and other militant groups to bombings and abductions.

The Institute of War and Peace Reporting in 2007 stated that, while international attention is mostly focused on the south of Afghanistan, in the northern parts of the country warlords use violence and intimidation to maintain their hold on civilians. It quoted human rights groups as saying that the government did not seem capable of resisting the power of the commanders, who constantly engaged in brutal assaults and abductions. There is limited information on the ethnic and religious affiliations of the victims of violence and human rights abuses in Afghanistan. However, based on the country's past record, it can be concluded that minorities are significantly affected by the violence, particularly in situations of anarchy where warlords/militia leaders are in control.

Limited reports indicate that ethnic tensions are also on the rise in volatile parts of the country. In mid-2007, several people were killed and hundreds displaced over clashes between nomadic Pashtun Kochis and Hazara settlers of Behsood District in Afghanistan's central Wardak province. The clashes were over access to pastures. In July a UN-brokered ceasefire was signed between the two groups, demanding that Kochis temporarily withdraw from the areas; but even UN officials warned that the agreement was a short-term solution.

Antagonism towards ethnic groups in Afghanistan exists at the highest political level, as was evident in the threats directed at the country's independent Human Rights Commission by parliamentarians. In September 2007, MPs in the lower house of parliament voted to restrict the Commission's autonomy, accusing the body of 'political and ethnic bias'. Amanullah Paiman, an Afghan MP, was quoted by the UN IRIN news agency as saying that the Commission repeatedly deviated from its mandate by favouring sectarian and political groups. The Commission leadership has however warned that Afghanistan would be in breach of its international commitment to human rights if the

MPs got their way. The fate of the Commission now lies in the hands of the upper house of parliament and the president.

A report released by the Afghan Human Rights Commission in August 2007 on economic and social rights showed that a large majority of the Afghan population suffered from glaring rights violations, including lacking the basics, such as the right to food, water, education and health. Minorities were included in the survey, although the findings were not ethnically disaggregated. The main finding that was specific to ethnicity was that 17 per cent of people who said they felt left out of development projects attributed it to their ethnic or tribal origin.

Kazakhstan

Despite President Nazarbayev regularly making public statements highlighting and praising the country's tradition of inter-ethnic and interfaith tolerance, Kazakhstan legislation renders it compulsory for all religious communities to register and the activities of unregistered religious organizations are banned.

In June 2007, 12 homes were forcibly demolished in a Hare Krishna community near Almaty and a Baptist pastor was jailed for three days in March for leading an unregistered congregation. A state crackdown on Baptist and Pentecostal Christians was described by police as 'the fight against terrorism and religious groups without registration'.

In April 2007 Kazakhstan's religious minorities expressed deep concern about a Justice Ministry booklet entitled *How Not to Fall Under the Influence of Religious Sects*. The Kazakhstan International Bureau of Human Rights and the Rule of Law said that the booklet provides 'the moral, or more accurately immoral, basis for officials to justify their negative attitudes towards non-traditional religions'. Among the booklet's claims is that 'transferring to other religious faiths represents treason to one's country and faith'.

Although the Russian language is deemed 'equal' to Kazakh under the constitution, legislation and programmes of 'Kazakhization' since 2001 are increasing the use of the Kazakh language as the main language of government. This is proving to be an obstacle to access to education and employment in the civil service for a large part of the Russian minority population.

Kyrgyzstan

Kyrgyzstan's Constitution prohibits discrimination based on religion or religious beliefs and provides for the separation of religion and state, yet Islam, which is the most widely held faith, is exerting a growing influence. According to the Institute of War and Peace Reporting, the human rights ombudsman, who is a devout Muslim, has openly declared that restoring religious values to public life will make for a more ethical society.

At the same time, Kyrgyzstan is part of the West's anti-terrorism coalition and is under pressure to maintain a close rein on militant Islamic groups. There is strong opposition to anything resembling extremism because of the recent history of instability in southern Kyrgyzstan and adjoining parts of the Fergana Valley. In a proposed state clampdown on radical religious groups, the director of the State Agency for Religious Affairs announced in July 2007 that his agency is drafting five laws that will tighten restrictions on religious activity.

In its August 2007 report, the Committee on the Elimination of Racial Discrimination (CERD) expressed concern for ethnic Uyghurs and Uzbeks, who, the Committee alleges, were forcibly returned to their countries of origin after seeking refugee status or asylum in Kyrgyzstan. Regarding the clashes that had taken place in February 2006 between Kyrgyz and Dungan communities living in Iskra, CERD recommended that the government brought those responsible to justice, provide compensation to the families that had been forced to leave, and that measures be adopted to promote dialogue and understanding between the two communities.

Language issues are prominent in Kyrgyzstan. The Kyrgyz authorities still refuse to acknowledge any increased use of or status for the Uzbek language, even with Uzbeks now surpassing Russians as the country's largest minority. Despite being used in some official areas, the Uzbek language does not have any official status, even in the Batken, Osh and Jalal-Abad provinces where the minority is concentrated, and this has indirectly led to the continued under-representation and even absence of Uzbeks employed in government offices. Demonstrations calling for an official status for the language and for some kind of proportional representation of Uzbeks in state administration in the southern provinces occurred in 2006, and property owned by prominent Uzbeks was seized in 2007.

Tajikistan

The situation of religious minorities is relatively better in Tajikistan than in some of its neighbouring countries. While religious groups must register, there are no reports of denial of registration of religious minorities, and Tajikistan permits the formation of political parties of a religious character, something no other country in the region permits. However Tajik lawmakers may be set to reverse this trend: a new draft religion law introduced in January 2006 and in the process of domestic review, was due to be sent to parliament in late 2007. The law on Freedom of Conscience, on Religious Associations and Other [Religious] Organizations would replace the current law on religion and add restrictions, such as increasing to 400 the number of petition signatures required to form a religious association; prohibiting religious education in private houses; prohibiting proselytizing; prohibiting religious associations from participating in political activities; and prohibiting political parties from having a religion-based ideology (which would effectively disallow the Islamic Renaissance Party of Tajikistan, a political party with two members in the lower house of the national parliament). In June 2007 representatives of 22 minority religious groups signed an open letter to the president and parliament expressing concern that the draft law would effectively outlaw minority religious groups in the country.

There is on the part of the government of Tajikistan, and the population at large, a significant fear of Islamic fundamentalism and this has led the former to ban one group, Hizb ut-Tahrir, though most outside observers describe it as a non-violent organization. Most of its activists who have been imprisoned since 2000 are members of the Uzbek minority.

There were reports in 2007 that the government had begun a 'transmigration' programme to bring Tajiks into strategic areas traditionally inhabited by members of the Uzbek minority. Tajik authorities started resettling some 1,000 Tajik families in November 2006 to a western region mainly populated by Uzbeks. Observers and members of the Uzbek minority claim that central authorities are trying to dilute the Uzbek percentage in a key industrial area. This raises issues of discrimination in relation to land rights and usage, among others.

The lack of educational materials in Uzbek, the increasing obstacles to Uzbek-medium education and even moves by authorities to convert schools which use Uzbek as medium of instruction into Tajik-medium schools continue to be issues that concern this minority, as does their near total exclusion from the higher echelons of political life and public administration. There is no provision for the use of Uzbek or other minority languages between state authorities and the public. All these raise issues of exclusion and discrimination against this minority.

Turkmenistan

Hopes that Turkmenistan's human rights record would improve after the demise last year of the country's autocratic president of 21 years, Saparmurat Niyazov, did not materialize in 2007. Local activists claim that emphasis on Turkmen national identity and persecution of minority religious groups persisted through 2007. Turkmenistan's 15 per cent minority population, including Kazakhs, Russians and Uzbeks, face wide-ranging discrimination from authorities – including being forced to study in Turkmen language, adopt Turkmen national clothing – thus marginalizing minorities and indirectly forcing them to give up their own ethnic roots.

Turkmenistan also has a worrying record of persecuting religious minorities. In September and October 2007, four prisoners of conscience were released on amnesty. A senior Islamic religious head, Nazrullah ibn Ibadullah, who was serving a 22-year sentence on publicly unknown charges, was among a group of prisoners released on presidential amnesty. Despite these releases, according to Forum 18, a Norwegian human rights organization working on issues of religious freedom, a 49-year-old Baptist pastor Vyacheslav Kalataevsky remains in police custody, amidst growing concerns he may be deported. According to the Forum 18 news site another Baptist pastor arrested with Kalataevsky, Russian citizen Yevgeny Potolov, was expelled from Turkmenistan in early July. Several Jehovah's Witness followers have also been given prison sentences in Turkmenistan for refusing military service on grounds of religious conscience.

In May 2007 the UN High Commissioner for Human Rights visited Turkmenistan as part of a visit to Central Asia with the aim of setting up a regional office there. During the visit she welcomed

Turkmenistan's ratification of the main human rights instruments and the submission of reports to treaty bodies, including the one monitoring racism. She welcomed educational reform initiatives in Turkmenistan and encouraged the government to engage in political, civil, social and cultural data aggregation to ensure that human rights in these areas are better protected.

Uzbekistan

Two years after Uzbekistan earned the wrath of the international community for massacring innocent protesters in an uprising in Andijan, the Uzbek government under President Islam Karimov continues its poor human rights record. The government's reputation for intolerance of political dissent and religious freedom showed little signs of change through 2007. Ahead of a European Union (EU) review of sanctions against the Uzbek government, international and local human rights groups urged Europe not to remove sanctions imposed against the government, citing continuous human rights violations, including torture, intimidation of human rights activists and persecution of minorities. A petition to the EU signed by journalists and human rights activists stated that the Uzbek government, in its crackdown on Islamic extremists, makes no distinction between such groups and the vast majority of Muslims. According to the petition, thousands of innocent Muslims languish in prison, facing long sentences and torture.

But in October 2007 the EU eased sanctions on Uzbekistan, primarily to suspend for six months the block visa ban on eight top Uzbek officials. The decision was heavily criticized by several local and international groups, which accused the EU of letting the Uzbek government off too easily for past crimes and for continuing violations, mainly the practice of torture. In November the UN Committee on Torture, in a report on Uzbekistan, said widespread torture was prevalent in the country.

According to Forum 18, a total ban on activities of Protestants in north-west Uzbekistan remains, while Christians in other parts of the country face severe persecution, including in some instances children being made to denounce their religion. In October 2007 the Uzbek police put out a nationwide 'wanted' announcement for a Pentecostal Christian. When Forum 18 inquired why there was a search for him it was said that a police officer had accused him of breaking the law by gathering people at his home for religious activities.

In north-west Uzbekistan 20 Protestant congregations and Jehovah's Witness congregations have arbitrarily been refused registration, Forum 18 reported. Under Uzbek law, unregistered religious activities are considered illegal and liable for prosecution. In August 2007 two members of the Peace Protestant Church in Nukus were fined a year's average earnings because they were unregistered.

Uzbekistan is also known to discriminate against ethnic minorities such as the Tajiks. Some Tajik cultural centres continue to have their registration rejected by authorities. There are complaints that books and other publications from Tajikistan are not allowed into the country. This ties in with complaints on the shortage of textbooks in Tajik, and with claims of discrimination in access to university-level education as the entrance tests are exclusively in Uzbek. For Tajiks, the continuing low level of recognition of the Tajik language – despite their now constituting the country's largest minority – means that many parents opt not to enter their children in Tajik-language schools, as they know that access to higher education and public employment will more likely be denied to them because of their non-Uzbek associations.

The term of Islam Karimov constitutionally ended in January 2007 but at the time of writing there has been no official announcement of an election. There is strong speculation regarding a possible December election. It is unclear if the current president, who is constitutionally in his last term of office, may manoeuvre parliament to enable him to run for an additional term. The International Crisis Group has warned that President Karimov's departure may lead to a violent power struggle.

South Asia

Political turmoil, return to conflict, and natural disasters defined most of 2007 for South Asia, and minorities were particularly affected. Nepal's much heralded peace process began to crack as the main protagonist, the Maoist rebels pulled out of the government. Sri Lanka's peace process was completely undermined throughout 2007 as the country slid back into war. In both countries ethnic minorities continued to be marginalized and affected by increased violence. Both Pakistan and Bangladesh were hit by political chaos and worsening security situations. The two countries were expected to face polls in 2007 but, after weeks of violent protest, Pakistan finally announced that the polls would take place in January 2008. The Bangladeshi interim government has said that elections will be held at the end of 2008, but no dates have been fixed.

Minority communities in the region were also affected by a series of natural disasters that swept across at least four of the seven countries in South Asia. Persistent rains caused devastating floods across Bangladesh, India, Nepal and Pakistan. Aid agencies made desperate calls for funds and relief as the death toll and displacement caused by the flooding began to escalate. Bangladesh in particular was devastated by cyclone Sidr, which hit the country in November leaving a trail of death and displacement affecting millions.

In Nepal's Terai region, only in September did flood waters begin to recede after three months of torrential rain. The Nepali government said 185 people were killed in the flooding and landslides that followed. Nearly 600,000 people were affected. A joint flood assessment report by UNICEF, the World Food Programme and Save the Children Alliance said the biggest impact of the floods was on livelihood and housing. The report also said the worst affected were minority communities such as Dalits, Madhesis, Tharu, Janjati and Muslims. Aid took longer to reach these communities, because they live in the poorest most underprivileged areas. Also, as a result of their general poor economic conditions, they found it much harder to cope financially with the rising cost of living.

In Pakistan, ethnic minority areas were severely affected by heavy rains and flash floods. The UN's humanitarian news site reported that, by the end of June, 300 people had been killed and 2.5 million affected by the floods. The UN Humanitarian Office said 800,000 houses had been destroyed in Pakistan. According to Save the Children Fund, in Baluchistan, the populous ethnic Baluchi province, some 200,000 people were in need of assistance, and in Sindh province, home to ethnic Sindhis, some 800 villages were submerged in water, displacing over 100,000 people. A month after the disaster, a report by the country's independent Rural Development Policy Institute said that 35 per cent of people in Baluchistan and 55 per cent in Sindh remained without basic shelter.

In India, the National Campaign on Dalit Human Rights reported that minority, low-caste Dalits were most affected by the floods in Bihar, which was the state worst hit by the rains. In its initial assessment report, the human rights group said that in the 51 villages they visited in Bihar, 80 per cent of those affected were Dalits. According to the report, aid was not reaching the Dalits and whatever they had access to was scant. Some 2,253 people lost their lives across India and 14 million were affected by the floods. In Bangladesh earlier in the year the country's national media reported that 40 out of 60 districts were impacted by flooding that killed more than a 100 people. But by November cyclone Sidr had, according to the Bangladeshi government, claimed 3,033 lives and affected some 6.7 million people.

Bangladesh

What should have been an election year in Bangladesh was marred by violence and a clamp-down on political opponents. During the course of the year, Bangladesh's care-taker government took stringent action against opposition leaders. Two former prime ministers and some 45 political leaders are amongst those detained on various charges, chief amongst them corruption.

Human rights violations have shown a rise in Bangladesh through the year. The European Union (EU) and the US have both shown concern about the situation in the country. Though the violence had no particular minority dimension, minorities were amongst those affected in the rising wave of human rights violations. In May, Amnesty International expressed grave concern over reports of alleged torture and death in custody following the imposition of emergency in early 2007. In March 2007, a leader of the Garo indigenous community, Richil, reportedly died in custody following torture carried out by military personnel, Amnesty said. The Garo community live in Modhupur and, since 2003, have been opposing the construction of a national park in their traditional homeland. The Garo community is also predominantly Christian.

Violence and discrimination against religious and ethnic minorities continued through 2007 a US government report on religious freedom said. The report, released in September, said Hindu, Christian and Buddhist minorities experienced discrimination and on occasion violence. It also

Climate change in Bangladesh

U-Sa-Chi-Master (pictured above), 53, is a fisherman from the Bay of Bengal. He is the head of Kansai Na Pyo Roa, one of the few minority Rakhain villages in the south of Bangladesh. His community is already experiencing the dramatic effects of climate change.

'As a child I used to walk along with members of my village to the sea shore and it was a 3-mile track through dense forest of weed and coconut tree, passing a Second World War, British military camp site. Now, after 40 to 45 years, I can hear the sound of the waves from the verandah of my house; the sea is just 400 metres from here. My family had water-buffaloes and they used to graze on the wetland, but now there are fewer of those animals as the grazing land is lost under the waves.

'There were three sand dunes on that now-submerged land, where we used to take refuge if there was a sea-surge. But now there is only one man-made embankment to protect us and nobody knows when it will disappear into the sea. The tides are higher now by the day.

'The weather has changed a lot. I have been fishing in the sea since I was 20 and we used to wait for the rainy season for the best catch. It used to rain heavily in the first phase of the rainy season but that has changed. Now the fishermen have to go farther from the shore to catch fish as the sea has become shallow near the coast-line: it is dangerous, with the chances of sea-surge, so I stopped fishing and rented out my boat and nets.

'My ancestors moved from the Arakan state of Myanmar (Burma) on boats a few hundred years back and settled here. It was a pristine beach then, with dense forest, but now it is populated densely. My community has lost much of its land over the time and our number has also fallen over the years, and we are struggling to keep our heritage alive in this place.

'I respect the scientists as they are wise and there must be truth in their words. I know very little about all this climate change or global warming, and few in my community understand it well. But we are already facing the true nature of these changes. I don't know where my grandson will grow up if this land is lost. Those who are doing this to nature, they need to think of the future of their own children.'

Interview by Abdullah Al Muyid

Photo by Abdullah Al Muyid

said that members of the Ahmaddiya Islamic sect faced harassment, and protesters demanded that they be declared non-Muslims.

Compared to most other countries in the region, the impact of natural disasters in 2007 was of added significance to Bangladesh because the country has been identified as under threat from climate change. According to environment experts 11 per cent of low-lying land, home to some 140 million people, may be permanently under water in the future due to rising sea levels. In Bangladesh too, minority and indigenous groups often face the biggest impact of natural disasters while aid and assistance to these groups is often too limited.

In late 2007, southern Bangladesh was ripped by cyclone Sidr, which impacted millions of people. Two weeks after the cyclone hit, while international and local aid agencies were struggling to get relief to those most in need, information on affected minorities and tribal groups was scarce. According to Bangladesh's Disaster Management Information Centre, two indigenous communities, the Munda and Mahato, in Sundarban area and the Rakhain community in Patuakhali were affected by the cyclone. The centre said that livelihoods had been badly damaged. Despite the Bangladeshi government, and local and international NGOs working in the area, two weeks into the disaster there was no proper assessment of how badly the minority and indigenous communities were affected and whether aid was reaching them properly. The Khulna and Barisal districts affected by Sidr are also areas that have a high concentration of minority Hindus.

India

During its 60th year of independence, India was slammed by the UN for failing to prevent caste discrimination. In March 2007 the UN Committee on the Elimination of Racial Discrimination (CERD) strongly criticized India for its treatment of its 165 million lower-caste Dalits. CERD accused India of widespread abuses against Dalits, saying they faced discrimination in housing, schooling and public positions. In a report released in New York, CERD said that Dalits, also known as 'untouchables', were made to work in degrading conditions. The UN report followed a resolution in the European Union (EU) Parliament in February, which found Indian legal protection of Dalits 'grossly inadequate'.

Violence against Dalits continued through 2007. According to the Dalit Freedom Network (DFN), every year 10,000 cases of violence against Dalits, ranging from attacks and rape to killings, are recorded. In August rioting broke out in Haryana province after a Dalit boy was gunned down by three unidentified gunmen. The World Organization against Torture, a coalition of international NGOs fighting against torture, in October issued a statement calling for urgent action against the harassment of Dalits in Kolathur, a village in Tamil Nadu. The villagers have been attempting to speak out against the health and economic impact of an illegally located aqua-farm in their village. In Bhilvara district in Rajastan, a Dalit man was murdered because he refused to withdraw a case against a person from a dominant caste for the rape of his wife, DFN said.

But 2007 also saw some significant political victories for the Dalits. In India's biggest state, Uttar Pradesh, Mayawati, who heads the Dalit Bahujan Samaj Party and is a Dalit herself, was elected Chief Minister for the fourth time. But this year's victory had added significance as her party gained a majority in the province without the support of bigger political groups. In January K.G. Balakrishnan, a Dalit, was appointed as Chief Justice to head the country's judiciary.

Like low-caste Dalits, India's tribal Adivasis also face issues of discrimination and inhuman treatment. November 2007 saw nationwide outrage sparked as the media reported that an Adivasi woman was stripped in public and assaulted during a demonstration in Guwahati in Assam. Adivasis had been protesting in Assam, calling for constitutional recognition as a 'scheduled tribe', which would give them greater legal status.

Religious minorities, mainly Muslims and Christians, in majority Hindu India, were also victims of violence and persecution in 2007. In May thousands of Christians took to the streets of India's capital New Delhi, calling on the government to stop violence against the religious minority. The DFN reported on its website that some 4,000 people had been arrested by police and temporarily detained during the protest.

Muslim minority groups in September launched protests against the government for its failure to implement recommendations of the Sachhar Committee report. The report, released in 2006, recognized the discrimination against minorities and called for a series of government measures to bring an end to it. In May explosions in a mosque, Mecca Masjid, in Hydrabad, killed 11 people. Police fired live ammunition and shot and killed five people in subsequent rioting that broke out in the city in protest against the government's failure to protect minority places of worship.

Another major concern for minority groups has been the adoption of anti-conversion laws in four Indian states. In October the state of Himachal Pradesh became the fourth to usher in 'anti-conversion' laws. The controversial Act requires any person wishing to convert to another religion to give prior notice of at least 30 days to district authorities. The laws are expected to largely affect non-Hindu religious minorities.

One major victory for minorities came from India's southern state of Tamil Nadu, which in September announced a 3.5 per cent quota for backward classes of Muslims and Christians in government and educational institutions.

Nepal

Prospects for peace in Nepal received a blow in September 2007 when the Maoists quit the government amidst looming threats of a return to conflict. In 2006 the Nepali government had entered into a peace agreement with the Maoists, ending years of conflict. In November 2007 the media reported on Maoists' warnings that they could take up arms again if the government did not meet their demand to scrap the country's monarchy.

Throughout 2007, Nepal was crippled by strikes and violent protests by ethnic groups, mainly the Madhesis, in the south of the country. Madhesis are amongst the poorest in Nepal and have faced years of marginalization and human rights violations. They are demanding greater representation in the peace process, guarantees of proportional representation and a federalist form of government. Strike action initiated by Madhesi groups shut down schools and businesses and crippled large areas of southern Nepal through most of April and May. In May, 27 people were killed when one such protest turned violent. In August 2007, the Nepal Red Cross Society said the strikes were hampering the distribution of aid to flood victims in the south.

Also in August, the Nepali government announced it had reached a crucial peace agreement

with one of the major Madhesi groups, the Madhesi People's Rights Forum. The deal aimed at granting Madhesis more autonomy and expanded their political and economic rights. Smaller Madhesi groups, however, dissociated themselves from the agreement, claiming it was signed only by one group. These groups also accused the government of failing to grant their main demands – for electoral reform and federalism – and accused the ruling party of attempting to divide and rule. Some Madhesi groups have also been accused of engaging in incidents of violence and human rights violations, including killings and abductions.

According to local human rights groups, violence between the Pahade and Madhesi ethnic groups left at least 18 people killed and more than 4,000 displaced between September and October 2007. In early September two little-known ethnic militant groups – the Terai Army and the Nepal People's Army – claimed responsibility for a bomb blast in the volatile Terai region that killed four people and injured 30. In May the Terai Army also claimed responsibility for a series of bombings that injured 14 people in Rautahat.

Nepal's low-caste Dalits, who have faced years of structural discrimination, were also seen to be mobilizing themselves politically through most of the year. Dalits, like Madhesis, are clamouring for a bigger role in the constitution-making process. The country's new constitution is expected to be drafted by a Constituent Assembly. In July 2007, over 20 Dalit leaders were arrested for protesting against a government policy to allocate 6 per cent of the 497 seats in the Assembly to Dalits. The protest came a month after the first-ever National Citizen's Assembly of Dalits in Kathmandu, where more than 2,000 Dalit activists voted to demand one-fifth of the Assembly seats for Dalits. They also agreed to launch a campaign to convince the government to agree to the demand.

On 7 August 2007, the government and the Nepali Federation of Indigenous Nationalities (NEFIN) signed a 20-point agreement that included ensuring the participation of all the listed ethnic communities in the elections for the Constituent Assembly.

Despite the rising violence and worsening security conditions, Nepal's Prime Minister Girija Prasad Koirala in mid-September assured ethnic minority and indigenous groups that he would hold polls as scheduled in November to elect the Constitutional

Sri Lanka

In *State of the World's Minorities 2007*, Farah Mihlar reported from Sri Lanka on that country's resurgent civil war and its impact on minorities. Here, she gives a first-hand account of how the crisis has deepened over the past 12 months

April 28, 2007, was a glorious day for Sri Lanka as the cricket-loving nation prepared to watch their national team play in the finals of the sport's biggest prize – the World Cup. Successive victories in the run-up to the finals had lifted the islanders' spirits, previously weighed down by rising violence following the collapse of a five-year ceasefire that had ended two decades of bloody conflict between the government and Tamil Tiger militants.

Late that night, as the match got under way in the Caribbean, the roads were deserted and people stayed home, glued to their radios and TVs. But just past midnight, as the game was at a turning point, a sudden power cut plunged the entire capital Colombo into darkness. Since the Tamil Tigers had conducted their first ever air-raid on the capital a month before, such blanket power cuts meant that key government targets were being shielded in darkness.

Fifteen minutes or so later, a massive blast rocked Colombo, quickly followed by a second. Within minutes anti-aircraft guns at key spots on Colombo's skyline began incessantly firing into the air. It was deafening yet constant, and lit up the night sky with red flares. On the streets, soldiers fired into the air, ensuring that a terrified public stayed indoors. The Sri Lankan capital had never been terrorized in this manner in more than 25 years of ethnic conflict. The Tiger planes that had bombed a military installation just outside Colombo returned safely to their jungle base in the north of the country. Over an hour later, after what seemed a never-ending night, the power supply was restored and televisions were switched on in time for Sri Lankans to see their team lose the match.

Return to war

But 2007 was marked by other, different, victories in Sri Lanka as the country plunged further into war. In August 2007 the government celebrated a major victory in its 'war on terror' – the capture from rebel control of the entire eastern province, which is part of the 'homeland' the Tigers want for ethnic minority Tamils.

But it came at a heavy human cost – some 3,500 deaths since April 2006 and close to 290,000 displaced.

Continuous military checkpoints and road-blocks greet anyone entering the newly captured areas of the eastern province. The main town in the east, Batticaloa, is highly militarized. Tamil militants belonging to the 'Karuna group', a splinter group of the Tamil Tigers now working with the government, are seen openly carrying their weapons amidst civilians. Their offices stand adjacent to government military sites.

The displaced

A little distance from the main town, we approached a sea of white tents. Displaced families, some with four or five children, live packed into each tent. Water and food were scarce. People related stories of how they got there, leaving their homes at the dead of night as army shells rained down on them. At a distance, explosions could still be heard, followed by mild vibration of the ground. Families spoke of their fear of returning. But even as we were interviewing them the government, responding to mounting international criticism over the high numbers of displaced, had begun repatriation plans. In June 2007, a fact-finding mission by a group of local NGOs, including the Centre for Policy Alternatives and the Law and Society Trust, found evidence that, contrary to international law, in some cases the return of displaced people to their homes was forced.

Human rights abuses

While the country grappled with a humanitarian crisis throughout 2007, human rights violations were accelerating. A majority of the victims of human rights abuses have been ethnic minority Tamils and Muslims. In June 2007, the government used anti-terror laws to evict close to 376 Tamils who were living in temporary accommodation in the capital city Colombo. The next day, the country's highest court ruled that the eviction was unlawful and the Tamils were allowed to return. The government has also liberally used tough new anti-terror laws to arrest and detain Tamils. Cordon-and-search operations and checkpoints are a constant occurrence, especially in the capital.

Throughout 2007, extra-judicial killings, abductions and disappearances have been on the rise. According to local human rights groups, some 662 people were killed in the first eight months of 2007, of whom a majority were Tamils. Only a few cases of abductions and disappearances are reported, but available statistics show 540 disappearances in the same period. International and local NGOs have blamed soaring human rights violations on multiple perpetrators – chiefly the government, but also the Tigers and other Tamil militant groups. In some cases, as in recent child conscription, the UN has accused the government of colluding with the Karuna group.

Muslims

The country's ethnic Muslims have not been spared. Earlier in the year, Muslim businessmen, because of their influential economic position and their minority status, were the targets of abduction and extortion in the urban city centres. In the conflict zone Muslims continue to be harassed, intimidated and extorted from, mainly by the Karuna faction. Muslims were among the 22,000 displaced in fighting between government forces and the Tigers, which had shifted to the north-west of the country. A vast majority of the displaced are Tamils.

Mrs Careem, a Muslim school principal, whose displacement we reported on last year, has returned to her home in Muttur in eastern Sri Lanka. Her family, however, faces severe economic difficulties because a Tamil family they did business with has been barred from returning to the town. A military high security zone in Sampur, close to Muttur, has left thousands of Tamil families homeless and has affected the interdependency that communities have with each other. The government has taken over an area of 35 square miles, covering 15 villages and barring 15,000 mostly Tamil civilians from their homes. The Muslims have not escaped being affected by security issues either: 67 families of the Arafa Nagar village, close to Muttur, were given an hour to leave by the military on 10 August 2007. They have subsequently been allowed to cultivate rice but cannot stay in their village because of security concerns.

Mrs Careem's son, abducted by the Tigers, is still missing.

The Bishop of Mannar, Rayappu Joseph, who last year spoke to us about the plight of Tamils caught up in fighting in northern Sri Lanka, in a statement to mark the killing of a fellow Catholic clergyman called for an end to 'this senseless war'. Father Nicholaspilai Packiyaranjith was killed by a landmine on 26 September 2007. Six minority religious leaders have been killed in the past year.

In August 2007, John Holmes, the head of the UN's humanitarian agency, said that Sri Lanka was one of the most dangerous places in the world for aid workers. Since mid-2006, up to 30 aid workers have been killed in Sri Lanka, all of them Tamils. Tamil and Muslim journalists are also victims of killings, attacks and threats.

By the end of 2007, the government continued to maintain its firm stance, resisting calls by local and international NGOs to allow urgent international human rights monitoring in Sri Lanka. In 2008 Sri Lankan will mark 60 years of independence. But the country enters this landmark year torn apart by war and facing a severe human rights crisis.

> **For more information** see MRG briefing paper 'One year on: counter-terrorism sparks human rights crisis for Sri Lanka's minorities'
> **www.minorityrights.org/?lid=4583**

Assembly. However, on 5 October the Nepali government, having failed to come to an agreement with the Maoists, announced that the elections were suspended indefinitely. The Maoists had threatened to disrupt elections if an agreement was not reached with the government. Minority and indigenous groups that had strong expectations of the Constitutional Assembly elections are likely to be most affected by the suspension.

According to local and international human rights groups even during the last year – post the 2006 peace agreement – major human rights violations, including torture and abductions, prevailed. In June 2007, Human Rights Watch and the International Commission of Jurists called for the speedy implementation of a Supreme Court decision to investigate the disappearance of thousands of Nepalese during the conflict. Later in the year a local human rights group, Advocacy Forum, said that even after the peace agreement more than 1,300 Nepalese suffered torture, mostly at the hands of the country's police. According to a report by the Oneworld website, a majority of those affected by torture in Nepal are from minorities. The report quoted Nepali rights groups as saying that the Dalits have historically been victims of police brutality and torture, and their increasing public agitation in 2007 made them more vulnerable.

Pakistan

As Muslim-majority Pakistan celebrated its 60th year of independence in 2007, ethnic and religious minorities criticized the government for failing to live up to the pledges of the nation's founding fathers to protect human rights. The All Pakistan Minority Alliance (APMA) on 11 August 2007 organized a historic mass rally to demand more religious freedom in the country. In a 30-point Charter of Demands to the government, the APMA called for adequate political representation of minorities in national and provincial legislatures, and the scrapping of laws that discriminate against religious minorities. The charter particularly referred to anti-blasphemy and Huddod laws, which put Pakistan's non-Muslim minorities under threat simply for asserting their religion.

During most of 2007, Pakistan's Christian and Hindu minority populations continued to face persecution, particularly at the hands of religious extremists. Just weeks after the charter was presented to the government, the media reported that a Christian Bishop Arif Khan and his wife were murdered in Islamabad. In the same month of August, websites promoting religious freedom and Christian news websites reported that Christians in Peshawar, the capital of the North West Frontier Province, were asked to convert to Islam or face death. Seven churches and five Christian settlements received the threatening letters. Earlier, in May, Christians in Charsadda, also in the North West Frontier Province, were given ten days to convert to Islam and warned of 'dire consequences and bomb explosions', said *Christian Today* newspaper, which has headquarters in London with worldwide correspondents. Minority political rights were also under threat in the province. In July 2007, APMA said that 18 per cent of eligible voters belonging to minorities were left out of the new voters' list in North West Frontier Province.

Both Hindu and Christian children have also been the victims of abductions and forced conversions. In August a South Asian News Agency, ANI, reported two missing children, forcibly married and converted to Islam.

Pakistan's minority Ahmaddiya community, who profess a different version of Islam, have also historically faced severe human rights violations amidst the rising trend of Islamism in the country. In 2007 Human Rights Watch issued a statement accusing the Pakistan government of pandering to fundamentalists and violating the rights of groups such as the Ahmaddiyas. The statement said police in Lahore had supervised the demolition of a boundary wall in an Ahmaddiya graveyard. Two Islamic groups had for some time exerted pressure on the provincial authorities to bring down the wall.

Laws discriminating against minorities remained in place through 2007. In May Pakistan's National Assembly overwhelmingly rejected proposed amendments to the blasphemy laws, which were tabled by a minority Member of Parliament, saying they were 'un-Islamic'. Under the existing blasphemy laws, a person can face indefinite imprisonment or the death penalty for criticizing the Prophet of Islam, Muhammad. The reforms called for the punishment for blasphemy to be reduced to a maximum five-year prison sentence and a fine. In a special report on Pakistan the Asian Centre for Human Rights (ACHR) said that in 2007 some 25 people, of whom 16 were Christian and 9 were women, were victims of the blasphemy laws. The report also said that on 30 May 2007, Younis Masih, a Christian, was sentenced to death under the law.

In August, Pakistan's Christian National Party, in a rare legal challenge, petitioned the Supreme Court to amend a law that reserves the office of president only for Muslims. The petition said that this particular clause in the constitution violates other sections that guarantee equal rights to all citizens.

In January 2007, 13 members of the Baluchistan Provincial Assembly appealed to international human rights organizations and the UN to ask the Pakistani government to halt ongoing military operations and stop the 'genocide' and human rights violations in the area. Following the killing of a government spokesman by the separatist group, the Balochi National Army, in Quetta, the town has come under intense military scrutiny with increased checkpoints particularly in Balochi areas, opposition MPs claimed. In the same month, media reports said police raided and arrested up to 100 people also in Quetta following the killing of a police officer. According to the AHRC report, on the morning of 30 March 2007, Pakistani soldiers cordoned off the villages of Lanju and Sagari in the Sui area, while air force jets and helicopter gunships fired at the village. Some 18 people, including women and children, were killed as a result of the indiscriminate use of force.

Ethnic tensions rose as political turmoil gripped the country through most of 2007. The sacking of the Chief Justice by President Musharraf led to weeks of violent street protests. The protests culminated in two days of carnage in the city of Karachi in May, when more than 30 people were killed and over 150 injured. Pakistan's Human Rights Commission (HRCP), in a statement issued soon after the incident, accused the government, the Mohajir Quami Movement (MQM) and provincial government for being responsible for the violence. Much of the fighting reportedly took place between the MQM, which the Commission accused of supporting the government, and ethnic Pashtuns. 'The events in Karachi indicate that the government, in collusion with the MQM wants to return Karachi to a state of ethnic hostilities,' the HRCP said in a statement. According to human rights groups, violence against lawyers continued in Sindh, including incidents of harassment and arrest, but no action has been taken by the central government.

As the year drew to a close Pakistan was submerged in political violence, protests and the arrest and detention of several human rights activists and opponents of the government. In November 2007 General Musharaff stepped down as head of the army but remained president. He has called for elections in January 2008.

Cross-border refugee problem
Another significant issue that affected the region was a cross-border refugee problem. Bhutan, India and Nepal were locked in the problem facing ethnic Nepalese who were born in Bhutan but were expelled or fled from there nearly two decades ago. In 1990,

more than 100,000 ethnic Nepalese, who faced severe discrimination in Bhutan, were expelled for protesting against their treatment by the state. They have since lived in impoverished conditions in Nepal. In May 2007, 80 refugees were injured and thousands attacked by Indian border guards as they attempted to cross through India to return to their birthplace in Bhutan. The refugees want to return to Bhutan as the country is heading for a transition from monarchy to democracy in 2008. The UN has said the Bhutanese refugees should be given the freedom to make an informed decision about their future.

South-East Asia

Islamic extremism has continued to have an overarching effect on the region during 2007, with government-sponsored crackdowns on militants in Muslim-minority states such as Thailand and the Philippines and continuing religious violence in Muslim-dominated countries such as Indonesia. Minorities in these states routinely experience severe curtailments of religious freedom, either by the authorities or by religious extremists acting in an atmosphere of impunity. Burma's ethnic groups continue to suffer at the hands of the authoritarian state, despite the country being the focus of the international community's attention following massive pro-democracy protests in September. Massive cultivation of oil palm – in an attempt to meet the increasing global demand for biofuels – is having a devastating effect on the territories and cultures of indigenous communities in Indonesia and Malaysia. Land grabbing and illegal logging are vastly reducing ethnic minorities' access to ancestral lands in Cambodia, Indonesia and the Philippines.

Burma (Myanmar)

The US State Department labels Burma one of the world's seven worst human rights violators, evidenced during the September 2007 bloody crackdown by the ruling military junta on pro-democracy and anti-government protesters led by Buddhist monks. Information on the involvement of ethnic minorities in the protests is hard to come by due to government restrictions on information flow out of the country. Also, ethnic minority populations are greater in rural areas and the majority of the protests took place in urban centres. However, groups such as the Karen, Karenni, Rohingya and Shan joined the protests on the Thai–Burma border and in the city of Sittwe in Rakhine State. In an October 2007 Associated Press article Karen National Union Secretary General Mahn Sha said: 'We need to work together with the Mon, other groups, the students, to oust the [junta]. We have a common enemy and common goals.'

The UN Security Council released a formal statement on Burma in October, criticizing the military government's crackdown on pro-democracy demonstrators. It called on the ruling State Peace and Development Council (SPDC) to hold talks with opposition leaders and hasten the release of political prisoners. The international community remains divided over the treatment of Burma – France, the UK and the US proposed tougher wording in the UN Security Council statement and

continue to call for harsh sanctions, yet China and Russia successfully argued to soften the language of the statement and consistently oppose sanctions. The two countries are key supporters of the military junta and in January vetoed a US-led UN Security Council resolution calling on the military junta to end the persecution of minority and ethnic groups.

The pattern of the Burmese military has been to eliminate all opposition and take full control of ethnic areas. As part of its strategy to curb the support of ethnic insurgent armies, it targets civilians it perceives as backers of the insurgent groups.

The Burmese junta's monitoring and control of religious activity within its borders has led the US Commission on International Religious Freedom

Below: Shan men relaxing having escaped from the Burma army in 1997. Forced at gunpoint to carry munitions to the frontline, these men had been away from their homes for two months. They escaped captivity by crossing Karenni minefields. Dean Chapman/Panos Pictures

(USCIRF) to designate it in 2007 as a 'country of particular concern', a title given to states that are the most 'egregious violators' of religious freedom in the world. The report documents the Burmese junta allowing or instigating violence against religious minorities and forcefully promoting Buddhism over other religions. It notes that ethnic minority Christians and Muslims have encountered the most difficulties in recent years.

According to Refugees International, the worst Burmese military offensive in 10 years has displaced at least 27,000 people in Karen State since November 2005. There are some 130,000 Burmese refugees living in nine border camps in Thailand. Many of them have been there for up to 20 years, having risked minefields and army patrols to get there. The US Committee for Refugees calls the Karen people 'one of the most ignored groups in one of the most difficult humanitarian emergencies'.

The Tatmadaw (military of Burma) appears to be able to violate the Karen's most basic human rights with impunity. There were no reports in 2007 of government prosecution of previous incidents of rape of Karen women, nor obvious steps by the government to address widespread reports of security forces burning Karen villages.

The right to property and use of their own land by the Karen continued to be disregarded by the Burmese authorities. Surveying work on the Hat Gyi hydroelectric dam began in 2007 and, because of the settlement of Burmese troops near the site of the proposed reservoir, thousands of mainly Karen refugees fled over the border to Thailand. Karen forced labour is reported to be have been used to clear the area near the dam and to build access roads to military and government camps near it.

Discrimination against the Karen remains deeply entrenched in state institutions: state education in schools in Karen areas, even where they are the majority of the population, is exclusively provided in the Burmese language, and government offices provide no access to services in Karen languages. Numerous reports continue to point out that government jobs in Karen areas appear to be increasingly the reserved domain of ethnic Burman.

The Burmese army has continued to conduct occasional raids in those ethnic Mon areas where the ceasefire has not held, and is accused of enforced labour, displacement, rape, murder and widespread land confiscation. As a result, there has been a mass exodus of Mon to Thailand. The SPDC's military presence has increased dramatically: the number of army regiments in Ye Township went from two in 2000 to ten by 2007.

In part as a result of increasing government restrictions, Médecins Sans Frontières pulled out after four years of work in Mon State. As a result, Mon resettlement sites appeared to have run out of basic medical supplies by mid-2007. Other UN and international agencies based in Rangoon continue to have very limited access to the Mon ceasefire areas.

The Mon continue to be vastly under-represented in most state institutions, which seems to be partially due to discriminatory government polices and practices in hiring and promotion processes, which favour ethnic Burman.

In his June 2007 report, the Special Rapporteur on Contemporary Forms of Racism, Racial Discrimination, Xenophobia and Related Intolerance highlighted the case of the Rohingyas, a Muslim ethnic minority living in northern Rakhine State, western Burma. According to the report 'the Rohingyas are targeted because of their ethnicity and suffer widespread discrimination at the hands of the authorities'. Rohingyas are unable to qualify for citizenship and their freedom of movement is severely restricted because they cannot afford to pay the fee needed for official authorization to travel outside of their villages; they are also unable to access medical and educational services.

In 1993 the military government set in motion the National Convention in order to write a new constitution, yet in September 2007 the process came to an end with a written constitution still lacking. According to Human Rights Watch, some ethnic national groups that had reached ceasefire agreements with the government on the premise that the National Convention would bring about true reforms have hinted that they may resume armed conflict against the government if their basic demands are not addressed. In October the junta set up a fresh committee to draft a new constitution, a decision which the generals call their 'roadmap' to democracy according to state media. The opposition is unrepresented on the new committee.

The area of Burma along the Chinese border, which once produced about 30 per cent of the country's opium, was declared opium-free in 2006 by the United Nations. Ethnic Shan and Wa groups have both been involved in eradication of poppy cultivation, although UN observers note that the area is becoming central to the production of methamphetamine and is the source of half of Asia's supply of the drug.

Cambodia

Despite a 2001 Land Law to recognize indigenous rights in Cambodia, not a single indigenous group had received title for the collective ownership of their traditional lands by 2007. Regulations crucial to the enforcement of this legislation have still not been approved, resulting in indigenous people being particularly vulnerable to state orchestrated 'land-grabbing' strategies. Following his 2007 visit, the UN Special Representative for Human Rights in Cambodia expressed his deep concern about the practice of 'land grabbing', illegal or coercive sales, and the granting of concessions, including mining licences. It is thought that illegal logging in Cambodia has reduced the country's forest cover from 70 per cent in the early 1970s to less than 30 per cent in 2007. Announcements in 2007 of the possible construction of two dams in Cambodia on the Sesan and Srepok rivers have caused concern because of the negative impact they will have on the livelihoods of affected indigenous peoples.

The almost exclusive use of the Khmer language in all fields of public life continues to disadvantage indigenous groups and to some degree other minorities such as the Cham. In localities where the Khmer Leou are a majority, local commune councils still operate exclusively in Khmer and not local languages, making the participation of indigenous peoples who are not fluent in Khmer all but impossible. All communication with higher echelons of state administration is conducted exclusively in Khmer. The government of Cambodia announced at the end of 2006 that it would offer some form of bilingual education for indigenous students up to grade three in five of the north-east provinces, but this does not appear to have been implemented beyond a few pilot programmes. Despite numerous statements by state officials that bilingual education is one way to address the low levels of school participation of many minorities, the country's second National Education for All Plan is actually silent on the goal of education in minority languages.

Indonesia

Rising religious tension in Indonesia, the most populous Muslim-majority state in the world, was reflected in the May 2007 report of the US Commision on International Religious Freedom. The state was placed on the Commission's 'watch list' for countries that require close monitoring, highlighting the Indonesian government's inability or unwillingness to hold those responsible for religious violence to account, and the growing political power and influence of religious

extremists in Central and South Sulawesi. At least nine Protestant churches, four Ahmaddiya mosques and one Hindu temple have been closed or damaged in areas of West Java, North Sumatra, South Sulawesi and West Nusa Tenggara as a result of the influence of 'extremist' groups, which incited mobs and/or intimated local officials in the last year, said the report.

In July 2007, 17 Christians were jailed under anti-terrorism laws for the murder of two Muslims. According to International Crisis Group, the two Muslim fishmongers were attacked in Poso, Sulawesi, in September 2006, by a mob angry at the execution in the same year of three Christians convicted of leading a group that killed hundreds of Muslims at a boarding school during inter-religious violence in Poso in 2000.

In its August 2007 report the Committee on the Elimination of Racial Discrimination (CERD) expressed concern that under Indonesian law individuals are obliged to mention their faiths on legal documents such as identity cards and birth certificates, and that those wishing either to leave the document blank or to register under one of the 'non-recognized' religions, reportedly face discrimination and harassment. CERD also noted that couples involved in interfaith marriages face great difficulties in officially registering their marriages, and that their children are not provided with birth certificates.

Oil palm development is one of the most significant new investments in Papua. The Indonesian government plans to establish up to 5 million hectares of new plantations in the state by 2012 in a drive to increase biofuel production. According to a July 2007 International Crisis Group report, these plans have raised discrimination concerns relating to indigenous property rights and deforestation in the absence of a clear legal framework for customary land rights, as well as the prospect of an influx of large numbers of non-Papuan settlers.

Environmentalists called on CERD to intervene in a mega-project being planned in Kalimantan (Borneo), which will allocate up to 1.8 million hectares (4.4 million acres) of land for oil palm plantations; they fear that the project will cause irreparable harm to indigenous people's territories and cultures. The area covers the ancestral territory of between 1 million and 1.4 million Dayak indigenous people. CERD responded by

Hmong – portrait of a persecuted people

Ethnic Hmong people belong to a highland tribe inhabiting Cambodia, southern China, Laos, Thailand and Vietnam. They arrived in Laos from south-eastern China at the turn of the nineteenth century and settled as farmers in the mountains of the north. Today, the Hmong in Laos number over 450,000 people, constitute 8 per cent of the population and are the third largest ethnic group in the country.

As the Vietnam war spread into neighbouring Laos, the Hmong became an integral part of a secret CIA-trained militia that helped to dismantle Pathet Lao (a Communist Laotian nationalist movement) supply lines. Fearing the worst when communists came into power in Laos at the end of the war, a third of the Hmong population left the country. However, some Hmong continued their armed struggle against the Pathet Lao movement, while tens of thousands of Hmong simply fled into the isolated remote mountainous jungles in order to avoid persecution and relocation camps.

Today, more than 30 years later, many of the descendants of those who fled into the jungles after the war still live in hiding in the Laotian jungle, persecuted because of their grandparents' decision to support the US army. Internally displaced and isolated, they face frequent military attacks and rarely remain in one place for longer than three weeks. Most of them are women and children. They constantly live in desperate need of food and medical care. The Society for Threatened Peoples documents that more than 400 Hmong surrendered to the Lao military on 13 December 2006. They were put onto military trucks and driven away – their fate is still unknown in 2007.

Fearing death, torture, rape or capture, many thousand Hmong Lao have tried to escape by fleeing over the border to Thailand. In a March 2007 report to the United Nations Human Rights Council, the Society for Threatened Peoples stated that there were over 8,000 Hmong refugees in a make-shift camp in Petchabun, Thailand. Many more refugees are believed to also be in hiding in Thailand.

According to Human Rights Watch, in May 2007 senior military officers from Thailand and Laos signed the Lao–Thai Committee on Border Security agreement, allowing Thailand to send Lao Hmong asylum seekers back upon arrival. Over the next month, 194 Hmong were forcibly driven back over the border into Thailand. The Lao–Thai Committee on Border Security met once again at the beginning of September to decide the fate of the Hmong refugees at the camp in Petchabun and agreed to forcibly repatriate them to purpose-built villages outside Vientiane, the Lao capital. The UN refugee agency and other international human rights groups have not been given access to them.

---

recommending that the government 'secure the possession and ownership rights of local communities before proceeding further with this Plan'. It also said that the state should ensure that meaningful consultation with the communities, with a view to obtaining their consent and participation, should take place.

Oil palm plantations and the ensuing floods that at times accompany deforestation are an increasing threat for Dayak communities, who are unable to effectively oppose these schemes. There are continuing reports of the army having been used to intimidate anti-logging Dayak activists and to protect loggers, or of community leaders being swayed by bribes or intimidation to approve these plantations.

Laos

About 60 per cent of the population of Laos is Theravada Buddhist – Buddhism being both encouraged and controlled by the state. It is estimated that there are more than 35,000 Evangelical Christians in Laos, most of them belonging to the minority Hmong, Khmu and other tribes. According to a March 2007 report submitted to the UN Human Rights Council by the Society for Threatened Peoples, ethnic minorities in Laos face limitations of their religious freedom. For instance, Lao Christians were arrested for sharing and spreading their beliefs among families and fellow villagers.

Already under construction, the Nam Theun 2 dam, located in the central Lao provinces of

Bolikhamzy and Khammuane, is one of the biggest and most controversial projects in the region, impacting a river system on which 130,000 people depend for their fishing and farming-based livelihoods. According to the International Rivers Network, 6,200 Lao Tai villagers have already been forced to move from their ancestral lands in order to make way for the dam's reservoir, which covers an area of 450 sq km.

Malaysia

The interplay between race and religion is a sensitive issue in Malaysia, where ethnic Malay Muslims form about 60 per cent of the population and Buddhists, Christians, Hindus and Sikhs make up the bulk of the ethnic Indian and Chinese minorities. Islam is the official state religion and people of non-Islamic faiths – about 40 per cent of the population – continue to report problems in 2007.

Friction between ethnic communities led to the filing of a lawsuit in London in August 2007 by Malaysian lawyers backed by the Hindu Rights Action Force. The suit, on behalf of Malaysia's 2 million ethnic Indians, is against the current British government and demands that the court hold the British colonial authority liable for shipping millions of Tamil-speaking South Indians to Malaya and later abandoning them without adequate safeguards for their rights. The lawyers are calling for compensation for every minority Indian in Malaysia for their 'pain, suffering, humiliation, discrimination and continuous colonization'.

In November 2007 the ethnic Indian community staged its biggest ever anti-government street protest in Kuala Lumpur, when more than 10,000 protesters faced riot police to voice complaints of racial discrimination. Ethnic Indians claim that the government's affirmative action policy in favour of majority ethnic Malays has marginalized them. The protest was politically significant ahead of the coming elections.

According to the independent news organization, The Irrawaddy, decisions in Malaysia in 2007 that effectively compelled Malaysians born as Muslims to stay Muslim have led leaders of the state's minority religions to appeal to the government to allow people to choose their faith. In her March 2007 report, the UN Special Representative on the Situation of Human Rights Defenders highlighted the case of a lawyer representing Lina Joy in the Federal Court of Malaysia. Ms Joy is a Malay woman who has renounced her Muslim faith and embraced Christianity. The case relates to whether she can renounce Islam and have the religious affiliation on her identity card deleted. The lawyer has received death threats from an unknown group, denouncing him as a betrayer of Islam because of his involvement in the case.

According to current legislation, Orang Asli (aboriginal tribal groupings whose existence on peninsular Malaysia pre-dates the arrival of the Malay peoples and who number about 110,000) can use ancestral land as well as the timber and other resources on it. However, Malaysian state governments claim legal ownership of the land and insist that they need not pay compensation for acquiring it. Under the constitution, native customary rights must be shown to have existed before the formation of Malaysia in 1958. Most indigenous peoples do not have access to colonial or government documents demarcating their areas before this date, or such documents simply do not exist for some areas. According to a February 2007 study carried out by the Malaysia National Human Rights Commission, throughout the country Orang Asli communities are facing a bleak future marked by institutional discrimination and the greed of private enterprise. The study said loss of land, sudden eviction and paltry cash compensation has seriously injured the Orang Asli community.

Disenfranchisement from the legislative system has led some indigenous communities to take the law into their own hands. In April 2007, the Penan, a nomadic indigenous people in Sarawak, re-established a blockade to stop the logging company Samling taking over their lands. According to Survival International, the Penan have been fighting back against logging for two decades but only now are their actions having results – some of the companies are now agreeing to stop logging in the area. However the Penan need to stay vigilant as many such promises have been broken.

The Philippines

The Philippines government's 35-year confrontation with Muslim separatists on its southern islands continued in 2007, despite ongoing peace negotiations with the Moro Islamic Liberation Front (MILF) and the Moro National Liberation Front (MNLF). According to a July 2007 Human Rights Watch report, violent Islamist groups in the

Philippines have killed or injured more than 1,700 people in bombings and other attacks since 2000. President Arroyo has received significant US military support for her campaign against militants in Mindanao, and around 120,000 people have been uprooted by the fighting on the island. Government crackdowns against both the MILF and MNLF in 2007 have displaced some 40,000 civilians on the island of Jolo and 7,000 in Basilan. Some hope was held out for peace in 2008, after the signing of a demarcation agreement in November between the government and the MILF to set boundaries for a Muslim homeland.

In 2007, 10 years after the granting of a form of autonomy for the Moro in parts of Mindanao, restrictions remain on teaching in Moro languages in public schools or use of the languages as co-official or working languages of administration. Given the very large numbers of non-native Filipino-speakers and their concentration in parts of Mindanao, this language policy continues to create a very real obstacle to the full participation of Moro Muslims in the country's public and political life.

In March 2007 the UN Special Rapporteur on the situation of human rights and fundamental freedoms of indigenous people noted that the efforts deployed by the National Commission on Indigenous Peoples to promote the recognition of Certificates of Ancestral Domain continues to be under-funded, and the rate at which titles are granted every year is still very limited in relation to the number of requests. However, even land recognized as indigenous under these certificates can still be lost to development projects, since they can be pursued if a certificate of 'Free, Prior and Informed Consent' (FPIC) is obtained from indigenous peoples. A number of indigenous groups have repeatedly claimed that they have been deceived, and some individuals have been threatened and even assassinated in the pursuit of FPICs. The Rapporteur noted that more than 75 cases of extra-judicial killings of indigenous individuals have been reported by NGOs recently, many of which have not been thoroughly investigated.

Thailand

A year after the coup that overthrew Thai Prime Minister Thaksin Shinawata, armed violence has continued to plague the Muslim Malay-majority southern provinces of Kala, Narathiwat, Patanni and Songkhla. According to a July 2007 Human Rights

Watch (HRW) report, in their efforts to establish an independent Islamic state in Thailand's southern border provinces, separatist groups have killed 2,463 people in bomb attacks, shootings, assassinations, ambushes and machete attacks since January 2004 (89 per cent of victims were civilians). HRW also says that: 'Thai security forces have carried out extrajudicial killings, disappearances and arbitrary arrests of those known or suspected to be involved with separatist groups.'

Despite the continued violence, in some ways the September 2006 coup in Thailand has led to improved management of the conflict in the south. The current military-installed civilian government, headed by former army commander General Surayud Chulanont, made an historic apology to southern Muslims for past abuses and announced an end to blacklisting of suspected insurgents. However, according to a March 2007 International Crisis Group report: 'attempts to accommodate Malay Muslim identity such as the introduction of the Patani Malay dialect as an additional language in state primary schools and to promote its use in government offices have fallen flat in the absence of high-level political support'.

Vietnam

The Vietnamese government maintains far-reaching control of religious activities and organizations through the process of recognition and registration, with unregistered religious activity illegal. In its May 2007 report the US Commission on International Freedom (USCIRF) cited continued arrests of individuals because of their religious activities and severe religious freedom restrictions targeting some ethnic minority Protestants and Buddhists, Vietnamese Mennonites, Hao Hoa Buddhists, and monks and nuns associated with the Unified Buddhist Church of Vietnam. USCIRF recognized some positive religious freedom developments in Vietnam, such as releasing prominent religious prisoners. However, since Vietnam joined the World Trade Organization, positive religious freedom trends have, for the most part, stalled, and Vietnam has initiated a severe crackdown on many religious leaders.

After the fall of Saigon, Montagnard (or Degar) guerrillas continued a separatist campaign in Vietnam's Central Highlands until the early 1990s, when they disbanded, put down their arms and took up Christianity. Vietnamese authorities have declared the form of evangelical Christianity followed by many Montagnards a political movement, not a religion, and made it illegal. According to the Montagnard Foundation, in 2007 Vietnam has continued to prevent human rights monitors from having unhindered access to the Central Highlands. Over 350 Montagnard prisoners of conscience remain in Vietnamese prisons under brutal conditions.

Minority and indigenous groups continue to be displaced from their ancestral lands in the name of development in Vietnam. In the highlands in the north, the International Rivers Network reports that close to 100,000 people belonging to 13 indigenous groups may be resettled under a programme which began in December 2005 and is expected to be completed by 2015 (1,000 families had been moved by the end of 2006) in order to make place for the Son La Hydropower Project, which is the largest dam project ever built in Vietnam.

East Asia

Minority rights are enshrined within the constitution of ethnically diverse China, and ethnic autonomy is allowed in certain regions, yet minorities are still failing to benefit from China's relentless economic development projects, which often favour the majority Han Chinese. The scanty information from North Korea continues to indicate that the state is one of the worst violators of basic human and minority rights in the world. The US Commission on International Religious Freedom (USCIRF), in its 2007 report, classifies North Korea a 'country of particular concern' and documents severe government repression of public and private religious activities. There was some improvement for indigenous peoples in Taiwan, where constitutional reforms are in progress to protect aboriginal cultural and land rights. The treatment of 'new minorities' and migrants is of increasing concern in Taiwan and South Korea, while in what is considered to be ethnically homogeneous Japan, beleaguered minorities continue to struggle for an end to years of racial discrimination.

China

As the world's 'last great multi-ethnic empire', the People's Republic of China has well over 100 million people belonging to minority nationalities, whose numbers have been increasing at a much faster rate than the Han majority. Most minorities inhabit the outlying areas of China: the north-

western plateau and desert, the north-eastern plains and hills, and the south-western remote sacred forests and mountains, where they have lived in a sustainable way for centuries. The country has unique natural resources, cultural heritage, ethnic diversity – and increasingly vulnerable ecosystems. The challenges and complexities of ruling a country that is undergoing extraordinary economic and social change, however, should not distract from the disdain the government has shown for political change, the lack of meaningful and inclusive political participation of minorities, and the intolerant attitude of the authorities towards any public criticism of its human rights record. The international community has expressed great concern over the continuing violations of Tibetans' and Uyghurs' religious rights and Mongols' cultural rights; bilateral human rights dialogues and the EU have also criticized China's human rights practices and raised issues of minority protection. Yet, despite the heightened international scrutiny of the country in the lead-up to the 2008 Olympics, the state marked the one-year countdown to the Games without having fulfilled the promise to conform to its human rights obligations.

Cracking down on ethnic minorities and the Ethnic Minorities Affairs 11th Five-year Plan
In February 2007, the State Ethnic Affairs Commission (SEAC) announced the Ethnic Minorities Affairs 11th Five-year Plan (2006–10), aimed at strengthening the protection of the cultural identity of disadvantaged ethnic minorities and bringing about positive change by investing in infrastructure development and the improvement of living standards in minority provinces. However, the plan also includes measures designed to monitor ethnic minority relations and report on 'ethnic strife' in targeted minority areas; thus, while it might foster potentially beneficial developmental reforms for some smaller ethnic groups like the Daur, the Ewenki and the Orogen, larger minority communities, such as Mongol pastoralists and farmers, harbour deep mistrust of what they perceive as Han designs for their subjugation and forced assimilation. They remain suspicious that, under the plan, the government would foster sanctioned or spontaneous 'ethnic swamping', facilitating the resettlement of dominant Han Chinese into minority areas and thereby reducing

the minorities' proportion of the population. By and large, minority groups fear that the plan will further prevent them from enjoying their rights as the government retains control over their affairs and the autonomous territories.

During 2007, the government remained very sensitive about ethnic unrest in strategic border areas and kept a tight rein on its national minorities. Freedom of religious expression and association remained highly circumscribed, with surveillance and execution of Uyghurs, persecution of Christians, and the enforcement of new rules for Tibetan Buddhists in the designation of their spiritual leader. The authorities implemented regulations restricting Muslims' religious teaching and activities, for example by confiscating for 'safekeeping' the passports of Uyghurs intending to undertake the *Hajj* (the pilgrimage to Mecca). Societal discrimination against ethnic minority women remained severe, with the government implementing a highly humiliating policy of forcible relocation of young and unmarried ethnic Uyghur women to work in factories in eastern China.

The government political slogan that advocates building a 'harmonious society', and the 'counter-terrorism' pretext, justified a crackdown on alleged ethnic 'splittism' to safeguard social stability in the Tibet Autonomous Region (TAR) and remove the causes of social tensions to ensure national security in the Xinjiang Autonomous Region (XUAR). In August, violent ethnic clashes occurred between Hui and Han in eastern Shandong, and Tibetan monks and Hui Muslims in north-western Qinghai. Such incidents, although not unknown, point at the growing level of social tension between minority communities segregated by religion and ethnicity in tightly controlled areas, while the dominant Han majority are resentful of the preferential policies favouring minority groups like the Hui, who, in turn, complain about being marginalized and discriminated against on the basis of their religion and customs. Therefore, while the new 11th Five-year Plan may contribute to lifting some ethnic groups out of poverty, it does not envisage the institutional safeguards necessary to protect minorities' traditional languages, customs, livelihoods and group values, which are increasingly threatened by the state's call for social stability, national unity and rampant economic development through a systematic process of devaluing and diluting minority nationalities' identities.

Marginalization in education and employment

Employment and education discrimination are interlinked, and while the Chinese government has made great strides in providing compulsory primary education to ethnic children, many are still marginalized, abused and exploited, forced to work long and gruelling hours for low wages at the expense of their education. China's minority nationalities therefore continued to be *de facto* discriminated against in the fields of employment, social security, use and teaching of minority languages, culture and housing. They resent the discriminatory practice that favours Mandarin-fluent Han seizing employment opportunities and taking up better-paid jobs, which results in their own exclusion and economic disempowerment. The government claims that the Employment Promotion Law (EPL, 2007), enacted to combat employment discrimination on the base of ethnicity, race, age, gender or religious beliefs, will contribute to tackling such bad practice. Yet the existing China Labour Law (1994) already contained such provisions but was not effectively enforced and, on paper, the EPL does not seem to offer any concrete measures of enforcement, penalties for employers or means for those discriminated against to seek redress and compensation. In order to improve education and preserve minority languages, the government responded with substantial financial commitment to support the education of minorities, expanding the enrolment of ethnic students into schooling, increasing the number of ethnic minority cadres, and dispatching more bilingual teachers to ethnic areas. In the past, however, achieving such targets has proved elusive; for example, measures passed in the TAR promoting literacy in Tibetan as a working language have rarely been implemented or have been withdrawn. Some minorities, such as the Shui in Guangxi, responded positively to the educational measures offered by the state, but others, like the Yi in Sichuan, have long been alienated from institutionalized education that fostered few ethnically related incentives for their participation. The reality is that minority children in China are still largely at a structural disadvantage in comparison to Han children, as, rather than instil respect for their own language, values and cultural identity, education is often used to convey a sense of inferiority in comparison to dominant Han culture and values. In this context, only limited optimism is warranted, as the government has yet to provide institutional incentives to promote the learning and use of ethnic minority languages, and internal displacement and resettlement plans put these languages at further risk of extinction.

Environmental challenges

China's environmental challenges are daunting and, in spite of the official commitment (the ambitious National Climate Change Programme, 2007) and the comprehensive set of laws, the state has been slow to support sustainable ecological construction and environmental protection of autonomous areas inhabited by disempowered ethnic minorities. Minorities have largely been excluded from the planning and implementation of environmental regulations that would impact greatly on their lives. They have also been intimidated and silenced by local authorities that substantially curtailed any opposition to economic development programmes. Local officials have also turned a blind eye to serious environmental threats, ignored or not enforced the high targets set by the central government policies and diverted allocated protection funds to other endeavours.

In 2007 there was some progress with the adoption of the Ethnic Minorities Development Plans (EMDPs) in provinces such as Guangxi and Sichuan; the plans ensured minorities some sense of 'ownership' through consultation processes to assess the social and cultural impacts of large projects on groups inhabiting those areas, and sought ways to minimize adverse effects through the identification of appropriate mitigation measures. By contrast, other initiatives led to a host of adverse consequences in the dry northern areas and in southern grasslands and forest reserves. In north-western Ningxia, ethnic groups have accumulated great experience in checking sand erosion by means of afforestation in their struggle against desertification. But local attempts undertaken to establish communal range management systems have been challenged by large-scale digging for medicinal herbs in the grasslands, creating serious conflicts between Han and Hui. In Guizhou, having held an over-optimistic view of tourism development as a 'quick investment return', the Miao lost control over their own resources due to lack of power and capital and ended up marketing their culture. Environmental neglect, industrial pollution and massive resource extraction continued

throughout the year, leaving much of the north-west seriously degraded, which has had a major impact on the traditional livelihoods of minorities. In summer, the impact of climate change and environmental degradation on subsistence-based communities challenged the existence of minority communities in the mountainous south-western areas of Yunnan, while north-western Gansu saw the forcible relocation of hundreds of thousands of Tibetan herders. The vicious cycle of climate change and pastoral poverty affected the fragile ecosystem and livelihoods of 33 minority groups on the pastoral Qinghai Plateau in the north-west. Impoverished minority communities along the Yangtze River in Hubei, in Sichuan and Chongqing Municipality have been badly affected by floods and landslides that destroyed thousands of homes, livestock and hundreds of thousands of hectares of land. This combination of high exposure to natural disasters, increasing livestock diseases, decline of pastoral productivity and resources exploitation inhibited both minorities' and the government's capacity to take preventive measures and to protect the environment at local and provincial level. More crucially, the environmental degradation and the economic exploitation of resources has prompted not only growing political disaffection, increasing protest and social unrest, but has also paved the way to eco-conflict for Han and non-Han alike. China's grand-scale urbanization plans aggravated matters in many areas, particularly in the TAR, where the discriminatory allocation procedures to resettle and house Han Chinese meant land seizure and expropriation, as well as forced evictions and the demolition of thousands of traditional Tibetan homes and neighbourhoods, often with little or no compensation. This practice in turn is generating internal and cross-border displacement, and migration of ethnic communities. This is alarming because, if minorities do not maintain their numerical majority status in significant contiguous areas, and are not guaranteed fair representation, the government risks undermining the delivery of a workable framework of genuine autonomy as articulated in the laws. The 'great leap forward to modernization' is steadily eroding the environments, cultures and social values of China's ethnic minorities, depriving them of their traditional means of subsistence and survival. The country faces enormous challenges – water scarcity, severe soil

erosion, high rates of desertification, massive floods, and excessive levels of water and air pollution – which impose enormous burdens on China's people and jeopardize long-term progress.
Contributed by Marusca Perazzi

Japan

Minorities make up 1.5 per cent of Japan's population and include the Buraku people – a caste-like minority among ethnic Japanese. The Buraku are descendants of outcast populations from feudal days who were perceived to undertake 'polluting acts' under Buddhist and Shintoist beliefs due to their assigned social functions of slaughtering animals and executing criminals. Other minorities are the Ainu and the people of Okinawa; and people from and descendants of people from the former Japanese colonies of Korea and China. Japan has traditionally considered itself to be ethnically homogeneous yet NGOs continued to claim in 2007 that minorities face harsh discrimination and are deprived of their distinct cultures.

The UN Committee on the Elimination of Racial Discrimination (CERD) and the UN Committee on the Elimination of Discrimination Against Women (CEDAW) have previously expressed their concern at the government's lack of data on the ethnic composition of the Japanese population, and on economic and social indicators reflecting the situation of minorities. Both Committees have requested that such data be provided, disaggregated by gender and national and ethnic group, and that data on the exposure to violence of minority women should be included. CEDAW has also requested data on the education, employment, social welfare and health status of minority women. However, the Japanese government has failed to act on these requests to date.

In response, minority women took the initiative themselves, with a coalition of Ainu, Buraku and minority Korean women working together in 2003, 2004 and 2005 to draw up and implement surveys containing a common set of 41 questions covering the areas of education, employment, social welfare, health status and exposure to violence, in addition to further questions specific to the particular circumstances of each group.

In September 2007 the results of these surveys, together with proposals for policies to address the issues faced by minority women, were presented to government representatives, including the Gender Equality Bureau, which is charged with formulating national policy on gender equality. Survey results highlighted issues such as the low levels of post-compulsory education for Ainu women, particularly those over 40 years of age; higher than average levels of reliance on public welfare among those in the Buraku community; and the importance to Korean minority women of continuing to practise traditional Korean rituals for ethnic and cultural solidarity. All groups proposed to the government the introduction of legislation prohibiting discrimination, implementation of a government survey of minority women, policies reflecting the views of minority women, ongoing consultative processes between government and minority women, facilitation of the participation of minority women in decision-making bodies, and respect for and promotion of minority culture.

Taiwan

There are 13 officially recognized indigenous peoples in Taiwan: the Ami, Atayal, Bunun, Kavalan, Paiwan, Puyuma, Rukai, Saisiyat, Tao (Yami), Taroko, Thao, Tsou and Sakizaya (the latter officially recognized as Taiwan's 13th aboriginal tribe on 17 January 2007), as well as a number of unrecognized smaller groups, some of whom continue to fight for official recognition.

The situation of Taiwan's indigenous peoples has in general been improving over the last few years. One of the main recent legal-political developments has been the drafting of a new constitution that embraces an explicit recognition of the rights of indigenous peoples. For instance, in November the Taiwan cabinet approved a bill specifying that the nation's 13 aboriginal tribes' autonomous areas should enjoy administrative status equal to that of a county, and any dispute between the autonomous regions and county governments should be referred to the cabinet for settlement. The bill still has to pass through the legislative process, however.

The Council of Indigenous Peoples (CIP) and Council of Agriculture jointly ruled in September that Atayal aborigines from the Smangus and Cinsbu sub-tribes in Hsinchu county are entitled to use natural resources within their traditional territories for cultural, ritual or personal purposes. The ruling is significant because it is the first time that aboriginal people's traditional territories have been recognized by the government.

The ruling also sheds light on the case of three aborigines from the Smangus tribe who were found guilty of theft in April 2007 for attempting to remove the trunk of a tree that fell in 2005, blocking the tribe's only connection with the outside world. The three defendants filed an appeal with the High Court, which was subsequently rejected; however their sentences were shortened from six months to three months and, according to reports in the *Taiwan Journal*, the CIP hopes that the recent ruling will persuade the court to amend its verdict to not guilty.

Taiwan Indigenous Television (TITV) was launched in July 2005and claimed to be the first TV station in Asia fully dedicated to an indigenous population. However, in September 2007, aboriginal producers protested that most programmes broadcast on TITV are made by non-aborigines and demanded that they be given priority in producing the programmes.

Pacific

The Pacific states are some of the most ethnically diverse in the world and differing trends in minority and indigenous rights were observed throughout the region in 2007. Both Australia and New Zealand's indigenous peoples have experienced troubled relations with their governments during this period, exemplified by both states' opposition to the signing of the UN Declaration on the Rights of Indigenous Peoples. Increased migration of Chinese citizens to island states such as the Solomon Islands and Papua New Guinea is causing friction between communities, although the main threat facing the indigenous communities of the latter is Aids, with up to 120,000 people thought to be affected by the disease. Fiji, which saw a coup motivated by simmering ethnic tensions in December 2006, remained relatively calm in 2007. Coup leader, Commodore Frank Bainimarama, continues as prime minister and, despite ongoing conflict with the Great Council of Chiefs, the State of Emergency on the island was lifted in May 2007.

Environmental disasters perhaps pose the greatest threat to communities on the thousands of low-lying islands in this region. In September 2007, Solomon Islands Foreign Minister Patteson Oti said the Islands 'faced a future of more violent storms, depleted fish stocks, bleached coral reefs and even annihilation if the world fails to deal with climate change'.

Australia

A minority of around 450,000 among a population of 21 million, Australia's Aborigines continue to suffer health and lifestyle problems more common to people living in developing countries. On average, they die almost 20 years earlier than other Australians and suffer significantly higher rates of drug and alcohol abuse, unemployment and imprisonment.

The landslide victory of Labor in the general election late in 2007 may present an opportunity for improved relations between central government and the nation's indigenous communities. But for the preceding months, indigenous communities found themselves under intense scrutiny and bore the brunt of new policy-making which some declared was frankly 'racist'. The spark was a report released in June 2007 – the result of a Board of Inquiry created by the Northern Territory government to investigate allegations of sexual abuse of Aboriginal children. The report revealed that Board had found cases of abuse in each of the 45 Aboriginal communities researchers had visited. Recommendations included the improvement of education services and the appointment of a children's commissioner. Greater cooperation with the police and awareness-raising campaigns on issues such as pornography, alcohol and gambling, were also advocated. However, John Howard's government immediately deployed officials, police and army personnel to remote communities and announced that the federal government would take over the administration of Aboriginal communities in the Northern Territory for the next five years so that new laws could be strictly enforced. He also introduced extensive alcohol restrictions on Northern Territory Aboriginal land (limiting the liberty of Aboriginals to purchase alcohol in some cases where white Australians and tourists are exempted from the ban) and linked welfare payments to child school attendance. The measures sparked widespread accusations by Aboriginal groups of racism and vote-scoring ahead of the November elections.

In August 2007, Indigenous Affairs Minister Mal Brough pushed a package of five bills through the House of Representatives and the Senate, sealing legislation on the statute books which rights activists say overrides the 1975 Racial Discrimination Act and gives the minister direct control of indigenous townships. Two months after the government's unprecedented intervention, the Aboriginal Legal

Rights Movement in Adelaide said that indigenous people remained suspicious that the intervention was a 'Trojan horse for the takeover of Aboriginal land'.

The government's opposition to the September 2007 signing of the United Nations Declaration on the Rights of Indigenous People, at a time when the country had become so acutely aware of the plight of Aboriginal communities, made a mockery of a supposed renewed commitment to addressing the welfare of indigenous Australians. Australia expressed dissatisfaction with references to self-determination in the Declaration and complained that it placed international customary law above national law.

In July 2007, the Queensland Supreme Court acquitted a senior police officer of manslaughter and assault charges in the death of an Aboriginal man, Mulrunji Doomadgee, in a police cell on Palm Island in 2004. The prosecution was the first such case in Queensland, and the first homicide trial conducted against a police officer for killing an indigenous person anywhere in Australia since 1983 – despite the Royal Commission into Aboriginal Deaths in Custody, which investigated the deaths of 99 Aboriginal people in police custody or prisons between 1980 and 1989.

In October 2007, the Australian National Audit Office panned the work of government departments handling indigenous affairs since the demise of the Aboriginal and Torres Strait Islander Commission. After the Commission was abolished in 2005, the federal government arranged for indigenous programmes to be delivered by mainstream government departments, but the report suggests that the approach makes life more difficult for many communities.

On a positive note, an agreement was reached between the Natural History Museum and the Tasmanian Aboriginal Centre for the return of remains removed from Tasmania in the nineteenth century during forced land clearances for European settlers. MRG presented evidence in the case at the United Kingdom's High Court in February; however the case was resolved by mediation and the remains were handed over in May to be buried in Tasmania according to Aboriginal custom.

In November 2007, after a general election landslide victory which swept John Howard from power, the centre-left Labor Party leader and prime minister elect Kevin Rudd pledged that his government would be the first in Australia to make an early formal apology to Aborigines for the 'stolen generation' of indigenous children snatched from their parents. Earlier in the year, in a ground-breaking case, Bruce Trevorrow, an Aboriginal man taken from his family as a baby under the policy, was awarded A $525,000 (US $447,000) compensation. He is the first member of the 'stolen generation' to win compensation.

New Zealand

Issues attendant on reconciliation between white settlers and the Maori community continue to be examined in 2007 by the Waitangi Tribunal, which was created by an Act of the New Zealand Parliament in 1975. The findings of the tribunal are not legally binding but its recommendations are generally respected by society. The progress of land claims before the tribunal in 2007 remained typically slow.

Maori Party representatives (who hold four of the seven designated Maori seats in the Parliament of New Zealand) accuse the government of 'eroding the relationship between the Crown and Maori'. They applauded the September 2007 recommendation of the New Zealand Parliament's Justice and Electoral Committee that the 2006 Principles of the Treaty of Waitangi Deletion bill not be passed. The bill, which was supported by all parties except the Green Party and the Maori Party, proposed to wipe the words 'Treaty of Waitangi and its principles' from New Zealand's law books. The August 2007 report of the Committee on the Elimination of Racial Discrimination concluded that the New Zealand government was acting to 'diminish the importance and relevance of the Treaty and to create a context unfavourable to the rights of Maori'.

The government also sent a clear message regarding its recognition of the status of Maori and Pacific Islanders, being one of only four countries that opposed the UN Declaration on the Rights of Indigenous Peoples in September. New Zealand Prime Minister Helen Clark defended the decision not to sign, saying the Treaty of Waitangi and common law already protected New Zealand's indigenous peoples' right to lands, territories and resources they have traditionally owned or used. Maori leaders meanwhile claimed they were 'ashamed and outraged' by the decision.

In July 2007 the New Zealand Law Commission began a project to develop a legal framework for

Maori who want to manage communal resources and responsibilities. Existing legal structures in New Zealand such as trusts, companies and incorporated societies do not cater well for the cultural norms of Maori groups and the 'Waka Umanga (Maori Corporations) Act' project proposes an alternative that allows tribes to interact with the legal system. Maori leaders, however, hold out little hope that the government coalition will support the bill in its unamended form.

In October 2007, police arrested a group of Maori activists in the eastern North Island on weapons and terrorism offences, alleging that the group had been training and preparing to commit acts of terrorism within New Zealand. Although they were initially arrested under the Terrorism Suppression Act, the Solicitor General decided against charging them under this Act, describing it as 'almost impossible to apply in a coherent manner'. However, the weapons charges remain. The Maori arrested were all members of Tuhoe, a tribe that did not sign the Treaty of Waitangi and seeks to create a Tuhoe nation within New Zealand. The police have been criticized for the manner in which they carried out the raids: cordoning off whole communities, detaining, searching and photographing individuals without charge and seizing property. There has been a series of protests and calls for an inquiry into the government's conduct over the police raids. ▪

ICELAND
ATLANTIC
OCEAN
NORWAY
SWEDEN
FINLAND
RUSSIA
ESTONIA
LATVIA
LITHUANIA
Kaliningrad
(Rus.)
BELARUS
IRELAND
UNITED
KINGDOM
DENMARK
NETHERLANDS
GERMANY
POLAND
BELGIUM
LUXEMBOURG
CZECH REP.
UKRAINE
SLOVAKIA
FRANCE
SWITZERLAND
LIECH.
AUSTRIA
HUNGARY
MOLDOVA
SLOVENIA
CROATIA
ROMANIA
BOSNIA
AND HERZE.
SERBIA AND
MONTENEGRO
PORTUGAL
ANDORRA
MONACO
SAN MARINO
SPAIN
Kosovo
BULGARIA
MACEDONIA
ITALY
ALBANIA
GREECE
BLACK SEA
GEORGIA
AZERBAIJAN
ARMENIA
AZER.
TURKEY

Europe

Eric Witte

Europe's rich patchwork of diverse peoples continued to face frequent challenges from agents of intolerance in 2007.

Yet in Europe the ongoing marginalization of many minority ethnic, linguistic and religious communities is challenged by perhaps the densest network of oversight organizations, monitoring mechanisms and legal infrastructure on any continent. These safeguards are most robust within the 27-state European Union (EU), but not always in every regard. For example, France joins non-EU members Andorra, Monaco and Turkey as one of only four of 47 member states of the broader Council of Europe not to have signed or ratified that body's Framework Convention on National Minorities (FCNM). Belgium, Greece, Iceland and Luxembourg have all signed the FCNM but have not ratified it.

Within the EU, by agreement of the Council of the European Union, in March 2007 the European Monitoring Centre on Racism and Xenophobia (EUMC) became the EU Agency for Fundamental Rights (FRA). The FRA is tasked with the development of policies relating to fundamental rights for EU institutions and member states, and maintains the EUMC focus on issues of racism, xenophobia and anti-Semitism. In its 2007 *Report on Racism and Xenophobia in the Member States of the EU*, the FRA noted that by the beginning of the year some states had not yet passed necessary domestic legislation to implement the EU Council's June 2000 Racial Equality Directive, namely the Czech Republic, Latvia and Malta. By banning discrimination in employment on the basis of race or ethnicity, Estonia and Poland had only implemented the directive in part.

In August 2007, former Foreign Minister of Norway Knut Vollebaek became just the third High Commissioner on National Minorities at the Organization for Security and Co-operation in Europe (OSCE). Addressing the OSCE Permanent Council for the first time in November, he stressed the importance of good governance and democracy for the protection of minority rights, and the importance of coordination within the international community in addressing minority issues and preventing conflict.

These needs were indeed borne out by developments in 2007. In Bosnia, Georgia and Kosovo, ongoing abuses of minority rights have raised the spectre of conflict, with the international community at times floundering in its attempts to respond in coordinated fashion.

High Commissioner Vollebaek also echoed his predecessors' long-standing mantra of the imperative to balance integration with respect for diversity. France and Turkey, which fashion themselves as homogeneous societies, are struggling to respect a diversity that they deny. Likewise, many countries continue to expect integration of minority religious communities, especially Muslims, and are intolerant of minority religious groups that continue to practise their faiths. At the other extreme, some European countries rationalize policies of Roma segregation as recognition of diversity. However, important victories for Roma rights at the European Court of Human Rights during 2007 may place new limits on this practice.

Another point highlighted by incoming High Commissioner Vollebaek was the need for states and the international community to include minorities in devising policies that affect them. For such Arctic peoples as the Inuit and Sami, whose livelihoods and traditions are threatened by climate change caused by greenhouse gas emissions around the world, this is the monumental challenge to protection of their rights.

The topics of religious intolerance, Roma inclusion and global warming are considered in greater detail below.

Religious intolerance

European religious minorities have confronted intolerance to varying degrees for centuries. Although today such organizations and monitoring mechanisms as the European Parliament, the Council of Europe, the OSCE and the European Court of Human Rights provide much more robust institutional advocates and safeguards for minority religious groups than in previous eras, recent years have seen an increase in religious tension and debate over the role of religious minorities in European society. The terrorist attacks of 11 September 2001, and subsequent attacks in Madrid and London in March 2004 and July 2005 clearly provided strong impetus for this, and the fall-out continued in 2007.

In Belgium, the nationalist Flemish party Vlaams Belang chose the sixth anniversary of the 11 September attacks to protest against the 'Islamization of Europe'. The event in Brussels, a city with a significant immigrant and Muslim community, led to party members clashing with police. Similar anti-Muslim sentiment remains strong in the Netherlands following the 2002 murder by Islamic extremists of right-wing politician Pim Fortuyn and that of film-maker Theo Van Gogh in 2004. A nascent movement of young former Muslims in the Netherlands, alienated by violence in the name of Islam, launched a campaign on 11 September 2007 to make it easier for Muslims to choose to renounce the religion. Although fractured between those advocating a strident anti-Islamic tone and those simply advocating freedom of religious choice, members of the Committee for Ex-Muslims fear that Islamic radicals could use violence in seeking to enforce literal interpretations of the Koran to punish apostasy.

Islam is at the centre of current issues of religious intolerance in Britain as well. Just over two years since the terrorist bombings in London, a poll in August 2007 found that Britons were more suspicious of Muslim communities than the populations of any other EU state. The survey found that 38 per cent of Britons viewed Muslims as a threat to national security. Comments from government officials may have played a role in forming distrustful views of Muslims. The leader of the House of Commons, Jack Straw, caused controversy in October 2006 with his comments on women wearing the Muslim veil, and in December 2006 Prime Minister Tony Blair stressed the importance of immigrants' integration. In a rhetorical shift, new Prime Minister Gordon Brown instructed his ministers not to use the word 'Muslim' when talking about failed car bombings attempted by Islamic radicals in London and Glasgow in June 2007 and instead to keep the focus on the criminality of the acts. A spokesman explained: 'There is clearly a need to strike a consensual tone in relation to all communities across the UK. It is important that the country remains united.'

As Europe confronts new issues of intolerance largely revolving around Islam, the Jewish community in Germany is experiencing a revival decades after its attempted extermination under Hitler. Despite sporadic incidents of anti-Semitism, especially in the eastern parts of the country, Germany now has the fastest growing Jewish community in the world. In a nationally televised ceremony in 2006, three rabbis were ordained in Dresden – the first ceremony of its kind in Germany since 1942. In August 2007, Germany's largest synagogue re-opened in Berlin following extensive renovations.

Arctic peoples and climate change

Rising global temperatures through the emission of greenhouse gases over more than a century are cause for alarm in many parts of the globe. In April 2007 a group of 250 UN-sponsored scientists released the *Arctic Climate Impact Assessment*, a four-year study that found the Arctic warming approximately twice as fast as the rest of the planet. The extent of the Arctic ice-melt in northern summer 2007 shocked scientists, and is having immediate impact on indigenous Arctic peoples.

In the self-governing Danish territory of Greenland, around 90 per cent of the population is Inuit. Over 4,500 years, the Inuit have survived by adapting to the icy environment, which has given broad definition to their unique culture. The accelerating melt of ice and permafrost has had a direct effect on their lives. Landslides and loss of permanent ice-pack have damaged infrastructure, including significant loss of housing and contamination of drinking water. The daily effect has been felt most acutely in northern Greenland. There, towns have never been connected by roads, and dog sleds were usually used to traverse the distances between them; as the snow and ice recedes, sleds are becoming useless in the newly exposed rocky landscape and towns are becoming more isolated. The north, in particular, is an area where many communities have long relied on hunting and fishing to survive. The Arctic melt is vastly reducing habitat for seals, polar bears and walruses, and warmer waters are leading to shifts in populations of fish species. Inuit hunters, who have long been secure in their ability to navigate the ice, are finding it difficult to read the new landscape and many hunters have been lost to accidents on thin ice.

Beyond physical threats, these rapidly changing environmental circumstances are placing Inuit culture in jeopardy. Activities including hunting, ice-hole fishing and dog-sledding are at the core of Inuit identity. Even though southern Greenlanders dabble in potato farming and sheep herding in adaptation to the milder climate, these new opportunities do not fill the hole of their cultural loss.

Aqqaluk Lynge is a leader of Greenland's Inuit people. The Inuit – and other Arctic indigenous groups – have campaigned internationally to draw attention to the dramatic impact of global warming on their natural environment.

'In my lifetime, we have seen a big difference in floes of ice and animal migration, and we have seen the weather change. My community is lucky it is not in Alaska, where a village is crumbling into the sea because of rising sea levels. The Alaskan state is supporting them to relocate.

'The Greenland ice cap is melting very fast and this will affect the rest of the world – that's why the Arctic is a barometer. We have known about it for a long time – before other famous people started talking about it.

'We need to study much more the effects of this on Inuits. We have existed for thousands of years and our culture and lifestyle have changed for lots of reasons, but because of climate change it will be over in two generations. We are asking scientists worldwide to study what will happen to human beings if the ice caps disappear.

'We know what the effect will be on polar bears, on whales and on fish stocks. But the heating of the sea is far worse than we thought. We have tried to adapt to new circumstances but any small change in sea temperature can change many things and now it is too high.

'Each community in the Arctic is isolated – connected only by sea, no roads, no air. My mission is to say that local matters are global as well. People know that what happens here today will have an effect tomorrow.

'The permafrost is also disappearing: the environmental things that make the rest of the world stable are now unstable in the Arctic.

'We are very nervous and sometimes we are angry that the decision-makers are not taking the right decisions. We have to wake up the governments to the reality of what is happening.

'We have a legal petition under way in the US at the Inter-American Commission of Human Rights, to look into the issues we are facing. The case is not to get compensation; we need support for decision-makers to understand that we are paying a great price for what others are doing to the environment. I hope the government realizes this and adapts for the future. We are small nations and we cannot afford to shut up.'

Interview by MRG's Preti Taneja

Other indigenous Arctic peoples are facing similar situations. The Sami of Scandinavia and Russia, for example, have noted that warmer temperatures have brought with them a large increase in the number of mosquitoes. Mosquito-borne parasites are increasingly infecting reindeer herds, and thus pose a potential threat to Sami traditional herding culture.

Arctic peoples have banded together to claim that the climate change affecting their lives and threatening their cultures is a human rights issue, and that governments are doing too little to cut emissions of such greenhouse gases as carbon dioxide. The global nature of the problem, however, has made it difficult for campaigners to target the roots of the problem.

In May 2007, Aqqaluk Lynge, a leading Inuit politician from Greenland, took a high-profile role in fighting the proposed expansion of London's Stanstead Airport, which would result in 2 million tonnes of additional carbon dioxide emissions annually. With greenhouse offenders ubiquitous, Lynge readily admitted that, by itself, stopping the airport expansion would mean little. However, he argued that failure to tackle such policies on an individual basis would be 'an excuse for doing nothing'.

In February 2007, Greenlanders, together with representatives from the US, Canada and Russia in the Inuit Circumpolar Council, argued in their latest hearing before the Inter-American Court of Human Rights that, by refusing to curb greenhouse gas emissions, Washington was violating the American Convention on Human Rights. With 5 per cent of the world's population, the United States emits around 25 per cent of the world's greenhouse gases and the Bush administration has consistently opposed aggressive proposals to reduce them.

Scientists expect global warming to continue and, absent a new willingness in such far-flung capitals as Washington, Beijing and Brussels to reduce greenhouse gases, it is not clear that the trend will be reversible or that Arctic peoples' traditional cultures can survive.

Roma

Widely dispersed Roma communities remain the most chronically marginalized groups across Europe. Roma largely remain mired in poverty, with widespread discrimination blocking paths to employment and Roma children often segregated into separate, inferior classrooms that fail to prepare them for entry into the job market. Discrimination often extends to housing, and many Roma routinely face the threat of eviction. Authorities too often tolerate rampant anti-Roma racism and violence, with police sometimes among the perpetrators. Roma women confront compounded discrimination, and in several countries have been subjected to forced sterilization. Roma communities generally have poor access to healthcare, and lower life expectancy rates reflect this. In many places there are obstacles for Roma seeking citizenship documents, which is one cause of the communities' scant political representation across Europe; grossly under-represented, Roma have found it difficult to bring adequate political attention to the many problems they face.

These problems remain acute in Central and Eastern Europe, where Roma live in the highest concentration. Although international attention has again focused on simmering tensions in the Balkans, there has been little new attention to Roma issues there. As negotiations over Kosovo's final status intensified over the course of 2007, Roma representatives were excluded from the talks between ethnic Albanians and Serbs. In Kosovo, Roma face widespread harassment for using their mother tongue, either Serbian or Romany, in majority Albanian areas. Many displaced Roma, accused by Albanians of complicity in Serbian atrocities during the 1998–99 war, remain encamped near the Trepca lead mine in the north. There, many children have suffered severe, sometimes fatal, lead poisoning from living next to piles of toxic industrial waste, worsened by some of their parents' smelting of lead from used car batteries; United Nations administrators have been slow to organize their relocation to new, unpolluted settlements.

In Bosnia and Herzegovina, Roma live in extreme poverty and, along with other non-Bosniacs, Serbs or Croats, fall under the ethnic category 'Others', which denies them certain rights to political representation and further marginalizes them in the country's polarizing political system. Likewise, in Macedonia, where Roma continue to face discrimination and exclusion in all spheres of life, politics are dominated by ethnic Albanian–Macedonian relations and Roma barely participate.

Across Central and Eastern Europe, pervasive anti-Roma sentiment often surfaces in the statements of government officials. General elections in 2006 in Slovakia returned the ultra-nationalist party of Jan Slota to government as a junior partner. Anti-Roma rhetoric during and after the campaign worried Roma rights advocates, especially in light of the continued problem of hate crimes directed at the community. Slovak statistics provided to the EU Agency for Fundamental Rights showed an average 45 per cent annual increase in recorded incidents of racist violence between 2000 and 2006, with a 55 per cent jump between 2005 and 2006. In 2007 a Czech senator and district mayor in the city of Ostrava openly called for Roma to be segregated behind an electric fence. And in May 2007, Romanian President Traian Basescu called a reporter 'a stinky Gypsy'; two months later, Romanian Prime Minister Calin Popescu Tariceanu reportedly made comments calling all Roma criminals.

Despite continuing grave problems for Roma communities, the EU accession process has provided an impetus for change in the region. Ahead of Bulgaria's accession in January 2007, the government adopted a number of measures aimed at improving Roma rights. A new health initiative, the training of Romani-language teachers, anti-segregation school regulations, and increasing Roma representation at the municipal level offer hope that Bulgaria is finally tackling the ongoing deep marginalization of its Roma community. Hungary, which joined the EU in May 2004, likewise has increased its efforts to reduce Roma marginalization. The Hungarian government has undertaken an aggressive initiative to desegregate schools, and has taken steps to enforce strong anti-discrimination laws; in 2006 the government began a programme of legalizing previously unregistered Roma settlements.

Domestic and international legal cases offer another avenue for improvements in Roma rights. In June 2006, an appeals court in Debrecen, Hungary ordered an end to *de facto* school segregation in Miskolc, which it found violated the rights of Roma children to equal treatment. In Serbia, a war crimes court convicted a former member of the Kosovo Liberation Army (KLA) for anti-Roma atrocities in 1999; meanwhile, the war crimes trial of KLA leader Ramush Haradinaj and others, charged with targeting Roma as well as Serb civilians, continued into 2007 at the International Criminal Tribunal for the former Yugoslavia. In 2006, the European Court of Human Rights

(ECHR) rejected a legal challenge to Roma school segregation in the Czech Republic, finding that the Roma organizations bringing the case had failed to prove the state's intent to discriminate. In January 2007, MRG backed the organizations' appeal before the ECHR's Grand Chamber, which in November 2007 issued a groundbreaking ruling in favour of the 16 Roma pupils. The Chamber made use of statistical patterns in finding that the Czech Republic had systematically discriminated against Roma by sending them to special needs schools. Roma rights organizations expected the ruling to have swift and sweeping effect on the education policies of other countries in the region. The ECHR ruled in two cases in July 2007 that Romania and Bulgaria had both failed to pursue justice for Roma victims of violent hate crimes, making clear that European governments must respond robustly to such acts.

The Decade of Roma Inclusion, launched by nine Central and Eastern European governments with support from the World Bank and Open Society Institute in 2005, committed signatories to 'work toward eliminating discrimination and closing the unacceptable gaps between Roma and the rest of society'. In June 2007, a coalition of European Roma rights organizations issued the first *Decade Watch* report on each country's progress toward fulfilment of its Decade Action Plan. Consolidated scoring for various aspects of the initiative showed that Hungary was making the most progress in implementing its plan across the priority areas of education, employment, housing, health and anti-discrimination. Bulgaria and Slovakia were placed second and third. Of the nine states, Montenegro scored lowest, with the report finding that it 'has yet to embrace responsibility for developing integrated programmes or policies backed up with budget financing'. Macedonia and Serbia also scored poorly.

Although EU accession has spurred some positive developments for Roma rights in Central and Eastern Europe, ongoing discrimination in older EU member states serves as a warning that accession alone cannot be expected to eliminate Roma marginalization. Amid a flurry of anti-Roma rhetoric in May 2007, the Italian cities of Rome and Milan approved 'Pacts for Security' that aim at the abolition of informal settlements and the eviction of 10,000 Roma and Sinti. In Germany, many Roma and Sinti who have been in the country for years, or were even born there, continue to be denied citizenship. Roma and Sinti are vastly under-represented in political institutions and, in the face of pervasive societal discrimination, members of the community are subjected to constant pressure to move elsewhere.

Country by country

Belgium

Disputes between Belgium's majority Flemish and minority Walloon linguistic communities brought the country to the brink of a break-up in 2007. The wealthier Dutch-speaking Flanders region resents subsidies for the poorer francophone Wallonia region. This resentment builds upon memories of historical French and Walloon political, economic and linguistic dominance that lasted to varying degrees until 1970.

Over five months after June 2007 parliamentary elections, Flemish and Walloon legislators still were not able to agree on a new government. At issue were Flemish demands for greater regional autonomy and a cut in financial support to Wallonia. Enacting these changes, opposed by Walloons, would require a two-thirds majority of parliament. Flemish parties were unwilling to agree to a government with parties rejecting the proposal, and Walloon parties were unwilling to join a government advocating the proposal.

In November, Flemish parties broke with a tradition of seeking inter-communal consensus and used their majority in parliament to split a bilingual voting district straddling bilingual Brussels and Flemish Flanders, so that henceforth Walloon voters in the Flanders part can no longer vote for candidates in Wallonia. In 2003 a Belgian constitutional court had ruled the bilingual status of this part of the district unconstitutional, but had not prescribed a solution. Walloon parliamentarians walked out of the November parliamentary session. As the crisis endured, several thousand Belgians rallied for national unity in Brussels in mid-November; while most of the demonstrators were Walloons, some were Flemish. Indeed, opinion polls showed that even as most Belgians expected the country to eventually split apart, majorities in Wallonia and Flanders preferred continued unity. Divorce scenarios were further complicated by the dispensation of Belgium's third region: bilingual Brussels.

Bosnia and Herzegovina

Over the course of 2006 and 2007, international officials have grown increasingly alarmed by the stalling of reforms in Bosnia and Herzegovina and a resurgence of nationalist rhetoric among the country's leading politicians. The Bosnian election system, created through the 1995 Dayton Peace Agreement, systematically strengthens nationalist candidates in a polarizing, vicious cycle because they must only seek votes from largely mono-ethnic electorates. Such was the dynamic again in the October 2006 general elections, and the poisoned atmosphere carried over into 2007. As a result, the three main ethnic groups of Bosnia and Herzegovina – Bosniacs, Croats and Serbs – all feel insecure in parts of the country where they live as minorities.

Bosnians who are not of these ethnic groups, including Roma and Jews, or who are of mixed ethnicity, are categorized as 'Others' under the Dayton structure, a formulation that is inherently marginalizing. In March 2007 the UN Committee on the Elimination of Racial Discrimination criticized Bosnia and Herzegovina for failing to reform its constitution to allow minority participation in the parliamentary House of Peoples and the country's presidency. The European Commission noted the same failure in its November 2007 assessment of Bosnia and Herzegovina's progress toward EU membership. In 2007 MRG supported the application of Jakob Finci, a Bosnian Jew denied the opportunity to run for the federal presidency on the basis of his ethnicity, to the European Court of Human Rights. The European Convention on Human Rights is binding, pre-eminent law in Bosnia and Herzegovina, and the case holds the potential to force far-reaching reform.

In 2006 and 2007, the international community continued to push for an overhaul of police structures in Bosnia and Herzegovina. Currently there are 14 police forces in the country, with criminals (sometimes linked to politicians) exploiting the uncoordinated, fractured jurisdictions. Although constitutional court rulings require that all areas of public administration reflect the ethnic proportions of the 1991 Census, to a large degree the various police forces remain ethnically homogeneous. For minorities returning to their pre-war homes, the presence of often-hostile police forces, in which their ethnic group is hardly represented, has been intimidating, and is one reason why most minority returnees quickly leave. Bosniac returnees to the country's Republika Srpska (RS) entity have also encountered perpetrators of the July 1995 Srebrenica massacre still on the police force.

Serb and Bosniac nationalist leaders rejected police reform in October 2007, and in response the European Commission refused to initial the country's Stabilization and Association Agreement, an important step toward EU accession. Following the failure, the international community's High Representative for the country, Slovak diplomat Miroslav Lajcak, used his powers to impose new laws making it more difficult for obstructionists in cabinet and parliament to block legislation through failure to participate. The RS prime minister reacted by threatening to withdraw all Serb representatives from state-level institutions, the Serb member of the country's three-person presidency resigned and Serb politicians again mooted a referendum on secession.

In February 2007, the International Court of Justice in The Hague determined that RS forces in Bosnia during the war had committed genocide against Bosniacs, although the justices ruled that they did not have enough evidence to find Serbia guilty of genocide for its supporting role. The ruling echoed previous findings from the International Criminal Tribunal for the former Yugoslavia (ICTY), notably in the Krstic case relating to Srebrenica. Until 2005, the RS had only prosecuted two criminal cases against Serbs suspected of committing atrocities during the war. At the end of 2005 the pace increased, parallel to war crimes proceedings at the State Court in Sarajevo, which is responsible for more sensitive cases. Meanwhile, as of December 2007, the most wanted Bosnian Serb fugitives from the ICTY, Radovan Karadzic and Ratko Mladic, remained at large.

France

In May 2007, France elected Nicolas Sarkozy as its new president. He faces distrust among many French Muslims for incendiary comments he made as Interior Minister about youth rioters in 2005 and 2006. At his inauguration, Sarkozy pledged to make human rights a priority, but a petition launched by French intellectuals in June 2007 lambasted his powerful new Ministry of Immigration and National Identity as a sop to the far right.

The centralized nature of the French state, and its emphasis on a unified identity, has long made action on minority issues difficult. The country is only one of four of the 47 members of the Council of Europe not to have signed its Framework Convention for the Protection of National Minorities (FCNM) and neither has it ratified the Charter on Minority and Regional Languages. On constitutional grounds, France has declared a complete reservation to the article on the rights of minorities in the UN Convention on Civil and Political Rights, claiming in effect that there are no minorities in France.

In short, French policies continue to reflect an assumption that minorities should assimilate into the majority culture. On a visit to France in September 2007, UN Independent Expert on Minority Issues Gay McDougall observed:

'Currently, there is a widespread feeling within the communities of new minorities that to become a citizen of France is not sufficient for full acceptance; that acceptance will be granted only with total assimilation that forces them to reject major facets of their identities. Only when a way is found to shed the colour of their skins, hide the manifestations of their religion or the traditions of their ancestors, only then will they be accepted as truly French.'

France's sizeable – mostly North African – Muslim community, estimated at 6 per cent of the population, felt the brunt of new policies instituted in the wake of the 11 September attacks on the United States, including police searches, in some circumstances without a warrant. Already widely ghettoized on the margins of large cities, these Muslim immigrant communities felt deepening marginalization amid rising popular Islamophobia fed by politicians and the media. Arab and other underclass immigrant youth riots erupted in November 2005, and in 2007 tensions continued to simmer.

Amid rising popular fear of Islam, in 2004 the French government banned the wearing of overt religious items in public schools. While the law has disproportionately targeted Muslim girls wearing head-scarves, it also applies to such items as the Jewish skullcap, heavy Christian crosses and the Sikh turban. In 2005, French courts upheld the expulsion from school of several Sikh boys who refused to remove their turbans for religious reasons. In June 2007 a Sikh organization lodged a challenge at the European Court of Human Rights following a French court ruling that, ostensibly for security reasons, requires Sikh men to be photographed without their turbans to obtain a driver's licence. The Sikh organization representing a man denied a driver's licence when he refused to remove his turban argued that the French law undermines freedom of thought, conscience and religion. MRG is providing legal advice in the case and helping to publicize the implications of the ban.

Georgia/Abkhazia and South Ossetia

In December 2006, Russian President Vladimir Putin stated that if Kosovo gains independence from Serbia, then Abkhazia and South Ossetia should be free to become independent of Georgia. As tensions between Georgia and Russia mounted in 2007, conditions worsened for ethnic minorities in Georgia's unrecognized break-away states of Abkhazia and South Ossetia. Exclusion of minorities in these regions threatened to push the region into conflict.

Soviet-era settlement of Georgians in Abkhazia and the demographic marginalization of ethnic Abkhaz led to their distrust of Georgia's drive for independence in the final days of the Soviet Union. With Russian assistance, ethnic Abkhaz defeated heavy-handed Georgian forces in a 1992–3 war that saw atrocities on both sides. Abkhazia lost over half of its population as an estimated 200,000 ethnic Georgians fled to Georgian-held territory, mostly in the neighbouring Zugdidi district. Abkhaz now form a plurality of the population, alongside sizeable Armenian and Russian populations. Those Georgians who remain are concentrated in Abkhazia's southern Gali district. Abkhaz authorities have gradually extended their *de facto* control over most of the territory. Talks remain at an impasse as Abkhazia insists on recognition of its independence as the first step in peace talks, while Georgia places priority on the return of displaced Georgians.

Displaced Georgians are not allowed to vote in Abkhaz elections. Those who have returned, estimated at 40,000, live mostly in the Gali district, where they are prone to gangsterism and intermittent upheavals and instability. Georgian-language education in Abkhazia remains a major area of contention. Abkhaz officials have been reluctant to make concessions in this area precisely because it would encourage Georgian return. The authorities also have taken pains to highlight the identity of remaining Georgians as Mingrelian, a

Georgian dialect sub-group prevalent in western Georgia, whose members resist seeing any conflict between simultaneous embrace of the Mingrelian and Georgian aspects of its identity.

Ethnic Abkhaz are of two minds regarding Russia's backing. Russia has gradually asserted control in the area through issuance of passports, introduction of the rouble, payment of pensions, attempted control of politics, and increasingly through language. While some Russophone Abkhaz join ethnic Russians and Armenians in generally favouring integration with Russia, Abkhaz speakers tend to favour a future of independence.

Rising tensions between Tblisi and Moscow are increasing the threat to the Georgian minority while making ethnic Abkhaz more reliant on Russia, whether Abkhazia becomes independent or not. Against the backdrop of Russian anger at Georgia's intention to join NATO and Georgia's 2004 expulsion of alleged Russian spies, in June 2006 Georgian military forces increased their presence in the Kodori Gorge, a part of Abkhazia still under divided control. In May 2007, Georgia established a 'patriot youth camp' in an area under its control near the ceasefire line, and refused access to UN observers. In response, Abkhaz authorities increased nearby patrols, as did peacekeepers from the Commonwealth of Independent States.

A similar situation exists in South Ossetia, where conflict with Georgian authorities in 1989–90 increased the desire of South Ossetians to work towards closer integration with Russian North Ossetia. While South Ossetians have set up a *de facto* government, Russians have provided most residents with passports. Although a 2004 ceasefire has held, near-daily shootings continue. In the conflict zone of Tskhinvali, ethnic Ossetian villages are interspersed with ethnic Georgian villages, as well as those of mixed ethnicity. If tensions boil over again, both groups stand to suffer. South Ossetian officials are largely looking to developments in Abkhazia to provide a precedent for finalizing their split from Georgia.

In August 2007, the Georgian government accused Russia of violating its airspace to fire a heavy missile (that failed to detonate) near South Ossetia. Russia denied the claim, accusing Georgia of staging the incident as a provocation. In September, military clashes occurred in both Abkhazia and South Ossetia. Georgian President

Mikhail Saakashvili, addressing the UN General Assembly, blamed these on Russia and accused Moscow of backing a 'mission of terror'.

Russia

Under President Vladimir Putin, Russia continued its slide into authoritarianism over the course of 2007, in parallel with the development of deepening xenophobia in Russian society and government policy. Although large-scale fighting in Chechnya was over for the time being, severe government violations of Chechen rights continued unabated.

SOVA, a Russian non-governmental organization (NGO) that monitors hate crimes, recorded 539 attacks on ethnic minorities, including 54 murders, over the course of 2006. A public opinion poll in December 2006 found that 54 per cent of Russians surveyed agreed with the statement 'Russia is for Russians'. Public officials have frequently stoked such chauvinistic sentiment. In November 2006, the deputy chief of the Russian migration service explained that ethnic minorities should not exceed 17–20 per cent of the population in any town, and that 'exceeding this norm creates discomfort for the indigenous population'. That same month, President Putin explained that planned restrictions on the employment of non-Russian citizens, including legal immigrants, would serve to 'ease tension on the labour market and make it more civilized'.

Putin's embrace of xenophobic sentiment has coincided with his consolidation of power at the expense of parliament and local government. Independent media and civil society organizations, both domestic and foreign, face increasing harassment. Indeed, Russian police are increasingly turning to violent disruption of peaceful, anti-government protests.

A youth movement, 'Nashi' ('Our People'), which is directly and indirectly sponsored by the Kremlin, is actively promoting Putin and an anti-European, anti-American agenda. Founded following the 2004 Orange Revolution in neighbouring Ukraine, Nashi (dubbed the 'Putinjugend' by some critics) now boasts some 10,000 members and 200,000 participants at its events. Senior members of the organization have received plum jobs in government or at Kremlin-friendly state enterprises. Some members have undergone paramilitary training specifically to learn techniques for breaking up opposition demonstrations. In October 2007,

Human Rights Watch wrote to the Moscow city police to express concern about the service's recruiting of Nashi members to help 'police' forthcoming human rights and other opposition demonstrations. Although awash with Russian nationalism, Nashi states that it opposes ethnic bigotry. Some civil society organizations worry, however, that this new, enthusiastic public arm of Kremlin power could yet follow the government's lead in adopting an increasingly xenophobic agenda.

Xenophobic sentiment in Russia is often directed at Chechens, on both ethnic and religious grounds. In Chechnya itself in 2007, major fighting has ended for the time being, following the June 2006 killing of Chechen resistance leader Sadullaev. Russian police killed another senior rebel, Rustam Basayev, in August 2007 in an ongoing campaign to 'liquidate' the remaining resistance leadership. Although Moscow is eager to portray the situation in Chechnya as completely under control, the Russian and puppet Chechen governments continue to inflict severe human rights abuses on the Chechen population, including disappearances and torture.

Human Rights Watch issued a report in November 2006 based on extensive interviews in Chechnya, finding that the Moscow-backed Chechen government and federal forces were employing the widespread and systematic use of torture, with no accountability for the perpetrators. The Council of Europe's Commissioner for Human Rights, Thomas Hammarberg, echoed those findings on a visit to Chechnya in March 2007, noting that every single prisoner he had spoken with had complained of abuse. In a landmark case in July 2007, the European Court of Human Rights (ECHR) ruled that the Russian government was responsible for the 'disappearance' and death of a young Chechen man, Khadzhi-Murat Yandiev, in 2000. It was the eleventh ECHR ruling against Russia for disappearances, deaths and disproportionate use of force stemming from the Chechen conflict; 200 similar cases were still pending. Moscow has not complied with the rulings. In June 2007, however, there was a rare conviction of four Russian soldiers in a domestic court for the killing of Chechen civilians in 2002.

The government remains sensitive to criticism about Chechnya. In August 2007 a court stiffened the suspended sentence for human rights activist

Stansilav Dmitrievsky, who in 2006 had been convicted of 'inciting racial hatred' for publishing articles by Chechen resistance figures, after Dmitrievsky assisted in the organization of peaceful anti-government demonstrations. While domestic criticism is quashed, foreign criticism of Russian abuses in Chechnya continues to be muted, as other issues and interests have dominated Russia's relations with the EU and United States.

Turkey

As detailed in a report from MRG in December 2007, Turkish attitudes and laws on minorities have progressed considerably over the past decade, but many reforms lie ahead if the country's legal framework and practice are to reach international standards. Minority groups including Alevis, Armenians, Assyrians, Caferis, Caucasians, Kurds, Jews, Laz, Roma, Rum (Greek Orthodox) Christians, and Yezidis still confront systematic repression in today's Turkey. Officially, the government still only recognizes Armenians, Jews and Rum Christians as minorities, but, as used in Turkey, this term denotes clear second-class status. All other groups have faced intense pressure to assimilate.

The January 2007 murder of Armenian rights campaigner and writer Hrant Dink offered a stark reminder of Turkey's ongoing failure to protect the rights of individuals from minority communities. Dink had been convicted and sentenced to six months imprisonment in 2005 under the notorious Article 301 of the Turkish penal code for 'denigrating Turkish identity'. This provision often has been used to suppress any discussion or acknowledgement of the 1915 Armenian genocide. Dink's offence was writing about Turkish–Armenian relations. Dink's assassin, a 17-year-old with 18 alleged accomplices, told police that Dink 'had insulted Turkishness'. Such concepts are not only enshrined in law; schoolchildren continue to learn negative stereotypes of Armenians and other minorities from their textbooks. At a hearing in October, the gunman's family accused the authorities of collusion in the killing; one co-defendant was a police informant who had notified the authorities of the plot, and Turkish media broadcast a recorded phone call providing further indication that police knew of the plan in advance.

As a large, unrecognized minority, Kurds continue to face systematic marginalization. Around 30,000 people have been killed in fighting between the Turkish military and the Kurdistan Workers Party (PKK) since 1984, and over 1 million people remain displaced in heavily Kurdish south-eastern Turkey. PKK attacks on the Turkish military from northern Iraq during 2007 raised tensions further, as Ankara massed troops in south-eastern Turkey for possible entry into Iraq.

The government continues to conflate any effort to promote Kurdish rights with support for 'PKK terrorists'. When in January 2007 the city council of the old-town section of the multi-ethnic south-eastern city of Diyarbakir agreed to provide municipal services in Arabic, Armenian, Assyriac, English and Kurdish, in addition to Turkish, the Ankara-appointed governor of the region removed the council, the old-town mayor, as well as the popular Kurdish mayor of the city. In July, prosecutors introduced charges against the two mayors and 17 council members on charges of 'abuse of office', and they may be jailed for up to three years if convicted. In February, the president and 12 members of a pro-Kurdish party received 6–12 month sentences for holding their party congress in the Kurdish language. On the basis of a vague 2006 anti-terror law, another Kurdish leader was convicted and sentenced in August for a speech he gave in March. Ahead of elections in 2007, government officials harassed one pro-Kurdish party's leaders through arrests, searches, seizures and prosecutions. Government harassment also targeted Kurdish media outlets.

Other ethnic minorities also continue to be targeted. In Afyon province in April, a mob attacked a Roma family and burned down several Roma houses. The police made no arrests. Religious intolerance remains a major shortcoming, too. In an attack in April on a publishing company that prints Bibles, extremists slit the throats of three Protestants. In May, the 2007 report of the US Commission on International Religious Freedom criticized restrictions on non-Muslim religious groups that prevent them from owning property or training clergy.

Two professors, Baskin Oran and Ibrahim Kaboglu, who drafted a report on minority rights on behalf of a human rights advisory committee affiliated with the prime minister's office in 2004, remain in legal jeopardy. The draft report, which

was leaked to the press but never published, called for a far-reaching overhaul of the country's constitution and statutes in order to achieve international standards. According to Agence France Presse, it described as 'paranoia' the notion that rights for Kurds and other groups would lead to the break-up of the state. Charges of sedition against Oran and Kaboglu were dismissed on free speech grounds by a court in 2006 but reinstated by an appellate court in September 2007.

In early 2007 the ruling AKP (Justice and Development Party) nominated Foreign Minister Abdullah Gul – a practising Muslim – for the largely ceremonial post of president in early 2007, sparking outrage among nationalists and the military. Incumbent President Ahmet Necdet Sezer warned that

Turkey's secularism was under threat, and told military officers they had a duty to protect the regime from a move toward radical Islam. A statement on the army website shortly thereafter warned that the army would defend the secular system, which many Turks interpreted as a threatened coup. Army Chief of Staff General Yasar Buyukanit also openly criticized the European Union (EU) and MRG for considering such groups as Assyrians and Roma as 'minorities'.

Nationalists launched mass demonstrations throughout the spring, with hundreds of thousands rallying in Turkey's largest cities against political Islam. However, early elections in July, spurred by the crisis, resulted in an absolute majority of parliamentary seats for Prime Minister Erdogan's AKP. For the first time since 1991, Kurds were

Turkish liberalism is creating new challenges for old-order nationalists and military-backed secularists. In response to the Dink murder in January nearly 200,000 protesters took to the streets of Istanbul carrying signs reading: 'We are all Hrant Dink. We are all Armenians.' New minority organizations are springing up and fighting for their groups' rights in domestic courts and the European Court of Human Rights. Liberal Turks shifted support away from secular parties and toward the moderate Muslim AKP party in the July elections. One academic liberal Turk who recently joined the AKP told the *New York Times* ahead of the elections, 'In 50 years, people will write that this was the time Turkey started to come to terms with its own people.'

The EU accession process has been a major catalyst for human rights reforms. In July, Amnesty International, in reporting on the continued practice of torture in Turkey despite the government's 'zero tolerance' policy, noted that the situation had improved following legal reforms prompted by the EU accession process. In its 2007 report on Turkey, the US Commission on International Religious Freedom stated that everyone interviewed for the report, from all religious communities in Turkey, 'stressed EU membership as the most promising means to advance religious freedom and other human rights protections and to drive democracy forward in Turkey.' Within the EU, however, some governments (notably France) and political parties (notably Germany's Christian Democratic Union) oppose Turkey's eventual accession on the basis of religion, which could undercut the impetus for further reform.

elected to parliament. Although receiving over half of the vote from the south-east in previous elections, their parties had failed to clear an onerous 10 per cent hurdle that has worked against all minority groups. This time Kurds ran as independent candidates, and 22 were elected, including one Kurdish activist elected from prison who was immediately released due to her newly acquired parliamentary immunity. Following previous criticism that no non-Muslims were represented in parliament, the AKP included four Alevis on their successful list.

Despite a renewed warning from General Buyukanit in August that the military would protect Turkey's secularism from 'centres of evil', the new parliament proceeded to elect reformist foreign minister Abdullah Gul as Turkey's new president.

Kosovo

On 17 February 2008, Kosovo's parliament declared independence. The move was swiftly backed by the US and some European states, including Britain, France and Germany, but attracted the opposition of others, including Spain, Cyprus, Greece and Bulgaria. Russia vehemently opposed the declaration, urging the UN Security Council to declare the move 'illegal', and signalling that it would block Kosovo's membership of the UN. In Serbia, there was anger and resentment, boiling over into attacks against a number of foreign embassies seen to have supported independence. While the declaration marks the end of one phase of Kosovo's existence, there is grave uncertainty for the future, particularly for minorities in the self-declared state, which for the time being will largely be administered by the EU.

Kosovo Albanians make up an overwhelming majority of the population. Ever since the Serbian assault of 1998–9, which cost around 10,000 mostly civilian Albanian lives, they have insisted that they could never again be ruled from Belgrade. However, the minority Serb population – thought to number about 120,000 – bitterly oppose an independent Kosovo. In the predominantly Serbian north-western corner of the country, daily demonstrations were organized against the move and NATO troops sealed the northern borders after hundreds of protesters stormed two crossing points. There have been mutterings that the Serbian stronghold in the north-west might secede from Kosovo.

In the run-up to the independence declaration, Prime Minister Hashim Thaci vowed to protect the rights of all minorities. But the concerns remain acute. Apart from Serbs, Kosovo's other minority groups include Ashkali, Bosniacs, Croats, Egyptians, Gorani, Roma and Turks and. These latter groups have been completely excluded from international discussions on Kosovo's status.

The minority situation in Kosovo is complex. Serbs and other minorities in Kosovo, including pockets of Albanians in majority-Serb northern Kosovo, face some of the most hostile conditions of any minorities in Europe. Following the withdrawal of Serbian forces in 1999, radicalized Albanians turned on minority communities, especially Serb and Roma. Pogroms in March 2004, hardly contained by NATO peacekeepers and UN police, claimed the lives of over 28 civilians and one NATO soldier, and wounded hundreds; 3,600 Serbs were displaced and 30 Serb churches destroyed, along with 200 Serb houses. Many minorities have fled Kosovo. Most Serbs who remain are still confined for their own protection to ethnically homogenized enclaves under international armed guard, or live north of the Ibar river in a Serb-controlled area that maintains close connections with Belgrade. Christian Orthodox churches south of the Ibar have

required the protection of NATO peacekeepers in order to prevent vandalism by Albanian nationalists. Serbs and other minorities face harassment and physical violence for being who they are, for living in their own homes if they belong to the 'wrong' community, and for speaking their own language. Kosovo government authorities, UN administrators and police, and NATO peacekeepers have been unwilling or unable to bring to justice many perpetrators of crimes directed at minorities.

Several years after the conflict, minority return to pre-war homes has barely occurred. In June 2007 the mission of the Organization for Security and Cooperation in Europe in Kosovo cited several reasons for this, including the failure to rebuild over 10,000 residential properties destroyed during or after the conflict, bureaucratic inefficiency in processing property and compensation claims, and widespread security fears among would-be returnees. Those who did return faced not only physical threats, but also widespread economic exclusion, including through discrimination in employment and provision of social benefits. In June 2007 the non-governmental organization Humanitarian Law Centre (HLC) released a survey of ethnic minorities conducted during 2006. While it found progress in majority Albanian acceptance of Ashkali, Bosniac, Egyptian and Turkish, minorities, including their improved freedom of movement, there was little improvement with regard to Serbs and Roma. The HLC survey reported that Kosovo's government had made no attempt to integrate Serb pupils into Kosovo's educational system; Serb and some Gorani children were attending a parallel school system financed and controlled by the Serbian government. Turkish and Bosniac children were being afforded education in their own languages within Kosovo-run schools, but in practice this has proved difficult due to an acute lack of textbooks and trained teachers. Roma-language education was unavailable in either the government or parallel Serb school systems.

In education and other areas, government and international UN administrators found it difficult to develop long-term policies due to the lack of clarity on Kosovo's final status. The status limbo has also had a more directly negative effect on minority rights by encouraging extremists on both sides of the Albanian–Serb divide to stake out maximalist positions and jockey for control of territory by driving out the other. Since 1999 the divided northern city of Mitrovica/Mitrovicë has been a particular flashpoint in this regard.

After eight years of international rule, Kosovo's Albanian and Serbian communities remain as divided as ever. As the UN mission in Kosovo starts to wind up, the European Union will begin to assume an even more important role. Their involvement will be based on the plan unveiled by UN envoy Martti Ahtisaari in February 2007. EU administrators will replace UN administrators, and extensive decentralization is planned, which will lead to six autonomous Serb districts, some of which would include majority Albanian villages. But much will depend on whether Kosovan Serbian leaders will cooperate with this plan, or whether they will continue to press for secession. ▪

Preventing conflict

In 2007, MRG laid out 10 practical steps which must be taken after an ethnic or religious conflict, to prevent violence re-occurring. These conclusions were based on research conducted for MRG's conflict prevention programme.

1 Stop violence against minorities and ensure a justice system that identifies and prosecutes perpetrators, especially the leaders. Ensure that all communities are free from attack, including minority women.

2 Ensure that minorities do not leave against their will by providing security and financial assistance. Provide conditions for minorities who have recently left to return as quickly as possible. Set up systems for identifying owners of property and returning these.

3 Prohibit and prosecute hate speech, especially in the media and education.

4 Create a political system based on equality. Remove (and do not insert any new) references to a country being based on a particular people, religion or constituent peoples.

5 If power-sharing is considered the only option, have a clause providing for a review or termination after a fixed period. Do not have any system that forces persons into ethnic groups.

6 Create an effective legal system that uses all languages in the country and is open to all. Ensure that minorities have financial means to use it.

7 Create a system to outlaw discrimination and give effective (legal and other) remedies against it.

8 If quotas are deemed necessary, make them temporary and ensure the discrimination is addressed first.

9 Ensure economic development does not marginalize communities, or destroy their identity. Ensure those involved in development understand discrimination.

10 Create an education system that ensures that all children can learn their community's language, religion and culture, but also creates common experiences and understanding. Ensure a shared history curriculum.

Report: *Minority Rights: The Key to Conflict Prevention,* **by Clive Baldwin, Chris Chapman and Zoe Gray.** To view/purchase full report go to www.minorityrights.org

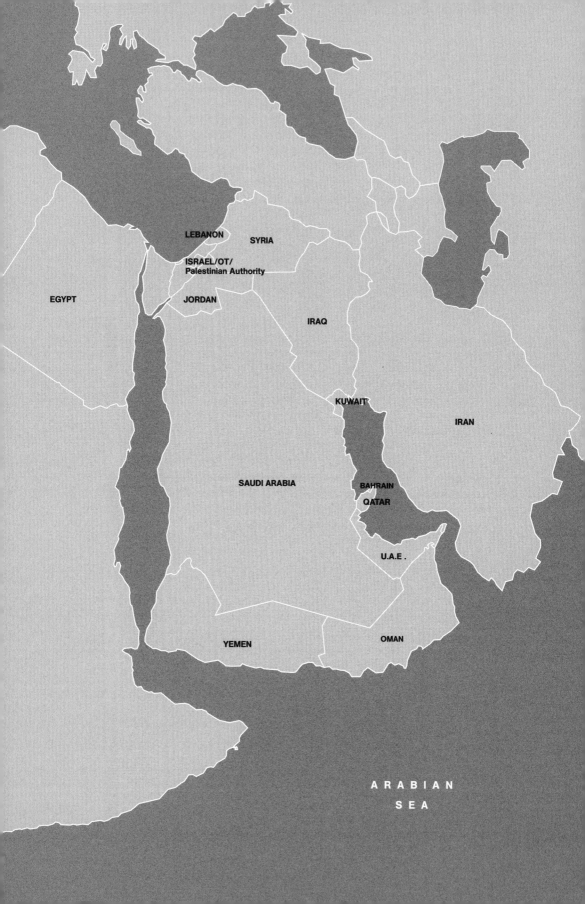

LEBANON

SYRIA

ISRAEL/OT/
Palestinian Authority

EGYPT

JORDAN

IRAQ

KUWAIT

IRAN

SAUDI ARABIA

BAHRAIN

QATAR

U.A.E .

YEMEN

OMAN

A R A B I A N
S E A

Middle East
East

Eric Witte

Violence against minority groups in Iraq continued at catastrophic levels in 2007, and the mounting impact has been felt region-wide. Sectarian and ethnic war has cost hundreds of thousands of lives, driven ancient minority communities to the edge of destruction, and sparked an exodus from Iraq of epic proportions. Hundreds of thousands of Iraqis have sought refuge in Middle Eastern countries, and have placed a particularly heavy burden on Jordan and Syria. The war in Iraq has also been one of the main reasons for a deterioration in the relationship between the US and Iran. Mounting tension has worked to the detriment of ethnic and sectarian minorities there, whom the government accuses of receiving Western assistance. Polarization between the Arab world and the West has also contributed to Lebanon's political crisis, in which alleged Syrian-backed assassinations of minority politicians have brought the country back to the brink of war. Meanwhile, efforts resumed to forge a peace between Israel and the long-marginalized Palestinians of the West Bank and Gaza, now controlled by rival factions Fatah and Hamas, respectively.

There is broad scientific consensus that human-induced climate change is affecting the Middle East, resulting in hotter summers, reduced rainfall and rising sea levels. By 2050 the amount of available fresh water per capita is expected to drop by half. In a region where conflicts have been sparked and exacerbated by an already acute shortage of fresh water, climate change presents a newly recognized threat to stability. In April 2007 the UN Security Council convened at the behest of the UK Council presidency to discuss the nexus between global warming and conflict. That same month a group of prominent retired American generals released a report on climate change as a national security issue, particularly noting its potential to exacerbate conflicts in the Middle East.

Although two major rivers, the Tigris and Euphrates, flow through it, Iraq already has problems with access to fresh water due to dam projects in Syria and Turkey. The Food and Agriculture Organization reports that 74 per cent of the irrigation water in central and southern Iraq suffers from salinity. With reduced rainfall expected due to climate change, on top of an expansion of Turkey's dam infrastructure, Iraq is facing a much drier future. This resource scarcity

could exacerbate a conflict in which minorities have suffered the most.

By Middle Eastern standards, Iran is relatively rich in fresh water. However, a severe drought in its south-east over the past few years has disproportionately affected the ethnic Baluchi minority concentrated in that region and provided fodder for accusations of government neglect. With global warming, Baluchis will face new environmental pressure to add to their discontent.

Country by country
Iran
Ethnic and religious minorities make up nearly half of the Iranian population. Discontent among various minority groups has risen sharply over the past two years. Since Iranian President Mahmoud Ahmadinejad came to power in August 2005, the government has more forcefully promoted the country's majority Persian and Shia Muslim identity. In contravention of formal guarantees in the Iranian Constitution and international commitments, in 2007 the government continued a crackdown on ethnic and religious minorities through methods including police repression, discrimination in education, and state media campaigns. There was significant overlap between minority rights abuses on ethnic and religious grounds in Iran, as nearly all ethnic Baluchis and Turkomans, most Kurds, and some Arabs practise Sunni Islam disfavoured by the regime.

Rising tension among Western governments over Iran's nuclear programme and alleged backing for Shia militias fighting American-led forces in Iraq have contributed to a poisoned environment for some minority groups within Iran. The government is wary of the large US and UK military presence in neighbouring Iraq and Afghanistan, especially given the steady flow of reports from Washington over the course of 2007 that senior members of the Bush administration are advocating military attacks on Iran. The government has accused disgruntled minority groups including Arabs, Azeris, Baluchis and Kurds of accepting covert support from the US, the UK and Israel. Reports of such assistance are murky, and it remains unclear to what extent, if any, they are true, or merely serve Tehran as a pretext to discredit and clamp down on regime opponents from minority communities.

Around 7 per cent of the Iranian population is Kurdish and concentrated in the north-west, along the borders with northern Iraq and south-west Turkey; another sizeable community of Kurds lives in the north-east, along the border with Turkmenistan. The Iranian regime has watched with alarm as Kurds have consolidated their autonomy within Iraq, and fears the establishment of a Kurdish state that would make claims on Iranian territory. An Iranian Kurdish militant group, the Party for a Free Life in Kurdistan (PJAK), which is affiliated with the Kurdistan Workers Party (PKK) of Turkey, operates in Iran from bases in the rugged mountains of Iraqi Kurdistan. Tehran accuses the US and Israel of supporting PJAK, and over the course of 2007 shelled northern Iraq indiscriminately in response. The regime has extended accusations of complicity with foreign enemies to other Kurds protesting, or even talking about Kurdish issues. In February 2007, Amnesty International reported that police allegedly killed three Kurds and injured dozens more during a demonstration for Kurdish rights in the town of Mahabad. Reporters without Borders announced in July that two Kurdish journalists had been sentenced to death in the town of Marivan. Both of the journalists had written on Kurdish issues for a magazine banned in August 2005, and the prosecution cited interviews one of them conducted with Voice of America as evidence of 'activities subverting national security' and 'spying'.

Ethnic Baluchis, who are mostly Sunni Muslims, live on both sides of the Iranian–Pakistani border and comprise around 2 per cent of the Iranian population. Baluchistan is the country's poorest region and in recent years has been plagued by severe drought. Baluchis complained of government discrimination and neglect following severe storms in June 2007 that cost over 20 lives, and claimed that the government response was inadequate. Since 2005 a Baluchi militia called Jondallah has claimed credit for attacks on government targets; Tehran also accuses it of attacks on civilian populations. Amnesty International reported that by August 2007, in the wake of a February bomb attack on a bus full of Iranian army troops claimed by Jondallah, around 50 Baluchis had been executed in the intervening months.

The ongoing war in Iraq has stirred unrest in the neighbouring Iranian province of Khuzestan, which in Arabic is called al-Ahwazi. High poverty rates among Ahwazi Arabs, despite their province's production of 90 per cent of Iran's oil revenue, have fuelled resentment, as has discrimination on cultural-linguistic grounds. Some Arabs are Sunni and not allowed to practise their faith publicly, or construct a single Sunni mosque. In January and February 2007 the Iranian government executed eight Ahwazi Arabs for alleged participation in 2005 sabotage of oil infrastructure in Khuzestan by the intentionally excruciating method of slow strangulation. Three UN rapporteurs deemed the one-day trial deeply flawed. The accused had not been allowed access to their lawyers and, when the Ahwazi lawyers complained, they were arrested. In September the government conducted three more such executions, sparking public protests on which police opened fire. In November 2007, eight additional executions appeared imminent, but an international advocacy campaign subsequently succeeded in removing two Ahwazi men from death row.

Azeris, who are Turkic-speaking Shias, make up nearly one-quarter of the population and are concentrated in north-western Iran, along the borders with Azerbaijan and Armenia. Of all of Iran's ethnic minorities, Azeris receive perhaps the greatest acceptance among Persian Iraqis; indeed, Iran's supreme leader, Ayatollah Khamenei, is ethnic Azeri. Nevertheless, Azeris continue to face discrimination and are denied education in their mother tongue. In February 2007 Iranian security forces arrested dozens of Azeris peacefully protesting for Azeri-language education in towns across the north-west. According to Amnesty International, some of those detained allegedly were mistreated in custody. In May, Azeris again demonstrating for language rights were arrested in their hundreds; these protests were timed for the one-year anniversary of a cartoon in a government newspaper that depicted a cockroach speaking Azeri.

Iran's largest religious minority, the Baha'i, also faces some of the worst government abuse. The estimated 300,000 Baha'i adherents are persecuted for their belief that other prophets followed Muhammad and, as followers of an unrecognized religion, are barred from public worship or contact with co-believers in other countries. Baha'i rights organizations reported an increase in government harassment in 2007. This included police raids on Baha'i homes and businesses in Tehran in February, criminal prosecution of group members for promotion of an 'un-Islamic' organization, and government orders to 25 industries in April to deny business licences to Baha'i. A 2006 government edict led to the expulsion of more than half of all Baha'i university students during the 2006–7 academic year, solely on the basis of their religion.

In November 2007 the UN General Assembly's Human Rights Committee narrowly approved a draft resolution expressing 'deep concern' at human rights violations in Iran. Among other provisions, the draft called on Iran 'to eliminate, in law and practice, all forms of discrimination and other human rights violations against persons belonging to religious, ethnic, linguistic, or other minorities'.

Iraq

The fifth year of war following the US-led invasion of Iraq was one of the bloodiest. The main fault line remains that between Sunni and Shia Arabs. However, within the broader war, small, often-forgotten minorities have been most prone to violent attack. The overall number of civilian deaths from the beginning of the conflict is disputed, but probably ranges in the hundreds of thousands. In July 2007 the Office of the UN High Commissioner for Refugees (UNHCR) estimated that 2 million Iraqis had become refugees and 2 million more internally displaced since March 2003. The agency further estimated that 2,000 additional Iraqis continued to be displaced every day. Most of the refugees have fled to Jordan and Syria, which have taken in some 500,000 and 1.5 million Iraqis, respectively – according to the UN, nearly a third of these refugees come from minority communities.

Iraqis fleeing insecurity and dire economic conditions have encountered new political and physical barriers at foreign borders. Some groups have found escape especially difficult, notably the Palestinian minority.

For the approximately 30,000 Iraqis internally displaced each month, new barriers also arose in 2007. In October, UNHCR announced that 11 of 18 Iraqi provincial governors had closed their territories to internally displaced persons from other provinces, and that any new arrivals would be denied government support for food and education.

Sectarian violence

Shia and Sunni Arabs living as numerical minorities among a majority of the other community face severe threats in all parts of the country, targeted by militias vying for power and land, or exacting retribution for attacks from the other side. Sectarian violence has been especially fierce ever since February 2006 when Sunni militants bombed one of the holiest Shia mosques in Samarra. Many in the Shia numerical majority are eager to consolidate control over the country, while long-dominant Sunnis fear persecution as a minority. The December 2006 hanging of Saddam Hussein following a war crimes trial deemed deeply flawed by human rights advocates did nothing to dampen those fears. In August 2007, the main Sunni bloc withdrew from Prime Minister Nouri al-Maliki's government, accusing him of sectarianism. By October, despite intense international pressure, the Iraqi government still had not reached agreement on how the country's oil revenues should be shared; Sunnis, predominantly from the country's oil-poor centre, fear efforts by Shia and Kurds to keep revenues in the oil-rich south and north.

In September 2007 the US Department of Defence claimed that death rates from sectarian violence had fallen compared with those of the previous year, however an analysis released separately by the politically independent US Government Accountability Office 'could not determine if sectarian violence had declined'.

Radical Shia militias have overt backers in government, and have infiltrated the Iraqi National Police and, to a lesser extent, the Iraqi army; from within the security services and without, death squads and militias continue to target Sunni civilians. They have also particularly targeted the Palestinian community in Iraq for abduction, torture and murder. Palestinians are Sunni, and under Saddam Hussein received privileged treatment in the country. The US alleges that Iran is providing support to some of the militants. In overwhelmingly Shia southern Iraq, Shia militias have fought each other for resources and power.

Many of the Sunni attacks on Shia have been perpetrated by foreign-led militias, including 'al-Qaeda in Iraq', and have often featured car bombs and suicide attacks. In February 2007, a bomb at a Shia market in Baghdad killed 137; in April five car bombs targeting Shia in Baghdad killed 200 people in a single day. As part of an announced offensive during the holy month of Ramadan, Sunni militants conducted a wave of suicide bombings and other attacks in September. During 2007, the US military began arming and training militias loyal to Sunni traditional tribal leaders, some of whom are hostile to foreign Sunni militants. Shia leaders have been wary of the tactic, worrying that support for Sunni militarization could eventually further sectarian attacks on their communities.

The ongoing sectarian violence has continued the process of segregation between Shia and Sunni Iraqis. In 2007 the government intervened to try to shore up the common practice of mixed sectarian marriage in Iraq by introducing cash bonuses for newly married, mixed Sunni–Shia couples. Meanwhile, Baghdad real-estate agents experienced a boom in arranging housing exchanges between Shia and Sunni minorities in Baghdad neighbourhoods. As the city and country become more segregated, life for remaining sectarian minorities has become more perilous.

International forces, mostly American, have been reluctant to take action on behalf of smaller minority groups, especially as political desperation to find a way out of the quagmire in Iraq has increasingly meant finding accommodation with the three dominant groups, elements of which are usually responsible for targeting smaller groups. Additionally, smaller minorities for the most part have no militias of their own, and must rely on police, who are often corrupt, or themselves perpetrators of ethnic and sectarian violence.

Attacks on non-Muslims
Iraq's Christian minorities, from the ancient communities of Chaldo-Assyrians and Syriac-speaking Orthodox Christians to the Armenians who fled to Iraq from the Ottoman Empire early in the twentieth century, are now all under severe threat. Across Iraq, Shia and Sunni Islamic extremists have singled out Christian families, often forcing them to pay protection money. When the funds run out, they are given a choice of converting, fleeing or dying. Among Christians who stay, women are forced to wear the Muslim *abaya* body covering. Death threats forced the last Anglican vicar, a British citizen, to flee Iraq in July 2007. He testified before the US Commission on International Religious Freedom (USCIRF) that in a single week earlier in July, 36 of his congregation had been kidnapped.

While many Christians have fled abroad, others have moved to the relatively calmer north. Reports indicate that 3,000 Christian families have left Baghdad and moved to the Kurdish territories, whilst another 4,000 have moved to the Nineveh Plains. The new arrivals often lack employment, schools and housing. There has been talk that some Christian communities – especially the umbrella Assyrian ones – are lobbying for a separate entity in the Nineveh Plains just north of Mosul. Discussions continue over the shape of any such entity and what degree of self-governance it would take on. While representatives of the Kurdistan Regional Government (KRG) have said they support the creation of a 'Nineveh province' within Kurdistan, the US government has opposed the idea, saying it would 'further sectarianism'.

The year 2007 was one of devastation for Yezidis, ethnic and linguistic Kurds who are adherents of a 4,000-year-old, pre-Islamic faith. Following a *fatwa*, or religious instruction from a Sunni militant group called 'Islamic State of Iraq' calling for the deaths of Yezidis, suspected Sunni militants pulled 23 Yezidi men from a bus and executed them in April 2007. The same group of extremists perpetrated the single most devastating terrorist attack of the Iraq war in August 2007; four truck bombs killed almost 500 Yezidis in two villages in the Nineveh Plains, along the Syrian border. The area is strategically important disputed territory. Following the US offensive against Sunni insurgents to the south, reports indicate that 'al-Qaeda in Iraq' has increased its presence in this region. Many Yezidis have fled the country and those who remain are now fearful of travel outside of their communities. Yezidi farmers are losing their livelihoods because they can no longer travel to markets to sell their produce. In October, the *New York Times* reported that security fears had led Yezidis to stop performing religious ceremonies.

Conflict in the north
The Kurds in the north have autonomous rule, with centres in Erbil and Suleimaniyyeh, and are drafting a local constitution for the Kurdish areas. Kurdish aspirations for an independent Kurdistan are anathema to Iran, Syria and Turkey, all of which have neighbouring Kurdish minorities who, they fear, would seek to join such a new state. Over the course of 2007, Turkey grew increasingly concerned about attacks on its territory conducted by militants of the Kurdistan Workers Party (PKK), which uses northern Iraq as a refuge. In August, Turkey and

Mandaean-Sabeans – bearing the brunt of warfare

The Iraq war has had a devastating effect on the Mandaean-Sabean community, which is being gradually driven out of its ancient homeland. Preti Taneja profiles the group, its history, beliefs and its prospects for survival.

The Mandaean-Sabeans are an ancient people whose faith dates back to pre-Christian times. It is estimated that only around 60,000 still exist, living in groups that, because of ongoing persecution, are scattered around the world, including in the Middle East in Syria, Jordan and Iran, and in Australia, North America and Europe. For more than two millennia they made their home in what is now southern Iraq, between the Tigris and the Euphrates rivers. The nearest city is Basra. Today, the community is under such extreme pressure that their religion, culture and language are in danger of disappearing forever.

The Mandaean faith is centred around John the Baptist. Mandaean baptism takes place regularly and often, as a form of spiritual cleansing. The person being baptized must submerge their head three times in the running water of a river, and in the presence of a Mandaean priest. The language is a form of Aramaic, the language of the New Testament. This language is still spoken by Mandaeans in Iran, but in Iraq it exists mainly in Mandaean liturgy. It is listed in the 2007 UNESCO *Atlas of the World's Languages in Danger of Disappearing*, but very little else has been done to formally protect it. Mandaeans are pacifists: the religion prohibits the carrying of weapons or taking of life. Although they are mentioned in the Qur'an as 'people of the book' this is disputed by some Islamic interpreters. Circumcision and marriage outside the faith is considered religious conversion for Mandaeans.

The Iraq war: Mandaeans targeted

Today, it is estimated that only 5,000 Mandaeans remain in Iraq, mostly in Baghdad, and in the area around Basra.

Since the US-led invasion of Iraq in 2003, Mandaeans have been the specific targets of violence. Mandaean women and children have been kidnapped and forcibly converted to Islam by rape, circumcision, physical beatings and even burning by bonfire. The community has suffered the looting and destruction of their homes and businesses. Specific instances have been well documented by MRG, Mandaean Crisis International, Mandaean Human Rights Group and Genocide Watch, among others.

Mandaeans do not have the protection of tribal structures, and their pacifism means they will not turn to violence, even in self-defence. Thus they are among the most vulnerable communities in Iraq. They daily face the harrowing dilemma: convert, leave or die.

Layla al Roomi, a Mandaean who is based in the UK and is now lobbying for the Iraqi community, said, 'In the last months, there have been further killings of Mandaeans in Iraq. Families are being separated, homes are being taken. It is worse than it has been so far. Despite the Bush administration saying that there is more security in Iraq, minorities are continuing to suffer.' In fact, she said, 'beneath the noses of the British and US troops in southern Iraq, including Basra, there has been a total cleansing of Mandaeans and Christians.'

Some Iraqi minorities have been resettled in the Kurdistan Regional Government (KRG) governorates in northern Iraq, and on the Nineveh Plains. But for most Mandaeans, who have few family or community ties in those areas, this is not an option. In the KRG only 20 or 30 Mandaean families with professional qualifications have found refuge. And the threat of Turkish military action undermines any sense of security these new arrivals might feel. Outside the KRG in northern Iraq, the few Mandaeans who have resettled still receive threats of kidnapping, forced conversion and death from religious fundamentalists.

Refugee life: hardship and loss of culture

The Mandaean Human Rights Group estimates that around 2,000 families (about 8,000 refugees) have fled to Syria and about 900 families (about 3,600 refugees) are now in Jordan. They live cramped in small apartments, sometimes five or six people to a room.

Basil, a 33-year-old Mandaean Iraqi, fled Baghdad 10 months ago with his parents. He trained to be an engineer. In Iraq, he worked for the United Nations before the headquarters were bombed in August 2003. Doing this work, he received death threats, and finally he left to work as an operations manager for a trucking company. The company had transport contracts with the coalition forces. 'That's what forced me to leave Iraq,' said Basil. 'I was almost killed. People were threatening me and chasing me – when they could not find me, they targeted my father. They knew that he was a dentist in Baghdad, they knew where his clinic was. They knew I dealt with the US army – they demanded I meet them and told me where to come. They knew so many things that we had to flee.'

Now, he lives with his parents in a small apartment in Damascus. Though he is glad to be alive, he is finding the situation he and his community are in increasingly difficult to bear. 'Sometimes I dream of going back to Iraq,' he says, 'despite the terror and the killings in Baghdad. There is no home, no comfort here.'

Refugees are not allowed work permits, and Basil confirms, 'It is hard to live in Damascus. There are no jobs, no future, you do nothing all day.' Instead he works as a volunteer for the Mandaean Association that has grown in the community. 'If you saw the circumstances we are living in, you would cry,' he said. 'People are running out of money, no one knows how they will survive when the New Year comes.' As the refugee population grows, rents increase even in the poorest areas where refugees are housed.

Living this way, Mandaeans cannot observe their religious rituals, including baptisms, weddings and funerals. Although they are free to worship in Jordan and Syria, there is no official area for them to do so and they are not close to the rivers that are so important to the faith. When members of the community die, Mandaean relatives have undertaken the perilous journey to bury them in Iraq, but, because of tighter visa restrictions for Iraqi refugees coming into the two countries, that is no longer an option.

The future

For most Mandaeans, return to Iraq is not an option. The religious climate, the difficulties in reclaiming homes and land, and the lack of political protection would make their situation highly dangerous and difficult. The Mandaean culture and language is at risk of being totally eradicated from Iraq.

As its members must adapt to survive away from their homeland, there is a chance that this ancient faith will eventually disappear completely. The US and UK have proved sympathetic listeners, but this has not translated into action. For Basil and for the rest of Iraq's Mandaeans, this is not enough. 'It makes it harder when we hear promises of protection. In the end they just seem to be lies.'

Read MRG's 2007 report: *Assimilation, Exodus, Eradication: Iraq's Minority Communities since 2003*, by Preti Taneja

Iraq signed an agreement on coordination of efforts to combat the PKK, but cross-border incursions by the PKK continued in September and October. In November Turkey moved 100,000 troops and heavy weapons to the border and the prospect of Turkish involvement in Iraq threatened to roil the relatively calm north, where small minorities have suffered the most from what violence has occurred in that region. Through intense US diplomacy with Turkey and pressure on the Iraqi Kurdish government to block support to the PKK, it was hoped that such a scenario could be avoided.

Violence between Kurds and Arabs increased during 2007, as a referendum slated for the end of the year on the future status of the oil-rich town of Kirkuk neared. The Iraqi Constitution provides for the referendum to decide on whether Kirkuk province will join the autonomous Kurdistan Region. In April the central government approved an incentive package for Sunni Arabs forcibly settled in Kirkuk under Saddam Hussein to return to their original homelands in the south. According to an Iraqi minister, by October around 1,000 Sunni Arab families had accepted the approximately US $15,000 payment to leave their Kirkuk homes. Yet, whilst Kurds view Kirkuk as the capital of Iraqi Kurdistan, many Arabs and Turkomans oppose this, and smaller minorities including Armenians, Chaldo-Assyrian Christians, Faili and Shabak have been caught in the middle. Forces of the Kurdistan Regional Government, along with Kurdish militias, have targeted Arabs and Turkomans, including through tactics of abduction and torture. Increasingly, Sunni Arab militants opposed to Kirkuk joining Kurdistan have launched attacks on Kurdish targets.

Turkomans view Kirkuk as historically theirs. Out of its opposition to the Kurds gaining control of Kirkuk and the likewise-disputed oil-town of Mosul, Turkey has provided backing for Turkoman militias that are confronting Kurdish forces. Apart from the competition for land, Turkomans have been targeted on sectarian grounds, with women being particularly vulnerable. In June 2007, four Shia Iraqi soldiers were charged with the rape of a Sunni Turkoman woman in Tel Afar – one of many such reported incidents. In July 2007 a marketplace bomb attack on Shia Turkomans killed between 130 and 210 civilians, mostly women and children.

Kurdish militants have also harassed the small ethnic Shabak community. In the interests of extending land claims in the northern Nineveh governorate, these Kurds assert that, despite Shabaks' distinct language and recognition as an ethnic group, Shabaks are really Kurds. Additionally, the majority of Shabak who are Shia have been targeted by Sunni militants. In July 2007 a Shabak MP claimed that Sunni militants had killed around 1,000 Shabak and displaced a further 4,000 from the Mosul area since 2003.

Faili, who are Shia Kurds, also face threats on sectarian grounds. A July 2007 truck bomb at a café frequented by Faili in the town of Amirli killed 105 and injured nearly 250 more. Journalists suspected that the bombing was linked to the forthcoming referendum on Kurdish autonomy.

Grim prospects

Despite the election of a parliament and the drafting of a constitution, the prospect of full-scale civil war between Shia militias and Sunni insurgents that threatens the existence of Iraq as a country, is still very real. A 'surge' of around 28,000 additional American troops in 2007 was meant to restore order in the country. Reported drops in levels of violence in Baghdad by the end of the year offered tentative hope – but clearly the country has a long road to travel before it climbs out of the post-invasion abyss. And the success of the surge strategy is by no means assured. Opposition to the war in the US has grown dramatically, and the Bush administration is facing ever stronger calls for force draw-down and withdrawal. In October, the British government announced that it would withdraw 1,000 troops, or 20 per cent of its force, from Iraq by the end of 2007.

Iraqi refugees

According to UN figures, nearly a third of the 2 million Iraqis who have fled the country come from the country's smaller minority groups. Beyond individual survival, these groups fear for the survival of their cultures.

According to a Kurdish government official in October 2007, at least 70,000 Yezidis, or 15 per cent of the group's population, have fled the country. Iraq's ancient and once sizeable Jewish community has all but entirely emigrated, with only a handful of Jewish people remaining in Baghdad.

Many Iraqi Christians also are emigrating in disproportionately large numbers. According to UNHCR, while Christians make up 4 per cent of the overall Iraqi population, they constitute 40 per cent of Iraqi refugees. According to the Iraqi non-governmental Christian Peace organization, a Christian minority of 850,000 in 2003 has been whittled down to under 600,000 today. In May 2007, USCIRF estimated that up to half of all Iraqi Christians had left the country.

For Iraqis fleeing the devastation of war, Syria has been a prime destination. Since March 2003 the country has taken in around 1.5 million Iraqis and, according to one Syrian non-governmental organization (NGO) estimate in August 2007, as many as 2 million. The refugees have swelled Syria's population by 8–10 per cent and the government estimates that the burden, including accommodation of Iraqi children in schools, has cost it US $1 billion each year. The influx has caused increases in the prices of housing and basic commodities. Assistance provided by UNHCR and other international agencies has not come close to covering the needs, and many Iraqi refugees are falling into poverty and despair. Homelessness is becoming a major problem, and some desperate Iraqis are turning to begging or crime to get by. Many of the Iraqi refugees are destitute widows, and some have turned to sex work to survive.

Since it allowed 300 Palestinian refugees from Iraq to enter in April–May 2006, the Syrian government has singled out this group for denial of entry. By May 2007, around 1,400 Iraqi Palestinians were camped at the Iraqi–Syrian border – fleeing Shia militia attacks at home and refused permission to enter Syria. Despite assistance from UNHCR and the International Committee for the Red Cross, Palestinians are living in squalid desert camps, exposed to blazing desert heat and sand storms, and lacking adequate water supplies. In May 2007 UNHCR appealed for international assistance in providing health care at the camps, noting that some Palestinian Iraqis were dying of treatable illnesses.

Jordan has admitted more Iraqi refugees per capita than any other country, with estimates ranging from 500,000 to 1 million. As in Syria, the influx has placed a heavy burden on the government, while driving up housing prices and the cost of basic goods. Many of the Iraqi refugees, disproportionately from Iraq's smaller ethnic and religious minority groups, live in poverty. Unemployment rates are high, in part because the refugees are ineligible for work in the public sector. With a higher cost of living, especially in Amman, increasing numbers of Iraqis have turned to begging.

Up till February 2007, Jordan still had no visa requirement for entry of Iraqi citizens, which helped make the country one of the prime destinations for those fleeing persecution. Beyond instituting a new passport requirement, ever since the 2005 suicide bomb attacks perpetrated by Iraqis on three hotels in Amman, the Jordanian government has feared the import of sectarian violence and routinely turned away Iraqi males between the ages of 18 and 45 and screened for Shia. In April 2007, Human Rights Watch documented the systematic rejection of Iraqi Shias at the border, as well as increasing police sweeps and repatriation of Iraqi refugees.

Although the US-led invasion triggered the conflict that has led to mass displacement, by July 2007 the US had only admitted 825 Iraqi refugees, while between 2003 and 2005 the UK had only let in 100. Iraqis working for these and other Western governments, international organizations, NGOs and international media outlets have been targeted by extremists; because many of the Iraqis willing to take such work are non-Muslims, these minorities have been disproportionately affected. As the number of Iraqis working at the US embassy killed or claiming asylum status abroad rose, in July 2007, the American ambassador pleaded with Washington to grant refugee visas to all local embassy staff and their families. A bill liberalizing the asylum process for Iraqis associated with US or US-backed institutions passed the US Senate in September, and included special allowances for Iraqis from minority religious groups. Sweden has admitted nearly half of the estimated 20,000 Iraqi refugees who have been allowed to settle in Western countries. Many of the thousands of refugees in Sweden are Assyrians and other Christians.

Israel

Israeli Arab citizens (or Palestinian citizens of Israel), who comprise nearly 20 per cent of the population, continued to face broad governmental and societal discrimination in 2007. In most cases where the government acknowledged discrimination against this group, it did so by citing the Jewish identity of the state and its security in the face of continued attacks from the Occupied Territories of the Gaza Strip and West Bank.

A 2006 report by Israeli Arab intellectuals titled *The Future Vision of the Palestinian Arabs in Israel* sparked controversy extending into 2007. The report, prompted by Israel's internal debate over a new constitution, called for Israel to abandon its identity as a Jewish state, stop treating its Arab citizens as 'enemies', and guarantee equal status for Jews and Arabs. One leading Arab academic, Dr Adel Manna, said in April 2007, 'The Israeli public doesn't want to understand that it is demanding that the Arabs become loyal but on the other hand it is not allowing them to do so.'

In March the UN Committee on the Elimination of Racial Discrimination (CERD) called on Israeli lawmakers to scrap a race-based provision blocking family unification in Israel for broad swathes of the population in the Occupied Territories; the ban, adopted out of concern over terrorist attacks, has

disproportionately affected Israeli Arabs who are more likely to have spouses from the West Bank and Gaza. Nevertheless, Israel's parliament, the Knesset, reauthorized the provision later in March, extending it until August 2008. Constitutional legal challenges to the law are pending.

Israel's 2006 war in Lebanon strained the relationship between the government and its Israeli Arab minority into 2007. An Arab member of the Knesset resigned his seat in April as it became known that he was under investigation for 'aiding the enemy' during the conflict, while he claimed that the government was persecuting him for his harsh criticism of its policies. In November 2007 the Knesset gave preliminary approval to a law that bans Israelis who visit 'enemy states' from taking seats in the Knesset. Supporters said it was aimed at ending meetings between Arab Knesset members and representatives of the Syrian government as well as such militant groups as Hezbollah and Hamas. Arab parliamentarians countered that the measure amounted to pure racism.

In September 2007 the Israeli Supreme Court ruled that the Jewish National Fund (JNF), established in 1901 to buy land for Jews in then-Ottoman administered Palestine, could no longer follow a policy of refusing to sell land to Arabs. The JNF administers around 13 per cent of all land in Israel, in part jointly with the Israeli Lands Administration. Anticipation of the ruling created pressure within the Knesset to make the continuation of such explicit discrimination legal. In June 2007 CERD criticized the government for impeding the land rights of Palestinians outside of Israel who wanted to return, calling on the state 'to assure equality in the right to return to one's country and in the possession of property'.

One subset of Israeli Arabs, the estimated 150,000–200,000 indigenous Bedouins of the Negev desert, continued their long-standing struggle for land rights. The government pursued into 2007 the repeated destruction of 45 unrecognized Bedouin villages, some of which pre-date the establishment of the Israeli state. The Israeli government denies Bedouin claims to the land for lack of documentation. Beyond bulldozing the shanties, the government has denied provision of electricity, water and sewage services to the unrecognized settlements that are home to around 80,000 Bedouins. In February the Israeli housing minister told the BBC, 'If they want their children to be educated, to grow up in the right environment, with all the culture and services, they cannot live in the desert.' Indeed, 120,000 Bedouins have moved into seven approved government towns. However these cramped settlements, with scant attached land, suffer shoddy design and were erected beginning in 1968 without Bedouin input. Forced urbanization has led to a loss of Bedouin traditional customs, high crime rates, drug problems and severe unemployment. Bedouin women have been especially affected, having lost their traditional social roles; added hurdles to mobility outside the home have contributed to near 90 per cent unemployment for women. In mid-July the government announced the establishment of a new agency to handle Bedouin issues.

Despite ongoing problems and setbacks, 2007 also saw some halting advances in Israel's acceptance of its Arab minority. In January the government of Prime Minister Ehud Olmert appointed Labour MP Raleb Majadele as a minister without portfolio – the first Israeli Arab ever to sit in a government cabinet. Over the objections of right-wing politicians, in July the government approved a history textbook that for the first time ever included Palestinian views on the 1948 creation of the state of Israel as a 'catastrophe'. However, the book was only for use in Israeli Arab schools.

A growing influx of Jewish settlers among Druze communities in northern Israel and the occupied Golan Heights further degraded the relationship between the state and Druze in the north in 2007. Druze and some in the established Jewish community complain bitterly of right-wing settlers bent on dominance of the local villages. In October, over 30 Druze and police officers were wounded in riots in the Golan Heights village of Peki'in.

Lebanon

Tolerance amid Lebanon's great religious diversity came under heavy strain in 2007 as a result of the July 2006 war between Israel and Lebanese-based Hezbollah militants, deepening regional Sunni–Shia tensions resulting from the Iraqi civil war, and a continuation of the long-standing divide in Lebanese politics pitting advocates of a pro-Western orientation against those favouring a greater alignment with Syria and the Arab world. Lebanon's

system of political confessionalism – the allotment of political offices to particular religious groups – continued to act as a catalyst for tension among various groups. At the same time, the divide between pro-Syrian and pro-Western sentiment created deeper divides within Lebanon's minority communities.

In the aftermath of the devastating war with Israel in 2006, Lebanon's recently booming tourist industry was left in tatters, and the country's sharp economic decline contributed to resentment among non-Shia Muslims of Iranian- and Syrian-backed Hezbollah, increasingly blamed for provoking the war. For its part, in late 2006, Hezbollah withdrew all Shia members of government and launched major protests in Beirut demanding a larger Shia voice in Lebanese affairs, commensurate with its share of the country's population. A backlash among Sunni Arabs, along with some Christians and Druze, further reduced what remained of Hezbollah's standing as a protector of the nation.

In May, the UN Security Council approved establishment of an international tribunal to investigate and prosecute those responsible for a string of assassinations of prominent Lebanese officials and journalists opposed to Syria's years-long influence, beginning with the February 2005 assassination of Lebanese Prime Minister Rafik Hariri. Pro-Syrian political factions in the opposition, most notably Hezbollah and Maronite Christian followers of former Maronite militia leader and current Member of Parliament Michel Aoun, viewed the development as one more element in an alleged pro-American, pro-Israeli plot to turn Lebanon against the Arab world.

Lebanon's key divide between advocates of closer relations with the Arab world or the West is mirrored within the Maronite Christian community. Maronite leader Michel Aoun was once an opponent of Syria's influence in the country, but is now one of the most prominent figures in the opposition to the current pro-Western government. Meanwhile prominent anti-Syrian Maronite Christians have faced the threat of political assassination. In November 2006, assassins gunned down Pierre Gemayel, a young MP and son of a former president, who was also active in opposing Syrian involvement in Lebanese affairs. Amid allegations of voting irregularities, a pro-Syrian Maronite Christian won a by-election for his seat in parliament in August 2007. A bombing in September 2007 killed another Maronite anti-Syrian MP, Antoine Ghanim, and six others in a mainly Maronite suburb of Beirut. As 2007 progressed, pro-Western and pro-Syrian factions in Lebanon focused their attention and energy on who would succeed current Maronite pro-Syrian President Emile Lahoud. Because the position is reserved for Maronites, the national divide animated divisions within the Maronite community. Leading contenders for the presidency, due to be chosen by parliament, were Michel Aoun and former President Amin Gemayel, the father of murdered MP Pierre Gemayel. A boycott by pro-Syrian factions delayed the vote three times, and Lahoud's term expired in late November. Parliament had failed to identify a successor capable of gaining the necessary two-thirds vote and in early December the office of president remained vacant.

With exception of Palestinians, most, but not all, Sunnis align politically with the pro-Western faction in Lebanon's main political divide, and prominent anti-Syrian Sunnis have been assassinated in recent years – most notably former Lebanese Prime Minister Rafik Hariri. A June 2007 blast killed Sunni politician and Syria critic Walid Eido along with nine others.

In the midst of Lebanon's political and sectarian crisis, the festering plight of the country's 250,000–300,000 Palestinian refugees erupted anew during 2007. The Palestinian community, refugees displaced by the 1948 creation of Israel and their descendants, continues to confront severe official discrimination in Lebanon, in part due to fears that integration of this large group of Sunni Muslims would upset the country's precarious sectarian-religious political balance. The growing refugee population has remained shoe-horned into 12 over-crowded camps whose confines have barely been allowed to expand since 1948. Palestinians are not allowed to own property, face tight restrictions on extending their homes, are barred from many professions, and are largely prevented from travel.

The Lebanese government accused Palestinian militants of the Fatah al-Islam faction of bombing two buses in a Christian town in February 2007, killing three; the attack was one day prior to the two-year anniversary of the Hariri assassination. The government also accused the group of several bank robberies throughout early 2007. Following arrests

of faction members for one such robbery in May, Fatah al-Islam militants holed up in the Nahr al-Bared refugee camp fired on Lebanese soldiers with rocket-propelled grenades and machine guns. The army responded with indiscriminate shelling and fighting lasted for the next 15 weeks. An estimated 35,000–40,000 Palestinian civilians fled the camp during the conflict, in which 40 civilians died along with 168 Lebanese soldiers; around 400 militants were captured or killed as the army eventually prevailed. In October the first of the camp's residents were allowed to return, many finding their houses destroyed and some complaining that the army had looted their property.

Syria

Instability in Iraq indirectly led to more violence between Syrian Kurds and state authorities in 2007. As Turkish anger over cross-border Kurdish rebel incursions from northern Iraq increased over the course of the year and Turkey massed troops at the frontier, Syrian President Bashar al-Assad visited Ankara to express his support. With the crisis mounting, in early November around 200 Syrian Kurds took to the streets in the north-eastern town of Qamishli, near the Turkish and Iraqi borders, to express their support for Iraqi Kurds. Government security forces broke up the rally with bullets and teargas, killing one young Kurd and injuring four others. Thousands of Kurds attended the funeral of the Kurdish youth the following day. The incident raised the prospect of clashes on the scale of those in 2004, when security services cracked down on rioting fuelled by resentment over the continuing stateless status of an estimated 300,000 Kurds in Syria. In the end, 38 Kurds were dead and some 1,000 arrested.

Saudi Arabia

State and societal intolerance of religious minorities continues to be standard practice in Saudi Arabia, although the government introduced some steps in 2007 to improve the situation. Saudi Arabia has no legal guarantees for freedom of religion. Beyond non-Muslims, Muslims who do not share ultra-conservative interpretations of Sunni Islam continue to face harassment, arrest and torture at the hands of the country's *mutawwa'in* religious police for practising their faith. In the past, this has particularly led to tension in concentrated areas of

Shia and Isma'ili Muslim practice, especially in Eastern and Najran provinces, respectively. Shia mosques are required to issue the Sunni call to prayers. According the US Commission on International Religious Freedom (USCIRF), extremist schoolteachers have berated Shia children about their alleged heresy and, in January 2007, a prominent cleric of the government's council of religious elders called for the expulsion of all Shia from Muslim countries.

Like all women, minority women are subjected to extreme Sunni interpretations of Islamic law (Sharia). This includes a strict conservative dress code, a ban on driving and the prohibition of 'illegal mingling' between unmarried or unrelated men and women. In October 2006, a Saudi court convicted a Shia woman who had been gang raped because she had been in a car with an unrelated male at the time they were both attacked and sexually assaulted. In November 2007 the court banished the female victim's lawyer from the courtroom and doubled her sentence, to 200 lashes and six months in prison, for 'her attempt to aggravate and influence the judiciary through the media'.

There have been recent incipient reforms to Saudi Arabia's religious regime. In December 2006, the government established a new Human Rights Council (HRC). According to USCIRF, whilst women are entirely excluded, the new 24-member body does include one Shia and one Isma'ili Muslim. It has a mandate to educate government institutions, including the *mutawwa'in*, about human rights and, by decree of the king, government ministries are required to reply to all HRC complaints within three weeks. Meanwhile, in Eastern province, the government eased restrictions on the public celebration of Shia holidays, and in March 2007 the government announced that schoolteachers espousing extremist views would lose their jobs.

Yemen

Yemen's Jews are the country's only indigenous religious minority. Once 50,000–60,000 strong, following the founding of Israel in 1948, most Yemeni Jews emigrated. The lifting of a subsequent travel ban in 1992 led to a further wave of emigration, and only 300–500 Jewish people remain in Yemen today. There are only two or three synagogues still active, as well as two private schools where Jewish pupils can learn Hebrew in addition to their Arabic mother tongue.

The Jewish community has long been widely accepted in Yemen, and its remaining members – many of them elderly – are reluctant to leave. However, in 2007 followers of the deceased extremist Muslim cleric Hussein Badr Eddin al-Houthi issued direct threats to the Jews of the Al-Salem village in northern Yemen. The al-Houthi group seeks re-imposition in the north of Zaydi clerical rule. Since 2004 al-Houthi militants have clashed with the army of predominantly Sunni Muslim Yemen. In January, al-Houthi members issued written warnings to the 45 Jews of Al-Salem, giving them ten days to leave. The government responded by relocating the threatened group to the nearby town of Sa'ada and launched an offensive against the militants. Amid increased fighting in the area, the government again relocated the displaced Jews, this time to the capital, Sana'a, and has provided them with housing and other assistance. Members of the group have expressed a desire to return to their village of Al-Salem. ∎

Reference

Compiled by Marusca Perazzi

Notes to Table 1

Sources of the indicators are as follows:

- *Conflict indicators*: The base data used was Monty G. Marshall, 'Major episodes of political violence 1946–2007' (Center for Systemic Peace, 2007) and, for self-determination conflicts, Monty G. Marshall and Ted R. Gurr, 'Peace and conflict 2005' (CIDCM, University of Maryland, 2005), updated for 2007 using figures from Center for Systemic Peace, MRG and the Heidelberg Institute for International Conflict Research. Self-determination conflicts in 2007 were ranked on a scale of 0–5 as follows: 5 = ongoing armed conflict; 4 = contained armed conflict; 3 = settled armed conflict; 2 = militant politics; 1 = conventional politics. Major armed conflicts were classified as 2 = ongoing in late 2007; 1 = emerging from conflict since 2004 or ongoing conflict with deaths under 1,000.
- *Prior genocide or politicide*: Harff, US Political Instability Task Force (formerly State Failure Task Force). 1 = one or more episodes since 1945.
- *Indicators of group division*: Failed States Index, Fund for Peace and the Carnegie Endowment for International Peace, 2007.
- *Democracy/governance indicators*: Annual Governance Indicators, World Bank, 2007.
- *OECD country risk classification*: Organisation for Economic Co-operation and Development, 'Country risk classifications of the participants to the arrangement on officially supported export credits', October 2007. Where no classification is given, a value of 8 was accorded.

Indicators were rebased as necessary to give an equal weighting to the five categories above, with the exception of the prior geno-/politicide indicator. As a dichotomous variable this received a lesser weighting to avoid too great a distortion to the final ranking. Resulting values were then summed.

The full formula is:

$$(A/2) + (B \times 1.25) + (C \times 2) + (D+E+F)/6 + (G+H+I)/-1 + (J \times 0.625)$$

Note that Israel/Occupied Palestinian Territories is ranked artificially low as some of the indicators only apply to the state of Israel and not to the OPT.

See the chapter 'Peoples under Threat' for a description of the methodology for the choice of indicators. Responsibility for the table and any errors or omissions remains with Minority Rights Group International.

Country	Group	Conflict indicators		
		A. Self-determination conflicts	B. Major armed conflict	C. Prior genocide/politicide

Table 1
Peoples under threat 2008

Country	Group	A. Self-determination conflicts	B. Major armed conflict	C. Prior genocide/politicide
Somalia	Darood, Hawiye, Issaq and other clans; Ogadenis; Bantu; Gabooye (Midgan) and other 'caste' groups	4	2	1
Iraq	Shia, Sunnis, Kurds, Turkomans, Christians, Mandaeans, Yezidis, Shabak, Faili Kurds, Baha'is, Palestinians	5	2	1
Sudan	Fur, Zaghawa, Massalit and others in Darfur; Dinka, Nuer and others in the South; Nuba, Beja	5	2	1
Afghanistan	Hazara, Pashtun, Tajiks, Uzbeks, Turkmen, Baluchis	4	2	1
Burma/Myanmar	Kachin, Karenni, Karen, Mons, Rakhine, Rohingyas, Shan, Chin (Zomis), Wa	5	2	1
Dem. Rep. of the Congo	Hema and Lendu, Hunde, Hutu, Luba, Lunda, Tutsi/Banyamulenge, Twa/Mbuti	2	2	1
Pakistan	Ahmaddiya, Baluchis, Hindus, Mohhajirs, Pashtun, Sindhis, other religious minorities	5	2	1
Nigeria	Ibo, Ijaw, Ogoni, Yoruba, Hausa (Muslims) and Christians in the North	5	2	1
Ethiopia	Anuak, Afars, Oromo, Somalis, smaller minorities	5	1	1
Chad	'Black African' groups, Arabs, Southerners	3	2	0
Sri Lanka	Tamils, Muslims	5	2	1
Iran	Arabs, Azeris, Baha'is, Baluchis, Kurds, Turkomans	5	0	1
Central African Republic	Kaba (Sara), Mboum, Mbororo, Aka	0	2	0
Lebanon	Druze, Maronite Christians, Palestinians, Shia, Sunnis	5	1	0
Côte d'Ivoire	Northern Mande (Dioula), Senoufo, Bete, newly settled groups	0	1	0
Uganda	Acholi, Karamojong	1	2	1
Angola	Bakongo, Cabindans, Ovimbundu, Pastoralists, San and Kwisi	4	0	1
Philippines	Indigenous peoples, Moros (Muslims), Chinese	5	2	1
Burundi	Hutu, Tutsi, Twa	0	1	1
Haiti	Political/social targets	0	2	0
Nepal	Madheshis (Terai), Dalits, linguistic minorities	2	1	0
Zimbabwe	Ndebele, Europeans, political/ social targets	2	0	0
Indonesia	Acehnese, Chinese, Dayaks, Madurese, Papuans	4	1	1

Indicators of group division			Democracy/governance indicators				Total
D. Massive movement – refugees and IDPs	E. Legacy of vengeance – group grievance	F. Rise of factionalized elites	G. Voice and accountability	H. Political stability	I. Rule of law	J. OECD country risk classification	
9	7.4	8.7	-2.07	-2.75	-2.53	7	22.81
9	8.3	10	-1.54	-2.89	-1.95	7	22.56
9.8	7.8	8.7	-1.76	-2.18	-1.33	7	21.56
8.9	8	8	-1.31	-2.29	-2.00	7	20.89
8.5	6.3	7.5	-2.28	-0.69	-1.45	7	20.10
8.9	9	9.1	-1.62	-2.31	-1.68	7	19.87
8.5	6.9	9.3	-1.17	-1.92	-0.82	6	19.16
5.6	6.5	8.3	-0.78	-1.99	-1.28	6	18.90
7.9	6	8.9	-1.08	-1.82	-0.64	7	17.77
8.9	7.1	9.4	-1.39	-1.81	-1.36	7	17.62
8.6	9.5	9.2	-0.35	-1.61	0.01	5	16.63
8.6	7.3	9.1	-1.33	-1.25	-0.78	6	15.71
8.4	8.8	10	-1.06	-1.69	-1.55	7	15.59
8.6	7.5	9.2	-0.51	-1.76	-0.49	7	15.29
8.3	7.7	9.1	-1.44	-2.09	-1.54	7	15.26
9.4	6.9	8.1	-0.54	-1.18	-0.5	6	15.25
7.5	6.3	8.1	-1.25	-0.85	-1.29	7	15.25
5.7	6.5	9.2	0.18	-1.26	-0.48	5	15.14
8.9	7.1	8.6	-1.04	-1.35	-0.96	7	14.83
4.2	7.7	8.5	-1.11	-1.54	-1.56	7	14.67
5.2	5.6	8	-1.15	-2.26	-0.68	7	14.48
8.7	6.4	7.9	-1.58	-1.18	-1.71	7	14.26
7.5	6.3	8.8	-0.25	-1.17	-0.82	5	14.07

Table 1 (continued)
Peoples under threat 2008

Country	Group	A. Self-determination conflicts	B. Major armed conflict	C. Prior genocide/politicide
Russian Federation	Chechens, Ingush, Lezgins, indigenous northern peoples, Roma, Jews	5	1	1
Uzbekistan	Tajiks, Islamic political groups, religious minorities, Karakalpaks, Russians	1	0	0
Bosnia and Herzegovina	Croats, Bosniac Muslims, Serbs, Roma	4	0	1
Serbia	Ethnic Albanians, Croats, Roma, Ashkali, Serbs and other minorities in Kosovo	4	0	1
Yemen	Zaydi Shia	0	2	0
Syria	Kurds	0	0	1
Colombia	Political/social targets, Afro-descendants, indigenous peoples	3	2	0
Equatorial Guinea	Bubi, Annobon Islanders	2	0	1
Rwanda	Hutu, Tutsi, Twa	0	0	1
Cambodia	Cham, Vietnamese, indigenous hill tribes (Khmer Leou)	0	0	1
Laos	Hmong, other highland peoples	4	0	0
Turkey	Kurds, Alevis, Roma, Armenians and other Christians	5	2	0
Bangladesh	Ahmaddiya, Hindus, other religious minorities; Biharis, Chittagong Hill Tribes	3	0	0
Azerbaijan	Armenians	4	0	0
Guinea	Fulani, Malinke	0	0	0
Algeria	Berbers, Saharawi	2	1	1
Djibouti	Afars	3	0	0
North Korea	Political/social targets, religious minorities	0	0	0
Tajikistan	Uzbeks, Russians	0	0	0
Kyrgyzstan	Uzbeks, Russians	1	0	0
Eritrea	Afars, Saho, Tigre, religious minorities	0	0	0
Cameroon	Westerners	2	0	0
Congo, Republic of	Lari, M'Boshi, Aka	0	0	0
Turkmenistan	Uzbeks, Russians, Kazakhs, religious minorities	0	0	0
Moldova	Trans-Dniester Slavs	4	0	0
Liberia	Dan, Krahn, Ma, other groups	0	0	0
China	Tibetans, Uyghurs, Mongols, Hui, religious minorities	4	0	1
Kenya	Borana, Kalenjin, Kikuyu, Luyha, Luo, Muslims, Turkana, Endorois, Masai, Ogiek, other indigenous groups	0	1	0
Georgia	Adzhars, Abkhazians, South Ossetians	4	0	0

Indicators of group division			Democracy/governance indicators				Total
D. Massive movement – refugees and IDPs	E. Legacy of vengeance – group grievance	F. Rise of factionalized elites	G. Voice and accountability	H. Political stability	I. Rule of law	J. OECD country risk classification	
5.9	7.5	9.2	-0.87	-0.74	-0.91	3	13.83
5.4	6.8	9.4	-1.86	-1.94	-1.44	7	13.73
8	8.6	8.7	-0.18	-0.52	-0.53	7	13.71
8	7.5	9.6	0.05	-0.69	-0.59	7	13.56
6.7	6.4	9.4	-1.06	-1.4	-0.98	6	13.52
8.9	7.5	8.2	-1.64	-0.88	-0.55	7	13.51
9.5	6.9	9.2	-0.25	-1.62	-0.64	4	13.24
2	6.3	9.8	-1.8	0.15	-1.21	7	13.15
7	8	8.9	-1.14	-0.53	-0.59	7	12.62
5.9	7.3	7	-0.98	-0.48	-1.11	7	12.31
5.5	6.3	9.7	-1.58	0.09	-0.98	7	12.28
5.8	7.3	9.1	-0.19	-0.65	0.08	5	12.27
5.8	7.6	8.7	-0.52	-1.4	-0.86	6	12.18
7.5	6	9.6	-1.14	-1.07	-0.86	5	11.91
6.5	6.1	9.2	-1.15	-1.72	-1.4	7	11.76
6.7	6.4	9.2	-0.83	-0.89	-0.63	3	11.74
6.5	5.5	6.9	-0.99	-0.2	-0.8	8	11.64
6	7.2	8	-2.19	-0.24	-1.28	7	11.60
6.1	6.2	9.5	-1.27	-1.3	-1.06	7	11.54
6.2	5.4	9.7	-0.7	-1.2	-1.18	7	11.37
7.1	5.4	9.2	-1.81	-0.87	-0.99	7	11.33
6.8	5.1	8.2	-1.02	-0.22	-1.02	7	11.27
7.3	6.8	7.2	-1.1	-0.97	-1.25	7	11.25
4.5	4.9	9.8	-2.00	-0.27	-1.44	7	11.24
4.7	7.3	7.5	-0.48	-0.48	-0.61	7	11.20
8.5	7.3	7.9	-0.55	-1.22	-1.16	7	11.16
5.1	7.4	8.4	-1.66	-0.37	-0.4	2	11.11
8	6.7	8.4	-0.18	-1.09	-0.98	6	11.10
6.8	7.6	7.8	-0.16	-0.86	-0.61	6	11.08

Table 1 (continued)
Peoples under threat 2008

Country	Group	A. Self-determination conflicts	B. Major armed conflict	C. Prior genocide/politicide
Ecuador	Afro-descendants, indigenous peoples	2	0	0
Thailand	Chinese, Malay-Muslims, Northern Hill Tribes	5	2	0
Niger	Djerema-songhai, Hausa, Tuaregs	3	0	0
Israel/OPT	Palestinians in Gaza/West Bank, Israeli Palestinians	5	2	0
Togo	Ewe, Kabre	0	0	0
Bolivia	Indigenous Highland, Indigenous Lowland, Afro-Bolivians	2	0	0
Guatemala	Indigenous peoples, Garifuna	0	0	1
Belarus	Poles	0	0	0
Venezuela	Indigenous peoples, Afro-descendants	0	0	0
Sierra Leone	All groups incl. Krio, Limba, Mende, Temne	0	0	0
Vietnam	Montagnards (Degar), other highland peoples, religious minorities	2	0	1
Nicaragua	Indigenous peoples, Creoles	3	0	0
India	Assamese, Bodos, Nagas, Tripuras, other Adivasis, Kashmiris, Sikhs, Muslims, Dalits	5	2	0
Cuba	Political/social targets, Afro-Cubans	0	0	0
Papua New Guinea	Bounganvilleans	3	0	0
Mauritania	Black Moors, Kewri	0	0	0
Libya	Political/social targets, Berbers	0	0	0
Macedonia	Albanians, Roma, Serbs	3	0	0

Indicators of group division			Democracy/governance indicators				Total
D. Massive movement – refugees and IDPs	E. Legacy of vengeance – group grievance	F. Rise of factionalized elites	G. Voice and accountability	H. Political stability	I. Rule of law	J. OECD country risk classification	
6	5.6	8.6	-0.35	-0.9	-0.96	7	10.97
5.8	6.3	9.2	0.5	-0.99	0.03	3	10.94
5.9	8.9	6	-0.24	-0.35	-0.87	7	10.80
7.9	9	7.2	0.68	-1.18	0.69	3	10.70
5.4	7	7.9	-1.24	-0.86	-1.03	7	10.67
3.7	7	8.3	-0.14	-0.93	-0.9	7	10.51
6	7.4	9.1	-0.29	-0.82	-1.02	5	10.42
4.6	7	9.4	-1.71	0.16	-1.16	7	10.35
5.2	6.8	7.2	-0.58	-1.24	-1.39	6	10.21
7.4	7.5	8.6	-0.43	-0.46	-1.21	7	10.18
5.9	5.6	6.4	-1.45	0.42	-0.43	4	9.99
5.1	6.4	7.2	0.22	-0.44	-0.76	7	9.97
3.2	5.4	6.8	0.35	-0.84	0.17	3	9.83
4.7	6.3	8.6	-1.55	0.12	-0.91	7	9.72
3.5	8	6.7	-0.05	-0.8	-0.94	5	9.45
6.2	8	7.9	-0.95	0.29	-0.43	7	9.15
2.6	5.6	8	-1.9	0.24	-0.74	6	8.85
4.7	7.1	6.4	-0.07	-0.66	-0.46	5	8.85

	International Convention on the Prevention and Punishment of the Crime of Genocide 1948	International Convention on the Elimination of All Forms of Racial Discrimination 1965	International Covenant on Civil and Political Rights 1966	International Covenant on Economic, Social and Cultural Rights 1966
Africa				
Algeria	■	■▶	■●	■
Angola			■●	■
Benin		■	■●	■
Botswana		■	■	
Burkina Faso	■	■	■●	■
Burundi	■	■	■	■
Cameroon		■	■●	■
Cape Verde		■	■●	■
Central African Republic		■	■●	■
Chad		■	■●	■
Comoros	■	■		
Congo		■	■●	■
Côte d'Ivoire	■	■	■●	■
Democratic Republic of the Congo			■	■
Djibouti			■●	■
Egypt	■	■	■	■
Equatorial Guinea		■	■●	■
Eritrea		■		■
Ethiopia	■	■	■	■
Gabon	■	■	■	■
Gambia	■	■	■●	■
Ghana	■	■	■●	■
Guinea	■	■	■●	■
Guinea Bissau		□	□	■
Kenya		■	■	■
Lesotho	■	■	■●	■
Liberia	■	■	■○	
Libyan Arab Jamahiriya	■	■	■●	■
Madagascar		■	■●	■
Malawi		■		■
Mali	■	■	■●	■
Mauritania		■		■
Mauritius		■	■●	■
Morocco	■	■▶	■	■
Mozambique	■	■	■	
Namibia	■	■	■●	■
Niger		■	■●	■

Status of ratification of major international and regional instruments relevant to minority and indigenous rights

as of October 2007

■ Ratification, accession or succession.

□ Signature not yet followed by ratification.

■▶ Ratification of ICERD and Declaration on Article 14.

■▷ Ratification of ICERD and Signature of Declaration on Article 14.

■● Ratification of ICCPR and Optional Protocol.

■○ Ratification of ICCPR and Signature of Optional Protocol.

□○ Signature of ICCPR and Optional Protocol.

Convention on the Elimination of All Forms of Discrimination against Women 1979	Convention on the Rights of the Child 1989	ILO 111 Discrimination (Employment and Occupation) Convention, 1958	ILO 169 Convention Concerning Indigenous and Tribal Peoples in Independent Countries 1989	International Convention on the Protection of the Rights of All Migrant Workers and Members of Their Families 1990	ICC Rome Statute of the International Criminal Court 1998	African Charter on Human and Peoples' Rights 2003	African Charter on the Rights and Welfare of the Child 1990
■	■	■		■	□	■	■
					□		
■	■	■		□	■	■	■
■					■	■	
■	■	■		■	■	■	■
	■				■	■	
■	■	■			□	■	■
■	■	■		■	□	■	■
	■				■	■	□
■	■	■			■	■	■
■	■	■		□	■	■	
	■				■	■	
	■				□	■	
	■				■		
■	■	■			■	■	□
■	■	■		■	□	■	■
	■					■	
	■				□	■	
■	■	■				■	■
■	■	■		□	■	■	■
■	■	■			■	■	
■	■	■		■		■	□
■	■	■		■		■	
■	■	■		□	□	■	□
■	■	■				■	
■	■	■		■	■	■	
■	■	■		□		■	□
■	■	■		■		■	
■	■	■			□	■	□
■	■	■			■	■	■
■	■	■		■	■	■	■
■	■	■				■	
■		■		■			■
■	■	■		■	□		
■	■	■			□	■	■
■	■	■			■	■	□
■	■	■			■	■	■

Status of ratification of major international and regional instruments relevant to minority and indigenous rights

as of October 2007

■ Ratification, accession or succession.

□ Signature not yet followed by ratification.

■▶ Ratification of ICERD and Declaration on Article 14.

■▷ Ratification of ICERD and Signature of Declaration on Article 14.

■● Ratification of ICCPR and Optional Protocol.

■○ Ratification of ICCPR and Signature of Optional Protocol.

□○ Signature of ICCPR and Optional Protocol.

	Genocide 1948	ICERD 1965	ICCPR 1966	ICESCR 1966
Nigeria		■	■	■
Rwanda	■	■	■	■
Sahrawi Arab Democratic Republic				
São Tomé and Príncipe		□	□ ○	□
Senegal	■	■ ▶	■ ●	■
Seychelles	■	■	■	■
Sierra Leone		■	■	■
Somalia		■	■	■
South Africa	■	■ ▶	■ ●	□
Sudan	■	■	■	■
Swaziland		■	■	■
Togo	■	■	■ ●	■
Tunisia	■	■	■	■
Uganda	■	■	■ ●	■
United Republic of Tanzania	■	■	■	■
Zambia		■	■ ●	■
Zimbabwe	■	■	■	■
Americas				
Antigua and Barbuda	■	■		
Argentina	■	■ ▶	■ ●	■
Bahamas	■	■		
Barbados	■	■	■ ●	■
Belize	■	■	■	□
Bolivia	■	■ ▶	■ ●	■
Brazil	■	■ ▶	■	■
Canada	■	■	■ ●	■
Chile	■	■ ▶	■ ●	■
Colombia	■	■	■ ●	■
Costa Rica	■	■ ▶	■ ●	■
Cuba	■	■		
Dominica			■	■

Convention on the Elimination of All Forms of Discrimination against Women 1979	Convention on the Rights of the Child 1989	ILO 111 Discrimination (Employment and Occupation) Convention, 1958	ILO 169 Convention Concerning Indigenous and Tribal Peoples in Independent Countries 1989	International Convention on the Protection of the Rights of All Migrant Workers and Members of Their Families 1990	ICC Rome Statute of the International Criminal Court 1998	African Charter on Human and Peoples' Rights 2003	African Charter on the Rights and Welfare of the Child 1990
■	■	■			■	■	■
■	■	■				■	■
						■	□
■	■	■		□	□	■	
■	■	■		■		■	
■	■	■		■	□	■	
■	■	■		□	■	■	■
	□					■	□
■	■	■			■	■	
	■				□	■	
■	■	■				■	□
■	■	■		□		■	■
	■	■				■	□
■	■	■		■	■	■	
	■	■			■	■	
■	■	■			■	■	□
■	■	■			□	■	■

						American Convention on Human Rights 1969	Additional Protocol to the American Convention on Human Rights in the area of Economic, Social and Cultural Rights 1988
■	■	■			■		
■	■	■	■	■	■	■	■
■	■	■			□		
■	■	■				■	
■	■	■		■	■		
■	■	■	■	■	■	■	□
■	■	■	■		■	■	■
■	■	■			■		
■	■	■		■	□	■	□
■	■	■	■	■	■	■	■
■	■	■	■		■	■	■
■	■	■					
■	■	■	■		■	■	

Status of ratification of major international and regional instruments relevant to minority and indigenous rights

as of October 2007

■ Ratification, accession or succession.

□ Signature not yet followed by ratification.

■▶ Ratification of ICERD and Declaration on Article 14.

■▷ Ratification of ICERD and Signature of Declaration on Article 14.

■● Ratification of ICCPR and Optional Protocol.

■○ Ratification of ICCPR and Signature of Optional Protocol.

□○ Signature of ICCPR and Optional Protocol.

	International Convention on the Prevention and Punishment of the Crime of Genocide 1948	International Convention on the Elimination of All Forms of Racial Discrimination 1965	International Covenant on Civil and Political Rights 1966	International Covenant on Economic, Social and Cultural Rights 1966
Dominican Republic	□	■	■●	■
Ecuador	■	■▶	■●	■
El Salvador	■	■	■●	■
Grenada			■	■
Guatemala	■	■	■●	■
Guyana		■	■●	■
Haití	■	■	■	
Honduras	■	■	■●	■
Jamaica	■	■	■●	■
México	■	■▶	■●	■
Nicaragua	■	■	■●	■
Panamá	■	■	■●	■
Paraguay	■	■	■●	■
Perú		■▶	■●	■
Saint Kitts and Nevis		■		
Saint Lucia		■		
Saint Vincent and the Grenadines	□	■	■●	■
Suriname		■	■●	■
Trinidad and Tobago	■	■	■●	■
United States of America	■	■	■	□
Uruguay	■	■▶	■●	■
Venezuela	■	■▶	■●	■
Asia				
Afghanistan	■	■	■	■
Bangladesh	■	■	■	■
Bhutan		□		
Brunei Darussalam				
Cambodia	■	■	■○	■
China	■	■	□	■
Democratic People's Republic of Korea	■		■	■
India	■	■	■	■
Indonesia		■	■	■
Japan		■	■	■
Kazakhstan	■	■	■○	■
Kyrgyzstan	■	■	■●	■
Lao People's Democratic Republic	■	■	□	■

Convention on the Elimination of All Forms of Discrimination against Women 1979	Convention on the Rights of the Child 1989	ILO 111 Discrimination (Employment and Occupation) Convention, 1958	ILO 169 Convention Concerning Indigenous and Tribal Peoples in Independent Countries 1989	International Convention on the Protection of the Rights of All Migrant Workers and Members of Their Families 1990	ICC Rome Statute of the International Criminal Court 1998	American Convention on Human Rights 1969	Additional Protocol to the American Convention on Human Rights in the area of Economic, Social and Cultural Rights 1988
■	■	■			■	■	□
■	■	■	■	■	■	■	■
■	■	■		■		■	■
■	■	■				■	
■	■	■	■	■		■	■
■	■	■		□	■		
■	■	■			□	■	□
■	■	■	■	■		■	□
■	■	■			□		□
■	■	■	■	■	■	■	■
■	■	■		■		■	□
■	■	■			■	■	■
■	■	■	■	□	■	■	■
■	■	■	■	■	■	■	■
■	■	■			■		
■	■	■			□		
■	■	■			■		
■	■					■	■
■	■	■			■	■	
□	□				□	□	
■	■	■		■	■	■	■
■	■	■	■		■	■	□
■		■			■		
■	■	■		□	□		
■	■						
■	■						
■	■	■		□	■		
■	■	■					
■	■						
■	■	■					
■	■	■		□			
					■		
■	■	■	■	■	□		
■	■						

Status of ratification of major international and regional instruments relevant to minority and indigenous rights

as of October 2007

■ Ratification, accession or succession.

□ Signature not yet followed by ratification.

■► Ratification of ICERD and Declaration on Article 14.

■▷ Ratification of ICERD and Signature of Declaration on Article 14.

■● Ratification of ICCPR and Optional Protocol.

■○ Ratification of ICCPR and Signature of Optional Protocol.

□○ Signature of ICCPR and Optional Protocol.

	International Convention on the Prevention and Punishment of the Crime of Genocide 1948	International Convention on the Elimination of All Forms of Racial Discrimination 1965	International Covenant on Civil and Political Rights 1966	International Covenant on Economic, Social and Cultural Rights 1966
Malaysia	■			
Maldives	■	■	■●	■
Mongolia	■	■	■●	■
Myanmar	■			
Nepal	■	■	■●	■
Pakistan	■	■		■
Philippines	■	■	■●	■
Republic of Korea	■	■►	■●	■
Singapore	■			
Sri Lanka	■	■	■●	■
Tajikistan		■	■●	■
Thailand		■	■	■
Timor Leste		■	■	■
Turkmenistan		■	■●	■
Uzbekistan	■	■	■●	■
Viet Nam	■	■	■	■
Europe				
Albania	■	■	■○	■
Andorra	■	■►	■●	
Armenia	■	■	■●	■
Austria	■	■►	■●	■
Azerbaijan	■	■►	■●	■
Belarus	■	■	■●	■
Belgium	■	■►	■●	■
Bosnia and Herzegovina	■	■	■●	■
Bulgaria	■	■►	■●	■
Croatia	■	■	■●	■
Cyprus	■	■►	■●	■
Czech Republic	■	■►	■●	■
Denmark	■	■►	■●	■
Estonia	■	■	■●	■
Finland	■	■►	■●	■
France	■	■►	■●	■
Georgia	■	■►	■●	■

Convention on the Elimination of All Forms of Discrimination against Women 1979	Convention on the Rights of the Child 1989	ILO 111 Discrimination (Employment and Occupation) Convention, 1958	ILO 169 Convention Concerning Indigenous and Tribal Peoples in Independent Countries 1989	International Convention on the Protection of the Rights of All Migrant Workers and Members of Their Families 1990	ICC Rome Statute of the International Criminal Court 1998		
■	■						
■	■						
■	■	■			■		
■	■						
■	■		■				
■	■		■				
■	■			■	□		
■	■				■		
■	■						
■	■	■		■			
■	■	■		■	■		
■	■				□		
■	■			■	■		
■	■	■					
■	■	■			□		
■	■	■					

						European Charter for Regional or Minority Languages 1992	Framework Convention for the Protection of National Minorities 1995
■	■	■		■	■		■
■	■				■		
■		■			□	■	■
■	■	■			■	■	■
■	■	■		■	□		■
■	■	■					
■	■	■			■		□
■	■	■		■	□	□	
■	■	■			■		■
■	■	■			■	■	■
■	■	■			□	■	■
■	■	■			■	■	■
■	■	■	■				
■	■	■			■	■	■
■	■	■			■	□	
■	■	■			■		■

Status of ratification of major international and regional instruments relevant to minority and indigenous rights

as of October 2007

■ Ratification, accession or succession.

□ Signature not yet followed by ratification.

■▶ Ratification of ICERD and Declaration on Article 14.

■▷ Ratification of ICERD and Signature of Declaration on Article 14.

■● Ratification of ICCPR and Optional Protocol.

■○ Ratification of ICCPR and Signature of Optional Protocol.

□○ Signature of ICCPR and Optional Protocol.

	International Convention on the Prevention and Punishment of the Crime of Genocide 1948	International Convention on the Elimination of All Forms of Racial Discrimination 1965	International Covenant on Civil and Political Rights 1966	International Covenant on Economic, Social and Cultural Rights 1966
Germany	■	■▶	■●	■
Greece	■	■	■●	■
Holy See		■		
Hungary	■	■▶	■●	■
Iceland	■	■▶	■●	■
Ireland	■	■▶	■●	■
Italy		■▶	■●	■
Latvia	■	■	■●	■
Liechtenstein	■	■▶		
Lithuania	■	■	■●	■
Luxembourg	■	■▶	■●	■
Malta		■▶	■●	■
Monaco	■	■▶	■	■
Montenegro	■	■▶	■●	■
Netherlands	■	■▶	■●	■
Norway	■	■▶	■●	■
Poland	■	■▶	■●	■
Portugal	■	■▶	■●	■
Republic of Moldova	■	■	■○	■
Romania	■	■▶	■●	■
Russian Federation	■	■▶	■●	■
San Marino		■	■●	■
Serbia	■	■▶	■●	■
Slovakia	■	■▶	■●	■
Slovenia	■	■▶	■●	■
Spain	■	■▶	■●	■
Sweden	■	■▶	■●	■
Switzerland	■	■▶	■●	■
The former Yugoslav Republic of Macedonia	■	■▶	■●	
Turkey	■	■	■○	■
Ukraine	■	■▶	■●	■
United Kingdom of Great Britain and Northern Ireland	■	■	■	■
Middle East				
Bahrain	■	■	■	■
Iran (Islamic Republic of)	■	■	■	■

Convention on the Elimination of All Forms of Discrimination against Women 1979	Convention on the Rights of the Child 1989	ILO 111 Discrimination (Employment and Occupation) Convention, 1958	ILO 169 Convention Concerning Indigenous and Tribal Peoples in Independent Countries 1989	International Convention on the Protection of the Rights of All Migrant Workers and Members of Their Families 1990	ICC Rome Statute of the International Criminal Court 1998	European Charter for Regional or Minority Languages 1992	Framework Convention for the Protection of National Minorities 1995
■	■	■	■		■	■	■
■	■	■			■		□
		■					
■	■				■	■	■
■	■	■			■	□	□
■	■	■			■		■
■	■	■			■	□	■
■	■	■			■		
■	■	■			■		■
■	■	■			■	■	□
■	■				■	□	■
■	■				□		
■	■	■		□	■	■	■
			■		■	■	■
■	■	■	■		■	■	■
■	■	■			■	□	■
■	■	■			■		■
					□	□	■
■	■	■			■	□	■
■	■	■			□	□	■
■	■				■		■
■	■			□	■	■	■
■	■	■			■	■	■
■	■	■	■		■	■	■
■	■				■	■	■
■	■				■	■	■
■	■	■			■	□	■
	■	■		■			
■	■	■			□	■	■
■	■	■			■	■	■
■	■	■			□		
	■	■			□		

Status of ratification of major international and regional instruments relevant to minority and indigenous rights

as of October 2007

■ Ratification, accession or succession.

□ Signature not yet followed by ratification.

■▶ Ratification of ICERD and Declaration on Article 14.

■▷ Ratification of ICERD and Signature of Declaration on Article 14.

■● Ratification of ICCPR and Optional Protocol.

■○ Ratification of ICCPR and Signature of Optional Protocol.

□○ Signature of ICCPR and Optional Protocol.

	International Convention on the Prevention and Punishment of the Crime of Genocide 1948	International Convention on the Elimination of All Forms of Racial Discrimination 1965	International Covenant on Civil and Political Rights 1966	International Covenant on Economic, Social and Cultural Rights 1966
Iraq	■	■	■	■
Israel	■	■	■	■
Jordan	■	■	■	■
Kuwait	■	■	■	■
Lebanon	■	■	■	■
Oman		■		
Qatar		■		
Saudi Arabia	■	■		
Syrian Arab Republic	■	■	■	■
United Arab Emirates	■	■		
Yemen	■	■	■	■
Oceania				
Australia	■	■▶	■●	■
Cook Islands				
Fiji	■	■		
Kiribati				
Marshall Islands				
Micronesia (Federated States of)				
Nauru		□	□○	
New Zealand	■	■●	■●	■
Niue				
Palau				
Papua New Guinea	■	■		
Samoa				
Solomon Islands			■	■
Tonga	■	■		
Tuvalu				
Vanuatu				

Sources:
http://www.achpr.org/
http://www.cidh.oas.org/
Treaty Office on http://conventions.coe.int/
http://www.iccnow.org/countryinfo/worldsigsandratifications.html
http://www.oas.org/juridico/english/Sigs/b32.html
http://www2.ohchr.org/english/bodies/docs/RatificationStatus.pdf
http://www.unhchr.ch/tbs/doc.nsf/Statusfrset?OpenFrameSet

Convention on the Elimination of All Forms of Discrimination against Women 1979	Convention on the Rights of the Child 1989	ILO 111 Discrimination (Employment and Occupation) Convention, 1958	ILO 169 Convention Concerning Indigenous and Tribal Peoples in Independent Countries 1989	International Convention on the Protection of the Rights of All Migrant Workers and Members of Their Families 1990	ICC Rome Statute of the International Criminal Court 1998		
■	■	■					
■	■	■			□		
■	■	■			■		
■	■	■			□		
■	■	■					
■	■				□		
■	■	■					
■	■	■		■	□		
■	■	■			□		
■	■	■			□		
■	■	■			■		
■	■						
■	■	■	■		■		
■	■						
■	■				■		
■	■						
	■						
■	■	■			■		
	■						
	■						
■	■	■			■		
■	■				■		
■	■				□		
	■						
■	■						
■	■	■					

Appendices
New Minority Protection Standards or Mechanisms in 2007

United Nations Declaration on the Rights of Indigenous Peoples

The General Assembly,

Guided by the purposes and principles of the Charter of the United Nations, and good faith in the fulfilment of the obligations assumed by States in accordance with the Charter,

Affirming that indigenous peoples are equal to all other peoples, while recognizing the right of all peoples to be different, to consider themselves different, and to be respected as such,

Affirming also that all peoples contribute to the diversity and richness of civilizations and cultures, which constitute the common heritage of humankind,

Affirming further that all doctrines, policies and practices based on or advocating superiority of peoples or individuals on the basis of national origin or racial, religious, ethnic or cultural differences are racist, scientifically false, legally invalid, morally condemnable and socially unjust,

Reaffirming that indigenous peoples, in the exercise of their rights, should be free from discrimination of any kind,

Concerned that indigenous peoples have suffered from historic injustices as a result of, inter alia, their colonization and dispossession of their lands, territories and resources, thus preventing them from exercising, in particular, their right to development in accordance with their own needs and interests,

Recognizing the urgent need to respect and promote the inherent rights of indigenous peoples which derive from their political, economic and social structures and from their cultures, spiritual traditions, histories and philosophies, especially their rights to their lands, territories and resources,

Recognizing also the urgent need to respect and promote the rights of indigenous peoples affirmed in treaties, agreements and other constructive arrangements with States,

Welcoming the fact that indigenous peoples are organizing themselves for political, economic, social and cultural enhancement and in order to bring to an end all forms of discrimination and oppression wherever they occur,

Convinced that control by indigenous peoples over developments affecting them and their lands, territories and resources will enable them to maintain and strengthen their institutions, cultures and traditions, and to promote their development in accordance with their aspirations and needs,

Recognizing that respect for indigenous knowledge, cultures and traditional practices contributes to sustainable and equitable development and proper management of the environment,

Emphasizing the contribution of the demilitarization of the lands and territories of indigenous peoples to peace, economic and social progress and development, understanding and friendly relations among nations and peoples of the world,

Recognizing in particular the right of indigenous families and communities to retain shared responsibility for the upbringing, training, education and well-being of their children, consistent with the rights of the child,

Considering that the rights affirmed in treaties, agreements and other constructive arrangements between States and indigenous peoples are, in some situations, matters of international concern, interest, responsibility and character,

Considering also that treaties, agreements and other constructive arrangements, and the relationship they represent, are the basis for a strengthened partnership between indigenous peoples and States,

Acknowledging that the Charter of the United Nations, the International Covenant on Economic, Social and Cultural Rights[1] and the International Covenant on Civil and Political Rights as well as the Vienna Declaration and Programme of Action,[2] affirm the fundamental importance of the right to self-determination of all peoples, by virtue of which they freely determine their political status and freely pursue their economic, social and cultural development,

Bearing in mind that nothing in this Declaration may be used to deny any peoples their right to self-determination, exercised in conformity with international law,

Convinced that the recognition of the rights of indigenous peoples in this Declaration will enhance harmonious and cooperative relations between the State and indigenous peoples, based on principles of justice, democracy, respect for human rights, non-discrimination and good faith,

Encouraging States to comply with and effectively implement all their obligations as they apply to indigenous peoples under international instruments, in particular those related to human rights, in consultation and cooperation with the peoples concerned,

Emphasizing that the United Nations has an important and continuing role to play in promoting and protecting the rights of indigenous peoples,

Believing that this Declaration is a further important step forward for the recognition, promotion and protection of the rights and freedoms of indigenous peoples and in the development of relevant activities of the United Nations system in this field,

Recognizing and reaffirming that indigenous individuals are entitled without discrimination to all human rights recognized in international law, and that indigenous peoples possess collective rights which are indispensable for their existence, well-being and integral development as peoples,

Recognizing also that the situation of indigenous peoples varies from region to region and from country to country and that the significance of national and regional particularities and various historical and cultural backgrounds should be taken into consideration,

Solemnly proclaims the following United Nations Declaration on the Rights of Indigenous Peoples as a standard of achievement to be pursued in a spirit of partnership and mutual respect:

Article 1
Indigenous peoples have the right to the full enjoyment, as a collective or as individuals, of all human rights and fundamental freedoms as recognized in the Charter of the United Nations, the Universal Declaration of Human Rights[3] and international human rights law.

Article 2
Indigenous peoples and individuals are free and equal to all other peoples and individuals and have the right to be free from any kind of discrimination, in the exercise of their rights, in particular that based on their indigenous origin or identity.

Article 3
Indigenous peoples have the right to self-determination. By virtue of that right they freely determine their political status and freely pursue their economic, social and cultural development.

Article 4
Indigenous peoples, in exercising their right to self-determination, have the right to autonomy or self-government in matters relating to their internal and local affairs, as well as ways and means for financing their autonomous functions.

Article 5
Indigenous peoples have the right to maintain and strengthen their distinct political, legal, economic, social and cultural institutions, while retaining their right to participate fully, if they so choose, in the political, economic, social and cultural life of the State.

Article 6
Every indigenous individual has the right to a nationality.

Article 7
1. Indigenous individuals have the rights to life, physical and mental integrity, liberty and security of person.
2. Indigenous peoples have the collective right to live in freedom, peace and security as distinct peoples and shall not be subjected to any act of genocide or any other act of violence, including forcibly removing children of the group to another group.

Article 8
1. Indigenous peoples and individuals have the right not to be subjected to forced assimilation or destruction of their culture.
2. States shall provide effective mechanisms for prevention of, and redress for:
(a) Any action which has the aim or effect of depriving them of their integrity as distinct peoples, or of their cultural values or ethnic identities;
(b) Any action which has the aim or effect of dispossessing them of their lands, territories or resources;
(c) Any form of forced population transfer which has the aim or effect of violating or undermining any of their rights;
(d) Any form of forced assimilation or integration;
(e) Any form of propaganda designed to promote or incite racial or ethnic discrimination directed against them.

Article 9
Indigenous peoples and individuals have the right to belong to an indigenous community or nation, in

accordance with the traditions and customs of the community or nation concerned. No discrimination of any kind may arise from the exercise of such a right.

Article 10

Indigenous peoples shall not be forcibly removed from their lands or territories. No relocation shall take place without the free, prior and informed consent of the indigenous peoples concerned and after agreement on just and fair compensation and, where possible, with the option of return.

Article 11

1. Indigenous peoples have the right to practise and revitalize their cultural traditions and customs. This includes the right to maintain, protect and develop the past, present and future manifestations of their cultures, such as archaeological and historical sites, artefacts, designs, ceremonies, technologies and visual and performing arts and literature.
2. States shall provide redress through effective mechanisms, which may include restitution, developed in conjunction with indigenous peoples, with respect to their cultural, intellectual, religious and spiritual property taken without their free, prior and informed consent or in violation of their laws, traditions and customs.

Article 12

1. Indigenous peoples have the right to manifest, practice, develop and teach their spiritual and religious traditions, customs and ceremonies; the right to maintain, protect, and have access in privacy to their religious and cultural sites; the right to the use and control of their ceremonial objects; and the right to the repatriation of their human remains.
2. States shall seek to enable the access and/or repatriation of ceremonial objects and human remains in their possession through fair, transparent and effective mechanisms developed in conjunction with indigenous peoples concerned.

Article 13

1. Indigenous peoples have the right to revitalize, use, develop and transmit to future generations their histories, languages, oral traditions, philosophies, writing systems and literatures, and to designate and retain their own names for communities, places and persons.
2. States shall take effective measures to ensure that this right is protected and also to ensure that indigenous peoples can understand and be understood in political, legal and administrative proceedings, where necessary through the provision of interpretation or by other appropriate means.

Article 14

1. Indigenous peoples have the right to establish and control their educational systems and institutions providing education in their own languages, in a manner appropriate to their cultural methods of teaching and learning.
2. Indigenous individuals, particularly children, have the right to all levels and forms of education of the State without discrimination.
3. States shall, in conjunction with indigenous peoples, take effective measures, in order for indigenous individuals, particularly children, including those living outside their communities, to have access, when possible, to an education in their own culture and provided in their own language.

Article 15

1. Indigenous peoples have the right to the dignity and diversity of their cultures, traditions, histories and aspirations which shall be appropriately reflected in education and public information.
2. States shall take effective measures, in consultation and cooperation with the indigenous peoples concerned, to combat prejudice and eliminate discrimination and to promote tolerance, understanding and good relations among indigenous peoples and all other segments of society.

Article 16

1. Indigenous peoples have the right to establish their own media in their own languages and to have access to all forms of non-indigenous media without discrimination.
2. States shall take effective measures to ensure that State-owned media duly reflect indigenous cultural diversity. States, without prejudice to ensuring full freedom of expression, should encourage privately owned media to adequately reflect indigenous cultural diversity.

Article 17

1. Indigenous individuals and peoples have the right to enjoy fully all rights established under applicable international and domestic labour law.
2. States shall in consultation and cooperation with indigenous peoples take specific measures to protect indigenous children from economic exploitation and from performing any work that is likely to be hazardous or to interfere with the child's education, or to be harmful to the child's health or physical, mental, spiritual, moral or social development, taking into account their special vulnerability and the importance of education for their empowerment.
3. Indigenous individuals have the right not to be subjected to any discriminatory conditions of labour and, inter alia, employment or salary.

Article 18

Indigenous peoples have the right to participate in decision-making in matters which would affect their rights, through representatives chosen by themselves in accordance with their own procedures, as well as to maintain and develop their own indigenous decision-making institutions.

Article 19

States shall consult and cooperate in good faith with the indigenous peoples concerned through their own representative institutions in order to obtain their free, prior and informed consent before adopting and implementing legislative or administrative measures that may affect them.

Article 20

1. Indigenous peoples have the right to maintain and develop their political, economic and social systems or institutions, to be secure in the enjoyment of their own means of subsistence and development, and to engage freely in all their traditional and other economic activities.
2. Indigenous peoples deprived of their means of subsistence and development are entitled to just and fair redress.

Article 21

1. Indigenous peoples have the right, without discrimination, to the improvement of their economic and social conditions, including, inter alia, in the areas of education, employment, vocational training and retraining, housing, sanitation, health and social security.
2. States shall take effective measures and, where appropriate, special measures to ensure continuing improvement of their economic and social conditions. Particular attention shall be paid to the rights and special needs of indigenous elders, women, youth, children and persons with disabilities.

Article 22

1. Particular attention shall be paid to the rights and special needs of indigenous elders, women, youth, children and persons with disabilities in the implementation of this Declaration.
2. States shall take measures, in conjunction with indigenous peoples, to ensure that indigenous women and children enjoy the full protection and guarantees against all forms of violence and discrimination.

Article 23

Indigenous peoples have the right to determine and develop priorities and strategies for exercising their right to development. In particular, indigenous peoples have the right to be actively involved in developing and determining health, housing and other economic and social programmes affecting them and, as far as possible, to administer such programmes through their own institutions.

Article 24

1. Indigenous peoples have the right to their traditional medicines and to maintain their health practices, including the conservation of their vital medicinal plants, animals and minerals. Indigenous individuals also have the right to access, without any discrimination, to all social and health services.
2. Indigenous individuals have an equal right to the enjoyment of the highest attainable standard of physical and mental health. States shall take the necessary steps with a view to achieving progressively the full realization of this right.

Article 25

Indigenous peoples have the right to maintain and strengthen their distinctive spiritual relationship with their traditionally owned or otherwise occupied and used lands, territories, waters and coastal seas and other resources and to uphold their responsibilities to future generations in this regard.

Article 26

1. Indigenous peoples have the right to the lands, territories and resources which they have traditionally owned, occupied or otherwise used or acquired.
2. Indigenous peoples have the right to own, use, develop and control the lands, territories and resources that they possess by reason of traditional ownership or other traditional occupation or use, as well as those which they have otherwise acquired.
3. States shall give legal recognition and protection to these lands, territories and resources. Such recognition shall be conducted with due respect to the customs, traditions and land tenure systems of the indigenous peoples concerned.

Article 27

States shall establish and implement, in conjunction with indigenous peoples concerned, a fair, independent, impartial, open and transparent process, giving due recognition to indigenous peoples' laws, traditions, customs and land tenure systems, to recognize and adjudicate the rights of indigenous peoples pertaining to their lands, territories and resources, including those which were traditionally owned or otherwise occupied or used. Indigenous peoples shall have the right to participate in this process.

Article 28

1. Indigenous peoples have the right to redress, by means that can include restitution or, when this is not possible, just, fair and equitable compensation, for the lands, territories and resources which they have traditionally owned or otherwise occupied or used, and which have been confiscated, taken, occupied, used or damaged without their free, prior and informed consent.
2. Unless otherwise freely agreed upon by the peoples concerned, compensation shall take the form of lands, territories and resources equal in quality, size and legal status or of monetary compensation or other appropriate redress.

Article 29

1. Indigenous peoples have the right to the conservation and protection of the environment

and the productive capacity of their lands or territories and resources. States shall establish and implement assistance programmes for indigenous peoples for such conservation and protection, without discrimination.
2. States shall take effective measures to ensure that no storage or disposal of hazardous materials shall take place in the lands or territories of indigenous peoples without their free, prior and informed consent.
3. States shall also take effective measures to ensure, as needed, that programmes for monitoring, maintaining and restoring the health of indigenous peoples, as developed and implemented by the peoples affected by such materials, are duly implemented.

Article 30

1. Military activities shall not take place in the lands or territories of indigenous peoples, unless justified by a significant threat to relevant public interest or otherwise freely agreed with or requested by the indigenous peoples concerned.
2. States shall undertake effective consultations with the indigenous peoples concerned, through appropriate procedures and in particular through their representative institutions, prior to using their lands or territories for military activities.

Article 31

1. Indigenous peoples have the right to maintain, control, protect and develop their cultural heritage, traditional knowledge and traditional cultural expressions, as well as the manifestations of their sciences, technologies and cultures, including human and genetic resources, seeds, medicines, knowledge of the properties of fauna and flora, oral traditions, literatures, designs, sports and traditional games and visual and performing arts. They also have the right to maintain, control, protect and develop their intellectual property over such cultural heritage, traditional knowledge, and traditional cultural expressions.
2. In conjunction with indigenous peoples, States shall take effective measures to recognize and protect the exercise of these rights.

Article 32

1. Indigenous peoples have the right to determine and develop priorities and strategies for the

development or use of their lands or territories and other resources.

2. States shall consult and cooperate in good faith with the indigenous peoples concerned through their own representative institutions in order to obtain their free and informed consent prior to the approval of any project affecting their lands or territories and other resources, particularly in connection with the development, utilization or exploitation of mineral, water or other resources.

3. States shall provide effective mechanisms for just and fair redress for any such activities, and appropriate measures shall be taken to mitigate adverse environmental, economic, social, cultural or spiritual impact.

Article 33

1. Indigenous peoples have the right to determine their own identity or membership in accordance with their customs and traditions. This does not impair the right of indigenous individuals to obtain citizenship of the States in which they live.

2. Indigenous peoples have the right to determine the structures and to select the membership of their institutions in accordance with their own procedures.

Article 34

Indigenous peoples have the right to promote, develop and maintain their institutional structures and their distinctive customs, spirituality, traditions, procedures, practices and, in the cases where they exist, juridical systems or customs, in accordance with international human rights standards.

Article 35

Indigenous peoples have the right to determine the responsibilities of individuals to their communities.

Article 36

1. Indigenous peoples, in particular those divided by international borders, have the right to maintain and develop contacts, relations and cooperation, including activities for spiritual, cultural, political, economic and social purposes, with their own members as well as other peoples across borders.

2. States, in consultation and cooperation with indigenous peoples, shall take effective measures to facilitate the exercise and ensure the implementation of this right.

Article 37

1. Indigenous peoples have the right to the recognition, observance and enforcement of treaties, agreements and other constructive arrangements concluded with States or their successors and to have States honour and respect such treaties, agreements and other constructive arrangements.

2. Nothing in this Declaration may be interpreted as diminishing or eliminating the rights of indigenous peoples contained in treaties, agreements and other constructive arrangements.

Article 38

States in consultation and cooperation with indigenous peoples, shall take the appropriate measures, including legislative measures, to achieve the ends of this Declaration.

Article 39

Indigenous peoples have the right to have access to financial and technical assistance from States and through international cooperation, for the enjoyment of the rights contained in this Declaration.

Article 40

Indigenous peoples have the right to access to and prompt decision through just and fair procedures for the resolution of conflicts and disputes with States or other parties, as well as to effective remedies for all infringements of their individual and collective rights. Such a decision shall give due consideration to the customs, traditions, rules and legal systems of the indigenous peoples concerned and international human rights.

Article 41

The organs and specialized agencies of the United Nations system and other intergovernmental organizations shall contribute to the full realization of the provisions of this Declaration through the mobilization, inter alia, of financial cooperation and technical assistance. Ways and means of ensuring participation of indigenous peoples on issues affecting them shall be established.

Article 42

The United Nations, its bodies, including the Permanent Forum on Indigenous Issues, and specialized agencies, including at the country level, and States shall promote respect for and full application of the provisions of this Declaration and follow up the effectiveness of this Declaration.

Article 43

The rights recognized herein constitute the minimum standards for the survival, dignity and well-being of the indigenous peoples of the world.

Article 44

All the rights and freedoms recognized herein are equally guaranteed to male and female indigenous individuals.

Article 45

Nothing in this Declaration may be construed as diminishing or extinguishing the rights indigenous peoples have now or may acquire in the future.

Article 46

1. Nothing in this Declaration may be interpreted as implying for any State, people, group or person any right to engage in any activity or to perform any act contrary to the Charter of the United Nations or construed as authorizing or encouraging any action which would dismember or impair, totally or in part, the territorial integrity or political unity of sovereign and independent States.

2. In the exercise of the rights enunciated in the present Declaration, human rights and fundamental freedoms of all shall be respected. The exercise of the rights set forth in this Declaration shall be subject only to such limitations as are determined by law, and in accordance with international human rights obligations. Any such limitations shall be non-discriminatory and strictly necessary solely for the purpose of securing due recognition and respect for the rights and freedoms of others and for meeting the just and most compelling requirements of a democratic society.

3. The provisions set forth in this Declaration shall be interpreted in accordance with the principles of justice, democracy, respect for human rights, equality, non-discrimination, good governance and good faith.

Adoption by a vote
Sixty-first General Assembly
13 September 2007

Human Rights Council Resolution 6/15. Forum on Minority Issues

The Human Rights Council,

Recalling the International Covenant on Civil and Political Rights and the Declaration on the Rights of Persons Belonging to National or Ethnic, Religious and Linguistic Minorities adopted by consensus by the General Assembly by its resolution 47/135 of 18 December 1992,

Taking into consideration article 27 of the International Covenant on Civil and

Political Rights as well as other relevant existing international standards and national legislation,

Recalling Commission on Human Rights resolution 1995/24 of 3 March 1995, Economic and Social Council resolution 1995/31 of 25 July 1995 and decision 1998/246 of 30 July 1998 on the mandate of the Working Group on Minorities of the Sub-Commission on the Promotion and Protection of Human Rights,

Recalling also Human Rights Council resolution 5/1 of 18 June 2007, which calls upon the Council to decide at its sixth session on the most appropriate mechanisms to continue the work of the former working groups of the Sub-Commission,

Taking note of the final report of the Working Group on Minorities (A/HRC/Sub.1/58/19), in particular the recommendations on the future of the Working Group, which emphasizes the need for a mechanism to serve as forum for dialogue and mutual understanding on minority rights issues,

Taking note also of the report of the Secretary-General on the rights of persons belonging to national or ethnic, religious and linguistic minorities (A/HRC/4/109), in which he invites the Council to consider ways to maintain mechanisms offering opportunities for the meaningful participation of civil society,

Commending the important work undertaken by the independent expert on minority issues and recalling the complementarity of her mandate with that of the former Working Group on Minorities provided for in Commission on Human Rights resolution 2005/79 of 21 April 2005,

Emphasizing the need for reinforced efforts to meet the goal of the full realization of the rights of persons belonging to national or ethnic, religious and linguistic minorities,

Affirming that effective measures and the creation of favourable conditions for the promotion and protection of the rights of persons belonging to national or ethnic, religious and linguistic minorities, ensuring effective non-discrimination and equality for all, as well as full and effective participation in matters affecting them, contribute to the prevention and peaceful solution of human rights problems and situations involving minorities,

Underlining the need to pay specific attention to the negative impact of racism, racial discrimination, xenophobia and related intolerance on the situation of persons belonging to national or ethnic, religious and linguistic minorities, and drawing attention to the relevant provisions of the Durban Declaration and Programme of Action adopted in September 2001 by the World Conference against Racism, Racial Discrimination, Xenophobia and Related Intolerance, including the provisions on forms of multiple discrimination,

Emphasizing the importance of dialogue among all relevant stakeholders on the promotion and protection of the rights of persons belonging to national or ethnic, religious and linguistic minorities as an integral part of the development of society as a whole, including the sharing of best practices such as for the promotion of mutual understanding of minority issues, managing diversity by recognizing plural identities, and promoting inclusive and stable societies as well as social cohesion therein,

Emphasizing also the importance of national processes aimed at promoting and strengthening dialogue between all relevant stakeholders on issues relating to the rights of persons belonging to national, or ethnic, religious and linguistic minorities with a view to ensuring the realization of their rights without discrimination and to help build stable societies,

1. *Decides* to establish a forum on minority issues to provide a platform for promoting dialogue and cooperation on issues pertaining to persons belonging to national or ethnic, religious and linguistic minorities, which shall provide thematic contributions and expertise to the work of the independent expert on minority issues.[1] The Forum shall identify and analyse best practices, challenges, opportunities and initiatives for the further implementation of the Declaration on the Rights of Persons Belonging to National or Ethnic, Religious and Linguistic Minorities;

2. *Also decides* that the Forum shall be open to the participation of States, United Nations mechanisms, bodies and specialized agencies, funds and programmes, intergovernmental organizations, regional organizations and mechanisms in the field of human rights, national human rights institutions and other relevant national bodies, academics and experts on minority issues and non-governmental organizations in consultative status with the Economic and Social Council; the Forum shall also be open to other non-governmental organizations whose aims and purposes are in conformity with the spirit, purposes and principles of the Charter of the United Nations, based on arrangements, including Economic and Social Council resolution 1996/31 of 25 July 1996, and practices observed by the Commission on Human Rights, through an open and transparent accreditation procedure in accordance with the Rules of Procedure of the Human Rights Council, which will provide for the timely information on participation and consultations with States concerned;

3. *Decides further* that the Forum shall meet annually for two working days allocated to thematic discussions;

4. *Requests* the President of the Human Rights Council to appoint for each session, on the basis of regional rotation, and in consultation with regional groups, a chairperson of the Forum among experts on minority issues, nominated by members and observers of the Council; the chairperson, serving in his/her personal capacity, shall be responsible for the preparation of a summary of the discussion of the Forum, to be made available to all participants of the Forum;

5. *Decides* that the independent expert on minority issues shall guide the work of the Forum and prepare its annual meetings, and invites him/her to include in his/her report thematic recommendations of the Forum and recommendations for future thematic subjects, for consideration by the Human Rights Council;

6. *Expresses its expectation* that the Forum will contribute to the efforts of the United Nations High Commissioner for Human Rights to improve the cooperation among United Nations mechanisms, bodies and specialized agencies, funds and programmes on activities related to the promotion and protection of the rights of persons belonging to minorities, including at regional level;

7. *Requests* the High Commissioner for Human Rights to provide all the necessary support to facilitate, in a transparent manner, the convening of the Forum and the participation of relevant stakeholders from every region in its meetings, giving particular attention to ensuring broadest possible and equitable participation, including, in particular, the representation of women;

8. *Requests* the Secretary-General to provide the Forum, within existing resources of the United Nations, with all the services and facilities necessary to fulfill its mandate;

9. *Decides* to review the work of the Forum after four years.

Adopted by consensus
Twenty-first meeting
28 September 2007

Who are Minorities?

There is no universally accepted definition of 'minorities', and the word is interpreted differently in different societies. The United Nations (UN) has failed to agree a definition of what constitutes a minority, beyond that implied in the title of the UN Declaration on the Rights of Persons belonging to National or Ethnic, Religious and Linguistic Minorities. Attempting a more precise statement has been fraught with difficulties: in some cases the motivation for a tighter definition has been to deny certain rights to certain peoples.

Minority Rights Group International (MRG) focuses its work on non-dominant ethnic, religious and linguistic communities, who may not necessarily be numerical minorities. MRG's work includes initiatives with indigenous and tribal peoples, migrant communities and refugees. These communities may not wish to be classified as minorities for various reasons. We also recognize that these groups are not homogeneous – some members face further marginalization due to age, class, disability, gender or other factors.

The groups MRG works with are among the poorest and most marginalized groups in society. They may lack access to political power, face discrimination and human rights abuses, and have 'development' policies imposed upon them. MRG seeks to protect and promote the basic rights of these communities. We believe that recognition of minority and indigenous peoples' rights is crucial to establishing and maintaining just and peaceful societies.

Notes

Climate change and minorities – by Rachel Baird

1. IPCC, *Fourth Assessment Report, Climate Change 2007: Synthesis Report.*
2. IFRC and Red Crescent, *World Disasters Report 2006*, Geneva, 2006.
3. Salick, J. and Byg, A., *Indigenous Peoples and Climate Change*, report of a symposium held on 12–13 April 2007, Oxford, Tyndall Centre for Climate Change Research.
4. For Hurricane Katrina see Brookings Institution, *New Orleans After the Storm*, Washington, DC, Brookings Institution, October 2005; NAACP, Gulf Coast Advocacy Center, Opportunity Agenda and Kirwan Insitute for the Study of Race and Ethnicity at Ohio State University, *Housing in New Orleans: One Year After Katrina*; for Indian floods see Divakar, N.P. (Convenor of the National Campaign for Dalit Human Rights), Letter to Shri R.S. Gavai, Governor of the State of Bihar, undated, URL: http://www.idsn.org/Documents/asia/pdf/Bihar GovernorLetter2007.pdf
5. All interviews for this chapter were carried out in September and October 2007.
6. See Salick and Byg, *op. cit.*
7. IPCC, *Climate Change 2007 – Impacts, Adaptation and Vulnerability – Contribution of Working Group II to the Fourth Assessment Report of the IPCC*, p. 374; see also chapter 7 on industry, settlement and society and chapter 17 on adaptation practices, options, constraints and capacity.
8. Divakar, *op. cit.*
9. Brookings Institution, 2005, *op. cit.*, pp. 16–17.
10. Steger, T., *Making the Case for Environmental Justice in Central and Eastern Europe*, Center for Environmental Policy, URL: http://inchesnet-work.net/p33.pdf
11. ACIA, *Arctic Climate Impact Assessment*, Cambridge, Cambridge University Press, 2004.
12. MRG, *From Conflict to Autonomy in Nicaragua*, London, MRG, April 2007.
13. See also Kimenye, D., 'Climatic changes in the Mandera district of Kenya', unpublished report commissioned by Christian Aid.
14. Tauli-Corpuz, V. and Tamang, P., 'Oil palm and other commercial tree plantations, monocropping: impacts on indigenous peoples' land tenure and resource management systems and livelihoods', paper produced for the UN Permanent Forum on Indigenous Issues, 6th session, May 2007.
15. Internal Displacement Monitoring Centre, *Resisting Displacement by Combatants and Developers: Humanitarian Zones in North-west Colombia*, Geneva, Norwegian Refugee Council, November 2007.
16. Perkumpulan Sawit Watch and 10 other organizations, 'Request for consideration of the situation of indigenous peoples in Kalimantan, Indonesia, under the United Nations Committee on the Elimination of Racial Discrimination's Urgent Action and Early Warning Procedures', submitted 6 July 2007.
17. Griffiths, T., *Seeing 'RED'? 'Avoided Deforestation' and the Rights of Indigenous Peoples and Local Communities*, Moreton-in-Marsh, Forest Peoples Programme, June 2007, p. 12.
18. Divakar, *op. cit.*
19. NACCP et al., *op. cit.*
20. Bukovska, B., 'Difference and indifference: bringing Czech Roma ghettoes to Europe's Court', 2002, URL: http://www.eumap.org/journal/features/2002/may02/czechromaghettoes
21. Simms, A., Magrath, J., Reid, H. and Working Group on Climate Change, *Up In Smoke?* London, New Economics Foundation and International Institute for Environment and Development, October 2004.
22. Magrath, J., Simms, A., and Working Group on Climate Change, *Africa Up in Smoke 2*, London, New Economics Foundation, October 2006.
23. See Ministry of Environment and Forest, *National Adaptation Programme of Action*, Government of the People's Republic of Bangladesh, November 2005.
24. Adger, N., Mace, M.J., Paavola, J. and Razzaque J., 'Justice and equity in adaptation', Tiempo Climate Newswatch, URL: http://www.tiempocyberclimate.org/newswatch/feature040926.htm
25. *Ibid.*
26. The UN Framework Convention on Climate Change website contains a lot of clear informa-

tion about the Convention and Kyoto Protocol, Convention bodies and documents, and meetings linked to Convention processes. It also includes a list of NAPAs and National Communications submitted by governments, URL: www.unfccc.int

27. *Ibid.*
28. Perkumpulan Sawit Watch, *op. cit.*
29. Inter-Agency Standing Committee (IASC), *Protecting Persons Affected by Natural Disasters: IASC Guidelines on Human Rights and Natural Disasters*, Washington, DC, Brookings–Bern Project on Internal Displacement, June 2006.

Tourism and Minorities: A Kenya Case Study – by Lucy Hannan

1. Additonal research by Judy Gitu.

How Can the Law Help? Minority Rights and Tourism – by Cynthia Morel

1. The Awas Tingni Case, Inter-American Court of Human Rights, (2001), para. 148.
2. *Ibid.* at para. 151.
3. Daes, E.-I., 'Indigenous peoples' right to land and natural resources', in N. Ghanea and A. Xanthaki (eds), *Minorities, Peoples and Self-Determination*, The Netherlands, Brill, 2005, p. 89 (emphasis added).
4. *Ibid.*, p. 89.
5. Case of the *Indigenous Community Yakye Axa v. Paraguay*, Inter-American Court of Human Rights, 17 June 2005.
6. 'Concluding Observations of the Committee on the Elimination of Racial Discrimination: Ethiopia', 20 June 2007 (CERD/C/ETH/CO/15).
7. *Ibid.*
8. Integrating Human Rights with Development: A UNDP Policy Document, United Nations Development Programme (1998), Sec. 2.
9. See General Recommendation 23 Concerning Indigenous Peoples (1997), UN Committee on the Elimination of Racial Discrimination, para 4(d) and 5.
10. *Mary and Carrie Dann v. USA* (2002), para. 136.
11. *Ibid.* at para. 140.
12. *Roy Sesana, Keiwa Setlhobogwa and Others v. The Attorney General of Botswana*, Misca. No.

52 of 2002, held at Lobatse High Court, 13 December 2006.

Africa – by Ishbel Matheson

1. Additional research by Andrew Manley.

United Nations Declaration on the Rights of Indigenous Peoples

1. See resolution 2200 A (XXI), annex.
2. A/CONF.157/24 (Part I), chap. III.
3. Resolution 217 A (III).

Human Rights Council Resolution 6/15. Forum on Minority Issues

1. Subject to review of the mandate of the independent expert, as foreseen in resolution 5/1 of 18 June 2007

Contributors

Rachel Baird is a journalist. She worked at the *Daily Express* newspaper for eight years, but has spent the last year as a climate change researcher at the charity Christian Aid.

Maurice Bryan is a Caribbean-born writer and communications consultant who has worked in a variety of countries in Latin America, the Caribbean, Asia and Africa.

Matilde Ceravolo was a Country Coordinator in Colombia, where she designed and supervised projects in support of IDPs and Children's Rights. From June 2005 to December 2006 she supported the Aka in their actions to promote human rights in the CAR. She currently works as a Fundraiser at MRG. She holds a master in Pacification and Administration of Regional Development.

Emma Eastwood spent over a decade working in the field of human rights protection in Latin America, as an international observer in Guatemala and Communications Officer with Peace Brigades International Colombia Project. She is the media and events officer at MRG.

Lucy Hannan is a foreign correspondent and film maker, covering the East and Horn of Africa. She has written books on the transition to democracy and the Kenyan justice system.

Kamila Hyat is human rights activist and former newspaper editor with a particular interest in the rights of disadvantaged groups in Pakistan. She writes on politics and current issues for publications both within and outside Pakistan.

Mark Lattimer is Executive Director of Minority Rights Group International. Formerly he worked with Amnesty International. Recent publications include (as editor) *Genocide and Human Rights* (Ashgate, 2007).

Wangari Maathai is the founder of the Green Belt Movements. In 2004, she was awarded the Nobel Peace Prize.

Ishbel Matheson was the BBC's East Africa Correspondent from 2000 to 2005. She has an LLM (with distinction) in International Human Rights Law from the University of Essex. She is currently the Head of Policy and Communications at MRG.

Farah Mihlar has worked as a journalist for several international media organizations. She covered Sri Lanka for more than 10 years, reporting extensively on the conflict. Since 2004 she has worked as a consultant media officer in human rights organizations including at the Office of the High Commissioner for Human Rights (OHCHR). She currently works as media officer at Minority Rights Group International. She holds a MSc in Social Policy from the London School of Economics.

Cynthia Morel has been MRG's legal cases officer since 2002, coordinating the Trouble in Paradise campaign since 2006. Previously she worked at the Inter-American Institute of Human Rights, and the Canadian Commission for UNESCO.

Marusca Perazzi is Programmes Officer and Executive Assistant to the Director at MRG. Specialized in Chinese language and Oriental cultures, international relations and global governance, she lived and worked with ethnic minority communities in north-west China.

Preti Taneja is Commissioning Editor at MRG. She is also the author of the recent MRG report *Assimilation, Exodus, Eradication, Iraq's Minority Communities since 2003.*

Eric A. Witte is a senior associate at the Democratization Policy Council and former political adviser to the chief prosecutor at the UN-backed Special Court for Sierra Leone.

Acknowledgements

A report of this size involves contributions from a large number of people – including MRG staff. Special thanks to Richie Andrew, for production coordination and Sophie Richmond for copy-editing. We wish to gratefully acknowledge the following individuals, who have contributed their thoughts, comments, advice and expertise to this edition of *SWM*.

Neil Adger, Qamar Agha, Yinka Adeyeye, Mohamed Adow, Thodoros Alexandridis, Clive Baldwin, Daniel Balint-Kurti, Tricia Barnett, Dr Ester Bianchi, Matilde Ceravolo, Chris Chapman, Olu Coker, Savelina Danova, Cezara David, Chizom Ekeh, Judy Gitu, Ray Hasan, Sally Healy, Madeleen Helmer, Seema Kazi, Samia Khan, Calos Ling, John Magrath, Lena al Malak, Oliver Marshall, Olav Mathis-Eira, Paul Mulindwa, Jouni Paavola, Dr Mark Pelling, Andrew Pendleton, Megan Rowling, Brice Sereckissy, Tadesse Tafesse, Tom Tanner, Claire Thomas, Fernand de Varennes, David Vinuales, Kumar Vishwanathan, Kathrin Wessendorf, Caroline Wood.